CROWD MONEY

A PRACTICAL GUIDE TO MACRO BEHAVIOURAL TECHNICAL ANALYSIS

BY **EOIN TREACY**

HARRIMAN HOUSE LTD

3A Penns Road
Petersfield
Hampshire
GU32 2EW
GREAT BRITAIN

Tel: +44 (0)1730 233870
Email: enquiries@harriman-house.com
Website: www.harriman-house.com

First published in Great Britain in 2013.

ISBN: 9780857193049

British Library Cataloguing in Publication Data
A CIP catalogue record for this book can be obtained from the British Library.

 Harriman House

PRAISE FOR *CROWD MONEY*

"Everyone has access to a chart program. Have you ever wondered about the thought process behind those charts? *Crowd Money* does just that. It reveals the human emotions that drive those charts, and the psychology that drives bull and bear markets. If you think you're good at reading charts you've just been given another tool that will enhance your skill set and make those charts more meaningful. But it gets better. Eoin Treacy reveals the new aristocrats of our globally linked markets. The companies that will dominate markets over the next decade. *Crowd Money* is a wealth of information for professionals and novices alike."

– James Puplava, CEO, PFS Group

"Although behavioural analysis has been applied in financial and economic circles, Eoin Treacy's book is the first attempt I've seen to apply behavioural principles to technical analysis. *Crowd Money* is a welcome addition to literature in both fields of analysis."

– John Murphy, author of Technical Analysis of the Financial Markets

"Eoin Treacy's new book is a treasure trove of ideas and insights from a serious student of today's markets."

– Bill Bonner, president of Agora Publishing and author of The Daily Reckoning

"The charts show the rhythm of the markets. Eoin Treacy explains why."

– Christopher Wood, chief strategist, CLSA

EXCLUSIVE READER OFFER

Thank you for buying *Crowd Money* and welcome to the **FT-Money** global community. To help you put the methodology discussed in *Crowd Money* into practice, please join us for a one-month **FREE** trial of the **FT-Money** service valued at **£55**.

You will enjoy unlimited access to the fully customisable **Chart Library** containing more than 12,000 equities, bonds, commodities, currencies, indices and funds as well as all our written and audio commentary.

Just visit **www.ft-money.com/crowdmoneyvoucher** and fill in the form using this code; **2013FTCM**

CONTENTS

Acknowledgements   vii

About the Author   ix

Foreword by David Fuller   xi

Preface   xiii

Introduction: The Next Generation's Outperformers   xvii

Chapter 1: The Four Pillars of Global Thematic Investing   1

Chapter 2: Chart Reading Versus Technical Analysis   11

Chapter 3: Group Formation (Me + Them = Us)   19

Chapter 4: How the Crowd Influences Our Personal Psychology   27

Chapter 5: Greed, Fear and Love –
Developing Emotional Intelligence   35

Chapter 6: Psychological Perception Stages of Bull
and Bear Markets   43

Chapter 7: How Past Support Becomes Future Resistance
(and Vice Versa)   77

Chapter 8: How Does a Breakout Occur?   87

Chapter 9: Consistency Characteristics   97

Chapter 10: Anticipating Price Action   113

Chapter 11: Moving Averages   131

Chapter 12: Targets, Contrary Indicators, Roundophobia and
Psychological Levels   141

Chapter 13: Stops and Money Control Discipline   149

Chapter 14: Trend Ending #1 – Acceleration and Key Reversals   163

Chapter 15: Trend Ending #2 – The Massive Reaction Against
the Prevailing Trend   177

Chapter 16: Type-3 Endings – Ranging, Time and Size   185

Chapter 17: Monetary Policy   195

Chapter 18: Governance is Everything   207

Chapter 19: The Regulatory Environment   215

Chapter 20: Crashes, Contagion and Opportunity   223

Chapter 21: Major Market Cycles   235

Chapter 22: How Supply and Demand Influence Price and
Vice Versa   247

Chapter 23: Themes for the Decades Between 2015 and 2025   257

Chapter 24: The Global Middle Class   267

Chapter 25: The Autonomies   275

Conclusion   367

FT-Money.com   369

Index   371

ACKNOWLEDGEMENTS

To David Fuller, the most generous mentor anyone could ever wish for.

To Lily, Aisling and Fiona for your patience.

To Sam Prather (a retired Silicon Valley high-tech executive) for his tireless support and encouragement.

To FT-Money's subscribers, to whom this book is dedicated. Thank you for your continued support.

FREE EBOOK VERSION

As a buyer of the print book of *Crowd Money* you can now download the eBook version free of charge to read on an eBook reader, your smartphone or your computer. Simply go to:

http://ebooks.harriman-house.com/crowdmoney

or point your smartphone at the QRC below.

You can then register and download your free eBook.

FOLLOW US, LIKE US, EMAIL US

@HarrimanHouse
www.linkedin.com/company/harriman-house
www.facebook.com/harrimanhouse
contact@harriman-house.com

 Harriman House

ABOUT THE AUTHOR

Eoin Treacy has spent a decade as a global strategist and partner at **Fullermoney.com**, where he has represented the service on sell-out speaking tours to the USA, Australia and Singapore. He is an expert in the firm's unique macro behavioural approach to financial market interpretation and has appeared on Bloomberg TV, CNBC, CNN, CNBC India, NDTV Profit and the BBC World Service as a commentator on equities, bonds, commodities and currencies.

As well as frequent appearances on Indian financial media, Eoin travels regularly to China to gain first-hand experience of the evolution of its market. He is a world-renowned speaker and has been invited to deliver talks to financially-minded associations in a host of countries, not least for the CFA Institute, the Market Technicians Association, Society of Technical Analysts in the UK and the Australian Technical Analysts Association. He is also a regular presenter at The World Money Show in London and at the Contrary Opinion Forum in Vermont.

Following a degree in Philosophy from Trinity College, Dublin, Eoin went on to spend more than three years at Bloomberg, teaching seminars across Europe on the interpretation of price action. He joined David Fuller at Fullermoney in 2003 to specialise in the service's approach to research – combining technical, fundamental and behavioural factors. He shares his views on markets in Fullermoney's Comment of the Day on a daily basis and regularly records the service's daily audio updates. As an active trader Eoin also details all of his personal trades and investments in the service. Finally, Eoin developed the Fullermoney Chart Library, which is fully customisable and includes more than 17,000 instruments, ratios, spreads and multiples.

In 2013 David Fuller and Eoin Treacy formed **FT-Money.com** to take their service to the next level and to enhance the product experience for their many subscribers.

Eoin is married and has two daughters. In his spare time he is a keen scuba diver.

FOREWORD BY DAVID FULLER

EOIN TREACY IS one of the best-known financial strategists of his generation. His initial career at Bloomberg, followed by his efficient use of behavioural technical analysis as developed by Fullermoney, has given him a rare insight on global financial markets. Eoin is skilled at monitoring any financial market on a top-down basis.

For instance, with stock markets he starts by categorising developed, emerging and frontier markets on the basis of relative strength or weakness, which he can view in both local currencies as well as any single currency such as the US dollar, for comparative performance. This initial ranking shows him very quickly which markets are in or out of fashion. By viewing them regularly on a systematic basis, he will also know when any market is gaining or losing relative strength.

Thereafter, by utilising Bloomberg's comprehensive fundamental data, Eoin can compare markets in terms of valuations, commencing with historic and perspective price earnings ratios, plus dividend yields. When a market appears interesting and he would like to see more fundamental data, he can drill down further by looking at any additional information that is useful for assessment, including comparisons with other markets. And since Fullermoney is an interactive service, Eoin will also have access to research reports and articles from our often-knowledgeable 'collective' of subscribers around the globe.

Good financial research begins with awareness, based on monitoring what markets are actually doing. On a fractal basis, this process can be expanded by looking at the performance of market sectors and then their individual shares of potential interest. It is a disciplined, informative, factual, fascinating and often profitable process.

In writing this introduction to Eoin's book, I tip my hat to him because I know how difficult it is to explain a behavioural analytical process without making it sound simplistic and mechanistic. I can assure you that it is not. But how can one explain in detail a methodology based on lifelong observation, especially as it involves thousands of different charts, revealing the moves of share prices, government bonds, commodities and currencies over time?

My answer is that a text book is also a form of introduction, which hopefully sparks your interest and analytical curiosity. Talking about money driven by sentiment is similar to describing the process of falling in love. Each of us knows what that feels like but try explaining it to someone else and it sounds emotional and perhaps even banal. The big trends – up and down – are all about the crowd falling in love with a market story, which they extrapolate to unrealistic levels, ensuring that they subsequently fall out of love with the same instrument when it no longer performs.

Price charts show us the changing flows of money, driven by events which influence crowd psychology. Monitoring market action on price charts is an efficient analytical process. It also makes sense, because for those of us who hope to understand what markets are doing, how could it not be helpful to actually look at graphic presentations of price trends? To the trained eye, the facts of price action reveal not only money flows but also the changing moods of investors across the panoply of emotions, ranging from uncertainty in choppy markets, to unsustainable euphoria in accelerating uptrends, and panic near the bottom of accelerated declines.

An analytical process based on opinions, without consideration of what price action is revealing, can easily err by telling the market what to do. Yet most of us know as investors that when someone does this, the market seldom cares. Additionally, investors face a daily barrage of financial media explanations, conveniently enabled by events of the day which may be of little influence or even totally unrelated. No wonder people find markets confusing!

Instead, we usually do better by paying less attention to the noise, and looking at what the market is actually doing. We can best observe the market efficiently, factually and accurately by looking at price charts. They are at the centre of Eoin's and my analytical process. And in looking at charts, we are only interested in technical facts, not theories.

I hope you will enjoy and learn from the examples in this first book by Eoin Treacy. Successful analysis and investing is a lifelong learning process. Each insight gained is an additional step along this fascinating journey. You will certainly hear a good deal more about Eoin and his market views in the years ahead.

David Fuller
London, 2013

PREFACE

IF YOU HAVE ever wondered how market interrelationships shape investment trends or how the psychology of the crowd changes perceptions of value, or have been disappointed by conventional market analysis, this book is for you. It is also for everyone who has ever attended the Chart Seminar, subscribed to the former **Fullermoney.com** or the present **FT-Money.com**, attended one of our talks, heard either David Fuller or me speak, seen us on financial TV channels or heard us on the radio.

I joined David Fuller in 2003 to help manage the evolution of the Fullermoney Global Strategy Service from print to online and to create its online chart library covering more than 17,000 instruments. In 2013 David Fuller formed **FT-Money.com** to enhance the service we provide to our global subscriber base and this is where our commentary can now be found.

The Chart Seminar has been held at venues all over the world for more than 40 years and has been attended by thousands of investors and traders from just about every major investment house. However, there has never been a book that detailed in one place the confluence of methods that form the basis of the seminar's macro behavioural technical analysis. Since we appear to be at a major turning point in the outlook for stock markets, commodities, bonds and currencies I thought that now was the most appropriate time to record in one place the methodology David Fuller and I use to reach our conclusions.

To do this I have broken the subject down into the four pillars of our method. These are:

1. price action / crowd psychology
2. liquidity
3. governance
4. theme / fundamental value.

While each of these individual strands can create powerful short to medium-term trends, it is the comparatively rare occasions when they combine to form secular bull and bear markets that are our primary concern. Major bull markets are where fortunes are made and where it is easiest to employ a trend-running strategy effectively. This book is therefore concerned with where to find the best trends and how to run them once identified.

PRICE ACTION / CROWD PSYCHOLOGY

The market is a mob and in order to profit from it we have to become part of it. We are conditioned by this process so it is useful to have an understanding of how groups form and what happens in terms of our personal psychology once we decide to participate. Price action tells us what people are doing with their money and represents reality for the macro behavioural technical analyst. We all have some strongly held opinions but unless they are supported by the action of the crowd they represent nothing more than conjecture.

LIQUIDITY

Every bull market thrives on liquidity so we need to have some way of monitoring both the supply and cost of money so that we can frame our investment strategy to take this information into account. David Fuller has long said that "*central banks have killed off more bull markets than all other factors combined*". Likewise the actions of central banks to support markets during times of crisis ensure that a bull market begins somewhere.

GOVERNANCE

In the West, the perception of political and regulatory governance has deteriorated considerably over recent decades so that citizens despair of it ever improving. The opposite is true in other parts of the world, where optimism towards standards of governance has been improving. However, it would be a mistake to assume that governance is either absolute or fixed. Governance is a relative consideration and has to be seen to be improving if investor perceptions of wealth creation are to improve. Even when governance deteriorates it can have short-term positive effects because it can increase the liquidity on which the market thrives.

THEME / FUNDAMENTAL VALUE

If we are to concern ourselves with long-term secular bull markets, a fundamental driver for such a move must be in place. If we define productivity as the product of labour, technology, energy and debt then a major improvement in any one of these factors can spur a secular bull market. When we see improvements in three of them, as is currently the case, the prospect for outsized gains multiplies.

David Fuller and I define the Autonomies as the companies most likely to benefit from the confluence of these factors. They are truly global in where they generate revenue, they dominate their respective niches and have globally recognisable brands that foster loyalty, they have strong balance sheets and many have lengthy records of dividend growth. An increasing number demonstrate that the investment crowd is coalescing around the idea that these companies represent value regardless of how one defines that term.

INTRODUCTION:

THE NEXT GENERATION'S OUTPERFORMERS

"Be not afeard; the isle is full of noises … "

– William Shakespeare

I HAVE A CONFESSION TO MAKE … I'm excited. I have that restive feeling I get when I find a market that has been doing nothing for a long time and looks like it is about to go haywire. The feeling that all the lessons people have learned over the last decade are about to be turned on their head as we go through a paradigm shift in perceptions of where value lies. The group of companies David Fuller and I define as Autonomies represent our best bet for those that are going to outperform over the next decade.

We all seek to learn from our experience but the most important lesson is that we are conditioned by those experiences. If we have lived through a disappointing period where returns have not met our expectations, the temptation is to withdraw from the market and to nurse our emotional wounds. The result is that without a disciplined approach to analysis we will not be open to new opportunities as they present themselves. Macro behavioural technical analysis is devoted to ensuring we learn the lessons market history is teaching us so that we can script how markets will perform in future.

There is always a healthy market in fear because investing is an inherently uncertain exercise. Volatility, disappointment, the apparent fickle nature of returns all contribute to anxiety. Additionally, human beings are inherently conservative. We just don't like change. And yet we do whatever we can to foster progress in the name of promoting productivity. The pace of technological innovation and the speed with which our lives are changing is greeted by many with apprehension and intensifies the uncertainty they feel. A broadly rangebound environment for many North American and European stock markets, declining faith in the political classes and some horrific financial crimes have exacerbated that feeling. I have met more than a few people who bought in the early 2000s and have nothing to show for a decade of investment except a sense that it is all going to end in tears.

However, even the most cursory appreciation of market history teaches us that optimism prevails over the long term. Generational long bear markets generally give way to generational long bull markets that exceed the peaks of the previous mania. The pace of technological innovation and improving governance in the world's population centres is such that the standard of living for billions of people is improving faster than ever before. The companies that help deliver what these new consumers want are likely to be among those that attract the greatest investor following and produce the greatest stock market returns.

This imbalance between optimism and pessimism is what creates market trends. In order to profit, we need a set of tools that allow us navigate the increasingly large quantity of information we are presented with; so we can see what truly matters. This is where the macro behavioural technical analysis pioneered by David Fuller proves invaluable.

Following a series of crashes in the decade 2000–2010 investors have become disillusioned with a monochromatic way of looking at markets. A purely fundamental perspective has not insulated advocates from the underperformance of equities. A purely technical perspective can often result in an over-reliance on indicators which obscures the reality provided by the market. Therefore a holistic approach which offers a fresh perspective on these topics by incorporating crowd psychology and the influence of monetary policy has obvious merit.

While behavioural finance and behavioural economics tend to be rather academic in their approach, macro behavioural technical analysis focuses on real-world problems and can be applied to any market over any time frame. The practicality of the method is perhaps its greatest strength. The simple test of any methodology is not whether it sounds good or appeals to our vanity but whether it succeeds in improving our investment results. I can unabashedly say that this is the case with my trading and investment. The Chart Seminar was developed by David Fuller in the late 1960s as a way of showcasing this behaviourally focused approach to markets. The course has been attended by thousands of investors and traders from just about every major investment house over the last 44 years and it was my pleasure to assume responsibility for presenting it in 2007. Since then I've been on sell-out tours to Europe, the USA, Singapore and Australia. The course remains as popular as ever because it offers a unique perspective on how the markets are likely to unfold.

The markets are the only subject that has ever come close to satisfying my intellectual curiosity. I am endlessly fascinated with the potential they offer not least because they reflect the entire range of human emotion, encompassing ambition, desire, avarice, love, fear, hope and more. Recognising the impact these emotions can have on our personal psychology and more particularly on the actions of the investment crowd lends us a competitive edge when compared to those with a linear view of the market.

During periods of market stress the temptation is to become increasingly problem-focused because we may have lost money or because we are incensed by the failings of the system as we see it. However, macro behavioural technical analysis ensures we adopt a solution-focused perspective so that as a problem intensifies we are aware of it and concentrating on the effect potential solutions may have on all asset classes. It is often said that there is always a bull market in something but ascertaining where the next bull market is likely to occur is where the application of macro behavioural technical analysis excels.

Macro behavioural technical analysis equips us with the tools to recognise the dawn of a new trend but more importantly the skills to recognise the rhythm and consistency of the move. These characteristics tell us how supply and demand are interacting and when they change we can only conclude that the interaction between these competing forces has evolved. We then have cause to reassess our strategy to ensure profits are protected.

David Fuller and I demonstrate the practical application of macro behavioural technical analysis via our daily assessment of market potential in written and audio format on **Fullermoney.com** / **FT-Money.com**. Using the methodology of macro behavioural technical analysis, we identify themes as they emerge on an ongoing basis. There has never before been a book which describes the particular way we perceive value in the markets so I thought the time had come for a more public exposition.

At the time of writing (mid-2013), powerful currents are coalescing to form the basis of a new secular bull market in equities. The greatest urbanisation in history, the greatest golden age of technological development ever, the revolution in unconventional energy supplies are three major interlocking themes that have the capacity to inspire investor interest for decades to come. The challenge in the short to medium-term is how the massive amount of debt built up by Western governments is going to be worked through. These are important issues where investors will make and lose fortunes over the coming decades. It will be important to be on the right side of these moves and to maintain emotional equilibrium as they progress.

CHAPTER 1:

THE FOUR PILLARS OF GLOBAL THEMATIC INVESTING

"If you board the wrong train, it is no use running along the corridor in the other direction."

– Dietrich Bonhoeffer

What we will cover in this chapter

A holistic approach to market analysis is likely to prove more productive than strictly adhering to any one theory.

It is easier to make money in bull markets so it makes sense to concern ourselves with how to identify where these may occur.

The four pillars of macro behavioural technical analysis are represented by an examination of:

1. *Theme / fundamental value* – a story capable of inspiring investor interest and which is grounded in sound fundamentals is required to fuel a major bull market.

2. *Liquidity* – bull markets thrive on liquidity. When central banks remove the punchbowl it is only a matter of time before a reversal occurs.

3. *Governance* – this is a relative value rather than an absolute consideration. When policies that enhance productivity are implemented, value is much easier to create.

4. *Price action* – we can feel passionate about our ideals and about our pet theories but if they are not supported by price action then we have to accept that our interpretation is incorrect. Price action is the ultimate reality check.

IT MIGHT SEEM SO OBVIOUS AS TO APPEAR facile but it is easier to make money in a bull market. Anyone who has ever taken part in a bull market that has persisted for any meaningful length of time has been pleasantly surprised by how well their investments do and how easy it all seems. The challenges lie in identifying it as it develops, employing a reliable trend-following strategy and having the emotional strength to identify when a market is topping and you should sell.

Everyone is familiar with at least some major investment themes if for no other reason than the bear markets that follow them. Today people talk about the tech bust of 2000 but often fail to mention the two-decade bull market that began in the early 1980s and created wealth for so many people. The 1929 crash remains a legendary event in the annals of stock market history, but people seldom associate the roaring 20s that preceded it with what had been a major bull market. Bull markets represent wonderful money-making opportunities if we equip ourselves with the tools necessary to benefit from them.

One of David Fuller's maxims since the 1960s has been that *financial markets are man-made resources for us to harvest when the timing is right*". Major bull markets represent times when a notable theme animates the investment crowd to such an extent that prices form rhythmic moves ideal for a trend-running investor. While we can become enamoured with any market we successfully interact with, it is worth remembering, that financial instruments only exist because of us. They depend on our participation and while they reflect real world phenomenon, how they perform is dictated by people, their perceptions and actions.

Investing is therefore a two-step process. On the one hand we need to equip ourselves with an appreciation of macro-economic conditions and fundamental value metrics. On the other we need to understand that how the investment crowd perceives this information will evolve over time, and this will affect how we can profit from the market.

As we approach the subject of how to identify major bull markets before they become celebrated by the media, the best way to profit from them, and the best time to exit before moving on to the next opportunity, we must first recognise that all bull markets have similar characteristics.

THEMES AND FUNDAMENTAL VALUE

Human beings are social animals and we thrive on stories. In psychological terms, we use stories to help us make sense of the world, to transmit ideas and to relate complex data to our individual experience. Therefore, when we are presented with an investment idea, it is more accessible if it comes packaged in a story that is easy to understand. For exactly the same reason politicians deliver stump speeches and are pleaded with by their handlers to 'stay on message'. An investment theme is therefore a complex idea based on facts that have been distilled down to a compelling message.

Given the right circumstances an investment theme can go on to form a major bull market and might even end in a mania phase where prices accelerate higher. The most successful investment themes promise to change the world. For example, the building of railroads in Europe and the USA allowed the transport of goods and services like never before. Railroads opened up huge new areas for cultivation because the time needed to bring products to market grew shorter. Leaps in technology created products and efficiencies that changed the way people lived their lives.

Japan's revival following World War II was nothing short of an economic miracle which was predicated on a collaborative and highly efficient management structure. The rest of the world went on to imitate this structure over the following decades. This represents another example of how productivity gains created value.

The swift pace of microchip development, the evolution of the internet and mobile phones among many other technological advances have created productivity gains where none were previously thought possible. All the promises about how technology would change the way we lived came true. And the pace of innovation continues. In the meantime, however, the prices of related instruments have moved both up and down a great deal as perception of the sector's potential varies.

Gold completed a lengthy bear market in 2002 following more than 20 years when it went from being the ultimate store of wealth to being considered, in Keynes' old phrase, a "barbaric relic". Following the dotcom bust in 2000, central bank money printing took off. Mines were forced to shutter production because of low prices. At the same time demand, particularly in Asia, began to trend higher. The stage was set for a major revival. All of these points are encapsulated in the typical beginning to any bullish story on the yellow metal: 'Gold is the only *real* money ... '.

All of these themes formed massive bull markets that have or will eventually end. There have, of course, been myriad other investment themes that have not persisted for nearly as long or had the wherewithal to change our lives in a truly meaningful way. In some cases it was because while the reasons to invest were compelling, the market was just not big enough to absorb the weight of money thrown at it. This is often particularly true of small, illiquid frontier markets or individual small cap shares.

It is not enough to have a good story. Any competent marketer can come up with an alluring sales pitch. For an investment theme to acquire the adherents necessary to spur a major bull market there must be fundamental value.

Value investors such as Benjamin Graham employed a method of discounting cash flows in order to come up with a fundamental value for a share then compared it to market traded prices in order to decide whether it was cheap or expensive. Warren Buffett has taken the premise further by, as he puts it, "finding an outstanding company at a sensible price". Deep value investing has been demonstrated to produce positive returns on a long-term (as in anything from three to 20-year) basis. However, because it ignores a timing component it is prone to underperformance until the wider market comes to share the investor's perception of value.

Value investors not only represent a major demographic within the investment community but their actions help to dictate at what point markets bottom out. They will often be early in buying during the typically lengthy base formations that precede more consistent uptrends and will often be too early in selling as bullish sentiment intensifies in the latter stages of major advances which are often characterised by upward acceleration in prices. Therefore, while value investing is a laudable endeavour, it should form a component in one's research rather than the basis for when to buy and sell.

When Sir John Templeton spoke of the best time to buy being "the point of maximum pessimism", he was referring to an emotional cue rather than a fundamental value.

LIQUIDITY

When we think about our reasons for participating in the financial markets it is to make money. Doesn't it therefore make sense to consider the nature of money when our ultimate goal is to get as much of it as we can?

Capitalist economic systems are set up to ensure that liquidity flows to assets with the most productive potential. These can be considered the assets with the best potential yield and/or potential for capital appreciation. When an asset class is considered to represent value and have a compelling theme it will inevitably begin to attract investor interest. Just how much money it attracts will be dependent on how much money is available for investment at that time.

When central banks ease the terms at which they are willing to make money available they follow three distinct policies. They lower the price at which money can be borrowed by cutting short-term interest rates. This simultaneously creates an incentive for those holding cash to spend or invest. They can increase the supply of money which helps to grease the wheels of commerce by ensuring availability of money for borrowers and increases the threat of inflation for savers. They can change the terms under which they are willing to lend by altering the regulatory framework. This increases the market for credit by making it available to more participants.

Any of these measures can be considered positive outcomes from a liquidity perspective. When all three are employed we can conclude that the money lent out by central banks will find its way into financial assets and will be multiplied as speculators take on leverage.

An important consideration is that while central banks have in the past and will again debase their currencies or neglect the interests of savers or, at the other extreme, impose austerity or actively curtail the flow of liquidity to a favoured asset, our opinion of these actions is irrelevant from an investment perspective. We might be angry, disgruntled, bemused, encouraged, happy or even delighted by central bank actions but that does not affect the influence of liquidity provision on asset prices. David Fuller has long said that "*we need to adopt the humility to accept the reality provided by the market*" and to resist the temptation to tell the market what to do.

When central banks begin to withdraw the proverbial punchbowl, credit becomes more expensive, less available and the conditions for access become stricter. As this process matures, it acts as a leading indicator for the next significant pivot in prices. Sentiment among the bulls trails this change in liquidity conditions but as David Fuller has long said "*central banks raising short-term interest rates have killed off more bull markets than all other factors combined*". Just as easy liquidity conditions are required to fuel a new bull market, as liquidity tightens it inevitably puts pressure on margins, speculators and other leveraged investors. In turn this alters the rhythm of the dominance of demand over supply upon which a bull market depends.

Central banks are in the unique position that they can create new money. However, there is still a large quantity of investable capital and this moves gradually from one asset class to another over time as perceptions of value evolve. During a major crash leverage is squeezed out of the system and investors flee to other assets vowing never to return. However as prices fall, value returns and, while it will take time, the fundamentals of the instrument readjust. When a compelling new demand story eventually develops, all those people with cash in another instrument represent potential investors who could be convinced to buy back into the original asset.

US Stock Market Allocations Stocks Index

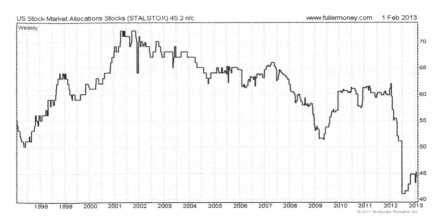

The Bloomberg US Stock Market Allocations Stocks Index offers a wonderful example of how trauma in one asset class affects the perceptions of how it will perform in future and therefore the decisions of investors in how they will allocate their assets. This chart depicts an average of the suggested allocation to equities among Wall Street strategists.

The index hit a peak near 72% in 2001; a year after one of the longest bull markets in history had ended. While the S&P Index spent the subsequent 13 years in a broad range, the perception of upside potential for equities continued to deteriorate so that by late 2012 the suggested allocation to equities was only 42%. A contrarian would look at this data and immediately conclude that just as it was incorrect to be overly bullish about expectations when prices had peaked it is most likely incorrect to adopt an overly bearish perspective about upside potential because prices have been rangebound for so long.

Above all else, this index exemplifies the tendency of investors to move with the latest fad. Their actions have a material impact on the flow of money in and out of various asset classes as perceptions gradually change. The nimble investor is best served by anticipating rather than following these movements.

GOVERNANCE IS EVERYTHING

To say that governance is everything may be something of an exaggeration but it does serve to highlight the fact that declining standards of governance are often a component of an inflating investment mania. Improving standards of governance are often a motivating factor that encourages investors to support a nascent bull market.

It would be inappropriate to speak of governance in absolute terms because there is no numeric way to measure this phenomenon. Instead we consider whether governance is improving or deteriorating. By removing an absolute comparison between countries, companies or regulatory systems and instead examining each individual asset class on its individual merits we put ourselves in a much stronger position to answer the question 'Are things getting better or worse?'.

When we address the prospects for an individual economy we look at fiscal policy, monetary policy, the regulatory framework, rule of law, minority shareholder protections and property rights. In making an appraisal we resist the temptation to compare the situation to other more highly developed or less-developed countries or indeed our home country. The more important question is whether the situation is improving and whether it is likely to continue to improve.

This is important for one simple reason. Improving standards of governance remove barriers to development and ease the way for productivity gains which create value. When a country's standards of governance improve it can have a material impact on the prospects for its bonds, currency and domestic stock market.

When a company that has been run for the benefit of its management rather than shareholders, or has been taking on more risk to enhance short-term earnings rather than focusing on creating long-term value, or expanding too quickly despite a saturated market, or paying record high prices to takeover questionable assets, we can conclude that governance has deteriorated. When managements change, the health of the balance sheet is prioritised, and the creation of value for shareholders is put ahead of short-term gains, we can conclude that governance is improving. This can have a material impact on pricing and sentiment towards a company.

If we concentrate on the trajectory of governance we can avoid complacency or self-satisfaction that a company or country's progress is 'good enough'. The simple truth is that governance can never be good enough. If value is to continue to be created there is always room for improvement. In fact, when governments or corporate boards engage in the hubris that they are perfect and have nothing to improve on we can conclude that standards of governance are more likely to deteriorate than improve.

PRICE ACTION

The determination of value can be a subjective practice because a market that we consider cheap can become cheaper. We might become enthralled with the story used to convey a bullish message. We might incorrectly consider that standards of governance are on an upward trajectory. To one extent or another these are subjective opinions. Price on the other hand is definite and can be regarded as a reality check. If price action does not support our hypothesis, we need to reassess.

An instrument's price tells us a great deal about how the competing forces of supply and demand are arranged. It tells us whether the trend of investment has been to support higher prices or to wait for lower prices. It allows us to sense the rhythm of the market and to observe how perceptions gradually change from disbelief to acceptance then euphoria and back again.

We need to have an appreciation of the fundamental basis for the market but once we understand the bull or bear case, the constituent arguments do not change all that often. Price changes a lot. The vacillation of the investment crowd and how it reacts to different stimuli will determine whether we make or lose money regardless of whether we have got the fundamental call on the market correct. For this reason alone I can say with absolute certainty that I never make an investment or trading decision without looking at a chart of price action first.

There would not be a financial market without human beings. Human beings are social animals and we thrive in groups. Price history gives us a graphic representation not of fundamental data but of how investors perceived it and reacted to it. A picture paints a thousand words.

David Fuller has long advised that investors should strive to *"view the market in the manner of a naturalist"*. We should attempt to view the investment herd as if we were looking in from the outside. If we are to profit from the market we need to participate. This eventually requires that we subject ourselves to the same allure of crowd psychology as everyone else. Put simply, as soon as we take a position our objectivity is compromised. Therefore in order to decipher what the price action is telling us we need to approach the market from a dispassionate perspective and employ a disciplined approach.

Just as with art, the tastes of buyers will differ considerably but those who interpret the works on display focus on facts such as composition, use of light and shade, texture and history. When we interpret price action on a chart we cannot simply rely on our gut feeling but must adopt an analytical process. We ask whether the market is trending or ranging, consistent or inconsistent. We identify what the consistency characteristics are. Once armed with this information we have a formula for monitoring the rhythm of the market. When this changes it signals that the interaction of supply and demand that has animated investor appetites has changed. We must then reassess our investment strategy.

CONCLUSION

No one method can be relied upon to frame our analysis of and participation in markets. A holistic approach where we are sensitive to fundamental considerations, aware of the effect on prices of liquidity, cognisant of the trajectory of governance and where we adopt a dispassionate interpretation of price action puts us in the strongest possible position to profit from financial markets.

When all four of these factors fall into place, when a major theme is developing and value is accruing, when liquidity is becoming more available, when the trajectory of governance is turning upwards and when the pattern of price action dictates that an asset is under accumulation, then we are presented with a high probability candidate for a trend running strategy that can persist for a number of years and possibly even decades.

CHAPTER 2:

CHART READING VERSUS TECHNICAL ANALYSIS

What we will cover in this chapter

- Technical analysis and chart reading are very often confused but are in fact two separate disciplines.

- Chart reading looks on price action as a reflection of how supply and demand are interacting, tells us which is dominant and allows us to imply the actions, objectives, motivations of market participants.

- Technical analysis looks at the relationship of price to itself and attempts to identify patterns to take advantage of.

- Chart reading allows us to take a dispassionate view of the market, enabling us to tailor our approach to the reality provided by the market and script how trends will eventually end.

DROWNING IN INDICATORS

I BEGAN MY CAREER IN THE FINANCIAL INDUSTRY as an account manager at Bloomberg, primarily covering the Netherlands, Belgium and Luxembourg from London. The team I was initially part of was mostly comprised of people who had previously worked in the fixed income sector either as traders or salespeople. On my first day they sat me down in front of the Bloomberg terminal and a pile of bond math manuals and told me to start reading and playing with the system. As you can imagine, bond math is a fairly dry subject and when I got to reverse repo calculation they told me I had covered enough. I spent the next couple of weeks getting to know the system and happened upon the charting package.

This was a revelatory moment. While I initially found the figures presented on the various calculators and spreadsheets to be fairly esoteric, the charts of price action appeared to be a language that contained discrete information if only I could learn to interpret it. I took on the task of learning about every available indicator in an effort to broaden my knowledge and to satisfy my intellectual curiosity. I quickly became known as someone who could talk to clients and answer their questions about technical analysis.

I subsequently went on to teach seminars all over Europe on the use of technical indicators and have to admit to feeling quite satisfied with myself, at least initially. However, after a while clients began to ask what seemed like an awkward question: "Why?" Why does technical analysis work?

This presented me with a problem because while I knew how to employ various indicators I could not explain why the vast majority of them worked. I began to whittle down the number of indicators I was willing to talk about to those I could explain in a rational, coherent way. The result was that having had an arsenal of almost a hundred indicators, I was left with a bare handful I felt could be explained in clear simple terms without relying on some abstract theory.

I was becoming disillusioned with the whole subject and began to think that I was wasting my time. A turning point in my analysis came when I met David Fuller in

2003. His focus on chart-reading rather than indicators was a light-bulb moment for me. His description of indicators as psychological crutches upon which we come to rely resonated with my experience of the field. His core belief that everything we need to know about supply and demand is right there on the chart if we are willing to allow ourselves to see it reawakened the passion I felt when I saw my first chart.

I had tried just about every technical indicator from momentum trackers to oscillators, from Elliott Wave to Fibonacci to DeMark and found them all wanting. They seemed to work some of the time and not others and I could not explain why. Some were better in a trending environment while others were better used in a range. Some were more reliable than others because of popularity. But none gave me a sense that I could rely on them. I even tried using them in conjunction so that if three indicators gave me a signal I would place greater significance on that. Still my results did not satisfy. Today, of all the technical indicators out there, the only one I use with any kind of regularity is the 200-day moving average (MA) because it represents the trend mean. The closest thing we have to a natural law of physics in the market is that when prices become wildly overextended relative to the trend mean, they will revert back towards the mean in due course. The 200-day MA is also one of the most widely used indicators and therefore often represents a self-fulfilling prophecy. For example, investors will be looking for support or resistance to be encountered in the region of the MA so they will adjust their actions to allow for such an eventuality. This simply increases the likelihood of its happening. In the fixed income futures and currency markets widely regarded Fibonacci levels have a somewhat similar influence.

RHYTHMS OF THE MARKET

As we approach the subject of chart reading it is important to accept that the interpretation of price action while useful is not a panacea. We can observe that the rhythm of a chart will persist until it breaks down and can tailor our investment strategy accordingly but it will not tell us at what level a market will eventually top or bottom. Nothing else can give us that information either. In an effort to increase certainty many people's first instinct when they consider price action is to think of it as a complicated subject. The first thing they want to do is draw trend lines or break up the data into what they consider manageable chunks. Still others deliberately complicate the subject in order to create the illusion that they have some privileged piece of knowledge they will share with you for a price. Others will complicate the subject in order to help justify their positions at financial firms. The reality David Fuller has expounded for nearly 50 years is that price action is simply the interaction of supply and demand. Nothing more than the price action is required in order to comprehend how the forces of supply and demand are aligned. Once we understand this we are in a better position to frame our interaction with the market.

While Benjamin Graham (1894–1976) could never be considered a chart reader, his thoughts on the complication of analysis (taken from *The Intelligent Investor*) are equally relevant here:

> "Mathematics is ordinarily considered as producing precise and dependable results; but in the stock market the more elaborate and abstruse the mathematics the more uncertain and speculative are the conclusions we draw there from. In forty-four years of Wall Street experience and study I have never seen dependable calculations made about common stock values or related investment policies that went beyond simple arithmetic or the most elementary algebra. Whenever calculus is brought in, or higher algebra, you could take it as a warning that the operator was trying to substitute theory for experience, and usually also to give to speculation the deceptive guise of investment."

When supply and demand are in balance markets range. When there is a difference between supply and demand prices trend until they come back into balance. We can observe this drama unfold via price charts. The dominance of demand over supply that creates an uptrend can just as easily be considered in terms of crowd psychology as an idea captures the imagination of ever more people and influences their actions. Every market is a crowd and while every crowd is different they all have common characteristics. By acquainting ourselves with the idiosyncrasies of the crowd we can measure our actions to the rhythm of that market.

THE AESTHETIC CASE

Most people are familiar with David Attenborough's documentaries or scenes from *Mutual of Omaha's Wild Kingdom*, and can envisage a herd of thousands of wildebeest flowing across the Serengeti in a mass migration. Such a sight offers a true sense of nature's wonder but it is also one of the best examples of crowd psychology at work.

Some might find it odd to have the financial markets described in aesthetic terms because they are more familiar with the venality of a certain class of banker or are disgruntled with having to foot the bill for various bailouts. However, there is unquestionable beauty in the way an idea captures the imagination of the investment crowd. If an investor can identify the market with the most aesthetic attributes, such as a clear trend of demand dominance coupled with improving governance and abundant liquidity, they are considerably more likely to profit from their participation than might otherwise be the case.

There is no denying that just as with the wildebeest, being a part of the investment horde can at times be a stressful experience. Individuals can get hot under the collar. It's hard to think straight when everyone around us is rushing towards some half-imagined goal. The precipice is difficult to visualise when all that one is presented with are other people heading in the same direction. We need to participate with the crowd if we are going to profit from it, but wouldn't it be better to adopt the position of the naturalist who is ready to get into the thick of the crowd dynamic but who can hold his own emotional participation in check?

Once we develop a sense of what to look for in a chart pattern, the simple truth that a beautifully trending market is easier to make money from than a violent choppy range becomes self-evident. Once we can identify the beauty and consistency of a well-defined uptrend then we are presented with an excellent opportunity to make money from a trend-running strategy over the medium to longer term.

For instance, compare the performance of Singapore's stock market index between 2003 and 2008 with its performance between 2008 and 2012. Ask yourself which market you find more attractive to look at. Then ask yourself which would have been easier to make money from.

Singapore Straits Times Index 2001–2007

Singapore Straits Times Index 2007–2013

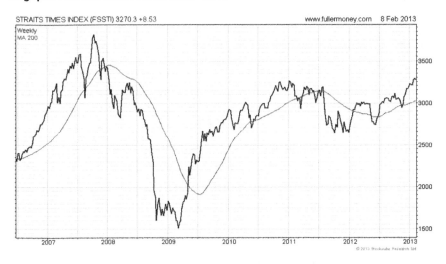

The period between 2003 and 2008 was remarkable for the consistency of the advance until the big pullback in late 2007. All one would have had to do was be invested to have made money. The subsequent period is completely different. There have been wild swings, huge volatility and lengthy ranging. The most nimble traders made money but investors have had a more difficult time. If we pursue a trend-running strategy we seek out the instruments with the most beautiful trends, hold them as long as they remain beautiful and move onto the next opportunity when their beauty fades.

It might not seem sporting but when investing, we all like to shoot fish in a barrel. We set out with the full intention of betting on the favourite because that is what has the greatest potential for making money. (This is where investing and gambling differ sharply.) Chart reading is not an intellectually difficult subject but it is emotionally subtle. It is easy to speak of such events but it is more difficult to put into practice because of the relationship we develop with our investments and the reliance we form on a market that has performed well for us. This is why we need to develop a disciplined approach to interpreting price action that relies on facts rather than esoteric theories.

DISCIPLINED AND RESPONSIVE INTERPRETATION

Price action tells us everything we need to know about the interaction of supply and demand. However, the interpretation of that information requires that we allow ourselves to become responsive to the cues offered by a chart. Long-term price charts demonstrate the movement of investment crowds in and out of markets. The evidence of accumulation and distribution of positions is evident in price history if we have the humility to recognise it without super-imposing our own assumptions. From the perspective of an investor, what we would call a beautiful chart will show a clear pattern of demand dominance that is recognisable from a quick first impression.

Japanese yen / US dollar 2008–2013

This chart represents the Japanese yen / US dollar cross rate. The yen trended higher against the dollar from 2007 until 2011. This trend was characterised by a series of ranges one above another. When the rate became overextended relative to the trend mean, a range ensued which allowed it to catch up. On pullbacks it found support in the region of the MA before rallying once more. This rhythmic pattern of demand dominance over a number of years changed in 2012.

The yen's strength over a number of years was progressively eroding the competitiveness of Japan's export sector, which was crying out for assistance. In early 2012 the yen posted its biggest decline in years. This move was clearly different to what had occurred previously because it was the first occasion that the rate failed to find support in the region of the trend mean. It subsequently failed to push back above it on a sustained basis. These two factors clearly signalled that the previous rhythm of the market had changed. The break below 0.012 in late 2012 confirmed the beginning of a new downtrend.

The evidence of change in the relationship between supply and demand is there on this chart if we allow ourselves to see it. However, when we have positions in a market which has rewarded us the temptation to see what we want or expect is intense. Therefore we need to develop a disciplined approach so that we can identify technical facts about how supply and demand are interacting before attempting to draw conclusions. Once we have facts, we can be responsive by assessing the maturity of the market via filter questions, and then decide whether the trend remains in motion or if there is evidence of trend-ending characteristics.

There wouldn't be a market without people so we should at minimum apprise ourselves of the characteristics common to every crowd regardless of class, race, colour or creed. Learning to spot extremes of emotion, the loss of a critical perspective, idolisation of the investment and other cues are invaluable in identifying major top and bottom characteristics. Equally important is how we are affected by the psychology of the crowd once we participate with it. Knowing ourselves and how we react to predictable stimuli is essential if we are to navigate our way to a wealthier future.

THE FINAL ARBITER

Chart-reading is an invaluable tool as part of a holistic approach to investing. As we develop sensitivity to themes capable of motivating investor interest and which have a solid fundamental basis, where we assess whether liquidity is expanding or contracting and whether the trajectory of governance is progressing or regressing, price action is the final arbiter. Dispassionate analysis will help us to identify investment opportunities, entry and exit points, major tops and bottoms. However the mental stability necessary to hold a position, maintain money control discipline and the strength of character to exit at an appropriate time are equally important attributes which need to be fostered if we are to be well-rounded, wealthy investors.

CHAPTER 3:

GROUP FORMATION (ME + THEM = US)

What we will cover in this chapter:

- The market is a mob. All mobs are psychological groups and have common characteristics. In this chapter we will look at the psychological conditioning that must occur for a group to form.

- *Fellow feeling* – the members have something in common and the group coalesces around this idea.

- *Segregation* – the 'you are either with us or against us' response.

- *Responsibility* – shared responsibility diminishes personal culpability for our actions.

- *Heightened emotional state* – we attend sports and music events because they produce a greater sense of occasion and more intense atmosphere than simply sitting at home. When we initiate investment positions there is no way to avoid the emotional intensity of the market.

- *Contagion* – if laughter is infectious so are fear, greed and anxiety.

- *Suggestion* – the temptation to believe that 'if it says it in the newspaper it must be true'.

I FIRST READ SIGMUND FREUD'S *Group Psychology and the Analysis of the Ego* (1922) at university, and while it resonated with me it wasn't until I stood on a trading floor for the first time that the principles came to life.

I realised that the market crowd was an identifiable, discrete grouping whose motivations and actions could be analysed if only I had the correct tools. I later came into contact with price charts and soon realised I had found the cipher which would allow me to interpret the emotions driving the crowd. The behavioural technical analysis pioneered by David Fuller opens up a great deal of additional information about the actions and motivations of market participants that would not otherwise be so accessible.

The crowd *is* the market. At important peaks and troughs the market is a mob. If we are to profit, we must participate with the mob but also be aware of how the mob affects us. When we do not have a position we have greater objectivity because we are analysing the behaviour of the crowd from the perspective of an outsider. When we take a position, regardless of whether it is long or short, our objectivity is compromised because we are no longer passive observers. We have a vested interest in the outcome.

In order to foster a disciplined approach we must equip ourselves with an understanding of some of the key factors evident in crowd formation. We will then be in a better position to recognise the changes in our own psychology that occur when we join a group. Becoming part of any group comes with advantages and disadvantages, depending on one's point of view. But every group formation shares similar characteristics.

FELLOW FEELING

Compromise is associated with the formation of all crowds. In order to cede personal authority to the group, the potential psychological rewards must be compelling. In the financial world the potential for financial rewards is also important. While taking a maverick approach to life and investing has the potential for reward, the lowest perception of risk and surest form of survival is to submit to societal norms which in turn entail compromise. In order for the group to form, the members must submit to a common purpose.

Regardless of what we decide to buy, the choice of instrument is a relative value decision. By backing one investment vehicle over another we are at once indicating that we believe the bullish case for this vehicle is more compelling than others. We obviously want to see it do well, but also to do better than other competing investments. This basic mechanism allows us to share a common and self-reinforcing bond with the other members of that investment community. William McDougall proposes a common-sense explanation of how a group forms in book *The Group Mind* (1920):

> " … these individuals must have something in common with one another, a common interest in an object, a similar emotional bias in some situation or other, and … some degree of reciprocal influence. The higher the degree of 'this mental homogeneity', the more readily do the individuals form a psychological group … "

A crowd always coalesces around a unifying idea. This can include religions, sports teams, musical genres or asset classes. A group can form around a person such as in a political party or when a person embodies an ideal. All groups, irrespective of the motivating idea, share common characteristics which we will deal with in a moment, but a sense of fellow feeling is the basic condition that must be met before these become relevant.

SEGREGATION

Talk to a teenager about music and they will wax lyrical about how inspired they are by the bands they admire. In the next breath they will tell you how the fans of other musicians are simply not the kind of people one should want to be associated with. Segregation is also widely observable in religion, where the advocates of one belief system believe wholeheartedly that the followers of another are at best worthy of pity. At worst, wars have been fought about such differences of opinion.

A crowd shares a common belief and its members differentiate themselves from others by being loyal to their fellows while highlighting the failings of those who are not members. This is equally observable in the financial markets. In a bull market, investors will very often refuse to accept the opinion of anyone other than someone else who holds long positions. They are just as likely to heap derision on those who express a contrary opinion.

LOWERED SENSE OF PERSONAL RESPONSIBILITY

Most people will have heard the saying 'there is strength in numbers'. This is no less true in the financial markets where 'weight-of-money' confers a perception of strength on a market, not least because prices tend to appreciate. The diminished sense of responsibility for one's actions that invariably becomes part of any crowd formation is abundantly evident in such scenarios.

The burden of decision-making is in part conceded to the crowd persona and the individual feels a sense of liberation. The crowd at once offers a sense of identification and anonymity because we have deferred authority to the group. This lends a sense a freedom while simultaneously requiring greater conformity to the group's accepted norms.

In a bull market, the knowledge that everyone we consider credible is long, acts as a powerful enabler as investors increase the size of their positions even when they know that by the simple law of averages they are closer to the end than they were. Anonymity and the diminished sense of personal responsibility is also empowering because participants have recourse to the ubiquitous 'everyone else was doing it too'. This phenomenon leads to the fund management maxim that the biggest mistake is to be wrong on your own. A common defence during the crash that followed the Lehman Brothers bankruptcy in 2008 was that no one else saw it coming either. This protected the majority from the criticism of their fellows. On the other hand, when a fund goes bust due to the opinions of the manager that ran counter to the mood of the crowd, schadenfreude is rife and ridicule is heaped on the individual concerned from all quarters.

HEIGHTENED EMOTIONAL STATE

Crowds are emotional. As anyone who has ever been at a sports event can attest, there are times when the crowd is relatively quiescent and others when it is particularly active. At a football game, supporters are most likely to be singing or shouting when their team is doing well or on the offensive. They are most reserved when their team has just conceded a goal. Occasionally in the course of any game, someone will attempt to start a chant in support of the team when they think the players need a boost but it will not take hold and quickly peters our. On other occasions, usually when their team is doing well, the chant is readily taken up by all the other supporters of the team. Supporters are often referred to as the *twelfth man* on a football field because of the effect a highly supportive crowd can have on the performance of the team.

These actions are mimicked in the financial markets. The crowd is most quiescent when the market is ranging. They are most likely to be come out in vocal support of the market when it is trending higher. When the market is in a range, occasionally a group of investors will begin buying in anticipation of a successful upward break but do not garner enough support to succeed. On other occasions, investors will begin buying and the market will run away from them as many more bulls join in the advance. When a market accelerates higher investors are forced to act quickly for fear they will need to pay more later. This raises the possibility that rash decisions will be made. The exact same situations occur in reverse during a downtrend.

These examples demonstrate that the crowd is capable of swift emotional shifts from one extreme to another dependent on changes in how the object around which the group has coalesced is perceived. In the financial markets, the fact that the crowd is driving prices onwards to new highs or lows has a transformational effect on sentiment, magnifying the emotional intensity of the crowd and attracting increasing numbers of investors into the bullish camp.

CONTAGION

Laughter is said to be infectious. Fear is often not only intoxicating but also contagious. In just the same way bullishness and bearishness are contagious. The contagion of emotional states contributes to the formation and growth of psychological groups.

Contagion is the *unconscious* transmission of an emotional state to another person. Of course, the more people feel the same emotion, the greater the effect on a single individual who comes into contact with the crowd. Here is Freud on the subject:

> "The greater the number of people in whom the same emotion can be simultaneously observed, the stronger does this automatic compulsion grow … lets himself slip into the same emotion. But in so doing he increases the excitement of the other people, who had produced this effect upon him, and thus the emotional charge of the individuals becomes intensified by mutual interaction … The coarser and simpler emotions are the more apt to spread through a group in this way."

An example most of us will be familiar with from the news is of a peaceful protest that turns violent and morphs into a riot. The diminished sense of responsibility will certainly play a part but the fact that individuals often end up doing things they would never contemplate in the course of their everyday lives and that their actions encourage the same attitude in others is evidence of contagion. Contagion is also readily observed in children when they feel distress because another child is crying or when we smile when we see someone else smiling.

Have you ever wondered why at a concert some people feel an uncontrollable urge to clear their throats? We might spend the whole day without sniffling but sit in a packed auditorium during a symphony and as soon as one person clears their throat there will invariably be a succession of additional people who feel the same compunction.

Another example of contagion at work is that if my neighbour leverages up to buy a second or third home, my perception of the risk attached to such an action diminishes.

If their actions are subsequently seen to have been correct then the perception of risk declines even further.

SUGGESTION

If contagion can be viewed as the unintentional swaying of someone else's emotional state then suggestion is similar but *intentional*. Stage hypnotists and magicians make abundant use of suggestion to awaken a desired response from the subject using unconscious cues. Advertising and marketing by definition seek to instil an attitude with regard to a product that one might not arrive at without it.

Any of us who have ever been involved in a bull market will have met, and to our chagrin might even have turned into, an investor turned proselytiser. This person will invariably have done well from an investment and will want to spread the benefit of their assumed foresight, knowledge and intuition to as wide an audience as possible. This might occur for the cynical reason of attempting to talk-up a losing position but more often it is because of an overinflated ego seeking to bask in the attention of others. In the investment sphere, while one might not like or believe this person, the very fact they are talking up the merits of an investment contributes to our own conditioning process. This evolution of a bullish or bearish attitude is compounded by the very real price action.

In the investment industry, suggestion is manifested by newspaper articles, blogs, financial TV channels, direct advertising, sponsorship of sports events etc. It is in every firm's interests to convince as many investors as possible to use their services. Where they are not outright attempting to sell an investment product they are often attempting at the very least to promote a positive attitude toward the company and its products or to foster a brand image. The suggestive qualities of advertising and marketing work on many different levels, ranging from selling products directly to product awareness.

The common perception of hypnosis is of the trance-like state where the subject gives over cognitive function to the hypnotist. However, hypnosis is not limited to this stereotype and skilled practitioners can implant suggestive cues in a subject's unconscious without their conscious knowledge. While this exact process does not take place in the financial markets, an approximation is evident in the attitude of investors to financial products.

We are more likely to accept suggestion when we are relaxed, comfortable and trusting. A stage hypnotist will emphasise that being hypnotised is a talent, stroking the ego of the subject. He will seek to build a rapport with the subject. Every business is focused on creating exactly the same conditions for potential customers. Sir John Templeton astutely identified the methods for retaining clients in a 1953 memo by saying:

"the influences on the psychological attitudes, decisions and beliefs of human beings are 90 per cent subconscious and only 10 per cent logical"

and

"it is human to be subconsciously influenced by appearances. Those banks which inhabit marble palaces usually attract the most customers ... The feeling of optimism and prosperity is contagious. The counsellor whose manner and words reflect uncertainty or disappointment will quickly give the same feeling to the client; and the counsellor whose manner and words reflect confidence and prosperity will quickly give the feeling of confidence to the client"
(both quoted in *Financial Times*, 18 April 2010).

In the investment industry, firms tend to emphasise their exclusivity, longevity, trustworthiness, expertise and responsibility in order to build trust and encourage potential customers to feel confident in handing over their savings. Showing off the accumulation of wealth helps firms to project that image of success to clients and bolsters the implication that they can do the same for you too.

In the modern age, investors are bombarded with information. Never have we had access to so much information and never has there been such a variety of investment products. Rationally, we know that the performance of investment products and investment managers focused on a particular market fits easily within a bell curve, with 10% outperforming impressively, 10% underperforming dismally and the rest somewhere in between. Even though the more important decision is which asset class of sector to invest in rather than the exact investment vehicle, investment companies spend a great deal of time and money attempting to sway investor attitudes in their favour. The same can be said of major household brands such as Coca-Cola. The reason they follow such aggressive marketing strategies is because they have been demonstrated to be effective in promoting a positive image of a product among current and potential consumers.

In summary, psychological groups form by coalescing around a shared attitude to an idea or object. The group offers the individual comfort by providing a lowered sense of personal responsibility. Attitudes towards the object or idea are magnified through processes of contagion and suggestion. The process of group formation is greatly enhanced by momentum in favour of the prevailing sentiment.

Having equipped ourselves with the characteristics of how groups form, we are in a better position to identify these influences on our own decision-making.

CHAPTER 4:

HOW THE CROWD INFLUENCES
OUR PERSONAL PSYCHOLOGY

What we will cover in this chapter:

- As a market move matures, the prevailing mood of the crowd intensifies. It exerts an increasingly powerful influence on our emotions. This creates a strong temptation to dispense with rational analysis and indulge in emotional responses to market events.

- Coincidence of contradictory ideas – 'earnings don't matter', 'everyone can hedge default risk', 'property prices only go up' and 'a currency union can function with one monetary policy and 17 fiscal policies' are all examples of where contradiction was not only evident in the financial markets but characterised the prevailing mood of the bull market prior to a crash.

- Crowds respect force – if you want to influence the market or make a name for yourself you need to make very bold forecasts in line with the trend in order to animate the crowd.

- Facts are unimportant to groups – crowds are emotional and therefore are much more likely to accept any idea that makes them feel better regardless of whether it is true or not.

JUST AS EVERY GROUP IS FORMED by the same process of empathy, identification, and shared purpose the characteristics of each crowd share important similarities. Writers in the 19th century such as Gustave Le Bon (1841–1931) and William McDougall (1871–1938) were heavily influenced by the events of their time and made liberal use of examples focusing on war and religion to illustrate the difference between what one is capable of in isolation versus as part of a group. They both tended to emphasise the base elements of the group persona because they had numerous examples to back up their theories.

History is replete with examples both of soldiers' heroism and degradation; sometimes in the same person. In the normal course of civilian life, one would never expect to experience such remarkable extremes of emotion. As an individual we would never commit actions that a crowd is capable of. The group contributes to an altered psychological state in the individual.

The same is true of how investors can act, particularly in major bull and bear markets or when using leverage. People take risks with their investment positions they would never normally countenance in their daily lives. They can experience the towering self-confidence of a winning position, terror of a sudden loss or the despondency of a losing position. Investors are not only capable of such varying emotional states but these are inextricably entwined in the psychological processes that come with participating in a group.

CROWDED OUT

If groups or crowds are capable of thoughts and actions not normally available to individuals, the question arises as to whether such extreme emotional states are common to all groups or do they differ depending on the members? Viewed from a certain perspective no two crowds are the same. The church-goer, soldier, concert-goer and football fan are all different manifestations of members of completely homogenous crowds but each of these groups share common characteristics. There is no contradiction in the fact that a single person can be a member of a number of distinct crowds. Any one of us can be a football fan, concert-goer and investor, giving emphasis to one or the other as required.

Here is Freud expressing his view of the individual in a crowd:

> "His emotions become extraordinarily intensified, while his intellectual ability becomes markedly reduced, both processes being evidently in the direction of an approximation to the other individuals in the group; and this result can only be reached by the removal of those inhibitions upon his instincts which are peculiar to each individual, and by his resigning those expressions of his inclinations which are especially his own."

These examples focus on the extremes of emotion evident in crowds. While the individual is capable of moderation, the group only responds to absolutes. The group exaggerates the original common attitude towards the object so that the members are transported to an ever-more intense emotional state. From the perspective of an investor, the extent to which one becomes immersed in the emotional life of the crowd will be dependent on the number of participants in the move, size of position relative to one's overall capital and leverage. If the move is relatively small or occurs intraday on an unleveraged position the effect on the crowd's mood is not going to be as strong as when the move has been going on for years, one's position is large relative to one's capital and leverage has been employed to multiply the potential return.

The intensification of emotion among the crowd is often indicative of how long or short they have become as more and more people align themselves with the prevailing trend. This is useful information but needs to be combined with additional factors if we are to base contrarian trading activity upon it. A quip attributed to John Meynard Keynes is apt in such a situation: "The market can stay irrational longer than you can stay solvent." The crowd is capable of moving to emotional extremes well beyond the imagination of the rational individual; often to such an extent that they begin to question whether it is they that are irrational and the crowd rational. Major bull and bear markets offer clear examples of where crowds can move to increasingly extreme attitudes and persist in such a manner for a prolonged period of time. The Nasdaq bubble, China's Shanghai A-Share Index, uranium prices, Saudi Arabia's stock market and various credit bubbles are examples from just the last decade.

As investors we seek to identify trends as they develop, implement trend-following strategies for as long as they remain consistent and aim to exit when they become inconsistent. Intellectually, this is a relatively simple formula but it proves to be emotionally subtle. Extremes of crowd sentiment are invaluable tools in the analyst's arsenal but crowds have a number of additional characteristics worth examining.

COINCIDENCE OF CONTRADICTORY IDEAS

People in groups are capable of believing wholeheartedly in quite contradictory ideas. By way of explanation let us examine the case of a new investor in the latter stages of a major bull market. This person might know they are not coming in early but they will often be thinking more of the personal benefit of participating in a market that is going to change the world rather than how they are going to sell.

During the dissection of the tech bubble, denigrators of the market latched onto and poured ridicule on the phrase which had been used to justify high share prices for low-functioning dotcom businesses at the time – 'earnings don't matter'. This phrase became synonymous with the psychology of the crowd that had allowed the bubble to inflate. As rational individuals we can look back today and think how silly the notion was – how could a company possibly survive with no product or customers and very little prospect of acquiring either? However, at the time no one was interested in such boring details as today's earnings because they were investing in dreams which were much more alluring. The fact remains that in the latter stages of a bull market people can quite easily hold two contradictory ideas without conflict for as long as the good news keeps coming. Here is Freud on the subject:

> "In groups the most contradictory ideas can exist side by side and tolerate each other, without any conflict arising from the logical contradiction between them. But this is also the case in the unconscious mental life of individuals, of children and of neurotics, as psycho-analysis has long pointed out."

During the credit boom that occurred between 2002 and 2007 the prevailing psychology could be summarised as 'risk doesn't matter'. Logically, if one keeps moving down the rating ladder in search of yield, one is by definition taking on more risk and the likelihood of experiencing a default rises. Rationally, we know that if we package together lots of mortgages that have little-to-no chance of ever being paid back, the risk attached to the mid to lower tranches increases rather than decreases. However, investors had been harvesting yield from lower quality instruments for a number of years and the prices for those vehicles had continued to go up so that spreads contracted even further.

The strategy had been demonstrated to work repeatedly and those who participated outperformed in no uncertain terms. Prospectuses stated the risks involved, particularly with the more exotic or esoteric collateralised debt obligations (CDOs), but investors either did not read them or dismissed the risk as the compulsory blurb that had to gloss all such vehicles. We can look back at these investment decisions and wonder how anyone could have bought such obvious garbage. But the lure of the prevailing sentiment at the time, as well as the very real career risk of avoiding such instruments, was powerfully in favour of ignoring the risk for the very real immediate profits. Again, two contradictory ideas existed side by side for as long as the good news lasted.

The exact same process is evident during bear markets. During the stock market collapse following the Lehman Brothers bankruptcy more than one pundit trumpeted the end of financial markets. Rationally we know that the stock market is a discounting mechanism and the farther an instrument's price falls the more of it we can buy. Abrupt panicky selloffs invariably create sound long-term buying opportunities. But that is not at all apparent to most investors when the decline is occurring. The contradiction of impending doom and accruing value exist together for as long as the prevailing bearish sentiment is dominant.

As a predictive measure, identifying contradiction can be a powerful harbinger of future opportunity. For example, at the time of writing the market is busy exploring the contradiction of the euro: that a currency union can exist with 16 different fiscal policies and no effective policing mechanism. This inconsistency was identified repeatedly before the currency came into being but a decade passed before the prevailing crowd sentiment was tested by the profligacy of the eurozone's banking sector and a number of peripheral countries.

Contradiction, then, is a common characteristic of financial market crowds. Identifying the inconsistency in the bullish or bearish argument holds the key to the rationale behind how the prevailing trend will eventually end. However, contradiction is not a timing tool. The crowd can persist in accepting a contradiction for a prolonged period. This is one reason why price charts are invaluable. They offer a window on the actions of the crowd. When the consistency of the chart changes, the crowd is changing and this is something we can use to our advantage.

CROWDS RESPECT FORCE

Anyone who has participated in the markets for any period of time will have noticed, particularly on financial TV stations, that analysts and pundits tend to compete with each other for the most bullish or bearish forecast. Anyone seeking to make a name for themselves or to drum up investor interest in their particular fund will invariably be successful by seeking to be the biggest bull or the biggest bear in the market. If one analyst says a share is going to fall 10% and another claims 20% and the share is still falling, the analyst saying it will go to zero will often get most attention of all.

This is one way of gaining more attention for themselves, but there will often also be the added motivation of attempting to help a position along by garnering more adherents. The most cynical will come out with major bullish or bearish forecast in order to liquidate their own position on favourable terms having encouraged new entrants to participate in line with the prevailing mood. Here is Freud on how to influence the crowd:

> "Anyone who wishes to produce an effect upon it needs no logical adjustment in his arguments; he must paint in the most forcible colours, he must exaggerate, and he must repeat the same thing again and again."

A clear example of someone painting in very bold colours indeed was Charles W. Kadlec's September 1999 book, *Dow 100,000*, which was hailed as prophecy by an adoring market crowd at the time. Similarly, when gold first moved to new highs in 2006 some of the more enthusiastic commentators predicted $10,000 as a potential peak price.

At major tops massive extrapolations of the prevailing trend are a necessary part of the psychological fuel that motivates new buyers to participate at already elevated prices. They will need to believe that prices are not only going to go up 10% but 100% in order for them to justify buying. During a major market bottom, progressively bearish extrapolations of the prevailing downtrend are necessary in order to create a state of such despondency among stale bulls that they feel compelled to liquidate their positions.

In both cases, by the time analysts are competing with each other for the most extreme view, it is almost invariably a signal that the move is in its latter stages because such extremes of emotion are not sustainable beyond the short term.

FACTS ARE UNIMPORTANT TO GROUPS

"Groups have never thirsted after truth. They demand illusions, and cannot do without them. They constantly give what is unreal precedence over what is real; they are almost as strongly influenced by what is untrue as by what is true."

– Sigmund Freud

In the aftermath of any major market burst commentators invariably talk about the irrationality of the bubble period and how if only investors would behave in a rational manner they would not get into these messes in the first place. However, groups are not rational entities. They are ruled by the raw emotions of the members. These are invariably reduced to a common denominator, resulting in only the basest of feelings having any effect on the mental life of the group. As the ashes of a bubble are picked through, there are a number of idioms which return to common parlance. Some of these are that the 'bull market was built on a lie' or that 'every big bull market hides a big crime'.

What in the end are heralded as the lies we allowed ourselves to believe during the bubble years never seemed so at the time. Regardless of how compelling the original story which helped fuel the bull market that morphed into a bubble, the reality couldn't possibly have hoped to fulfil the ambitions of the participants. As with any other part of our lives the Platonic ideal is unattainable. Investors who lost money in the inevitable bust will feel cheated. They will have bought into a dream, allowed hopes to soar and indulged their greed only for it all to be revealed as ethereal. When the internet investment bubble burst, the sector had succeeded in changing the world, so the promise was not entirely a lie. However, the investment implications of having bought in the latter stages, failing to identify the topping characteristics which were evident, was to have bought into the belief that all dotcom stock prices could only go up. In its simplest sense this is a lie that is common to every investment mania regardless of asset class.

The cynicism of the investor who has lost money as a result of a bull market rolling over into a bear market is often reinforced by the inevitable crimes that come to light following a bust. It is not too difficult to understand how crimes can go unnoticed during a boom: everyone is making money and the motivation to question is diminished. In such circumstances criminals who are not playing by the rules can continue for quite a long time before they are discovered. Traders who have undeclared losses, those running Ponzi schemes or exploiting the gullibility of investors all attract much greater scrutiny when the credit on which their models rely disappears or voters start pressuring politicians to find someone to blame.

When society at large accepts the prevailing emotional state of the crowd, people are less likely to question and more likely to accept conjecture as truth. In the latter stages of such a phase more than a few will have succumbed to an extreme emotional state and have paid little attention to the inconsistencies that will later become obvious in the bullish argument.

In a bear market we know for a fact that since prices are falling, the instrument is by definition getting cheaper. We could argue about whether one is getting additional value following the bust by buying, but an incontrovertible truth is that the farther something falls the closer it is to the bottom. Nevertheless, a large fall engenders a more pronounced bearishness among investors. Things are rarely quite as bad as some of the most vociferous bears claim. However, holders of stock often liquidate their positions in anticipation of even deeper losses. Those who have already sold are emotionally invested in seeing the market fall further to prove their actions right. Short sellers are financially invested in prices falling even further. However, we know for a categorical fact that very few instruments actually go to zero. Meanwhile the bottom is closer than it was before.

CONCLUSION

Crowds are fickle, emotional, aggressive, gullible, accepting of contradiction, irrational, extreme and can only be swayed by considerable force. However, if we are to participate in the financial markets we have to accept the likelihood that we will experience some or all of these states and rise to the challenge of identifying them in ourselves as they appear.

CHAPTER 5:

GREED, FEAR AND LOVE –
DEVELOPING EMOTIONAL INTELLIGENCE

What we will cover in this chapter:

- If we can become wedded to an idea we can form relationships with our investments.

- The vast majority of financial commentary concentrates on emotions such as greed and fear because they fit succinctly into a simplistic characterisation of investor actions. However, *love* is the only emotion that comes close to describing the relationship we can develop with our investments.

- Love answers the question of why it is so exciting to buy and so difficult to sell.

- The 'jilted lover' explains the ambivalence people feel towards a market they have been disappointed by. Having once been rewarded for faithfulness, we are punished for holding on. We then take the opposite position and hope for a negative outcome.

- If love can be described as putting someone else's interests ahead of our own then panic occurs when we return to a purely self-interested state.

- Self-recrimination is manifested in every major decline and is amplified by the size of the loss endured. While the most rational approach is to reform our own character, the emotional response is to spray blame around and most particularly on anything associated with the instrument that has proved to be such a disappointment.

THE AGONIES OF THE LOVESTRUCK

IN 2008, A DELEGATE AT ONE OF MY SEMINARS mentioned that he finds it much more difficult to sell than to buy. He said that when he opens positions it is usually with an enthusiastic opinion of the future but when they don't work out he dithers and ends up holding them indefinitely. Most people will understand this issue, so let's work through the emotional cues that create this phenomenon.

A running discussion is evident in the financial media about whether greed or fear is the more powerful emotion in the markets. Both are important powerful emotions we need to hold in check if we are to maintain our emotional equilibrium, but understanding love is, I believe, more important. Love offers a more accurate description of how we deal with both conditions because like it or not, we often end up in a relationship with our investments.

Love is exciting. When we begin a new relationship, we wish to spend more time with the other person, we hang on their every word, we idealise their good points and ignore their shortcomings. We are willing to tolerate failings and mistreatment at the hands of the other person we would not tolerate in normal circumstances. Love gives us all we need as long as it lasts.

Love can also be unnerving. Our sense of insecurity can increase and we can strive for the approval of our loved ones. We can overcompensate in our desire to fix a problem. When we fall out of love, revenge, spite, schadenfreude and depression are common emotional responses.

The 'loved object' for an investor will always be an investment vehicle and the development of a sentimental attitude towards it is an important subject. If one doubts that one can love an object, think of the love some men have for their cars or the love some women have for their shoes and bags. In the same way that we build up emotional ties with objects we are in frequent contact with, we can all too easily develop similar ties to our investments.

HOW DOES THIS TYPE OF ATTACHMENT DEVELOP?

This attachment develops because trading and investing is an uncertain profession. We constantly lurch from confidence to self-doubt depending on the success of our positions. We all know there is no such thing as the perfect investment but that does not stop us wishing that whatever we buy only goes up and whatever we sell only goes down. And there is a strong temptation to compensate for this uncertainty by imposing the emotions we wish to feel on the attributes of our investments. Freud refers to this process as "introjection of the object into the ego".

Let us take a simple example of an investor who opens a long position which moves into a profit. We have identified ourselves with the market crowd and with the object by taking up an attitude of bullish appreciation. This process is manifested both by the positive light in which the investment is seen and emotionally by transferring the positive aspects we wish to possess onto the object of our identification. In a bull market, bravery, fortitude, fidelity, strength and consistency are all attributes that we might imagine the investment vehicle to possess because they represent personal attributes within our ego or because they are ideals to which we aspire.

We often refer to our spouse as our 'better half'. This implies that the other person is not only a part of ourselves but that they contain all the attributes we wish we had. In the movie *Jerry Maguire*, Tom Cruise's titular character declares his love for Dorothy (played by Renée Zellweger) by telling her "You complete me". This resonates with many people because it is the translation of a narcissistic wish to be complete. We wish to become whole by absorbing the perceived emotional strengths of a loved object – whether it's a person or an investment.

This explains the love between two people who at first identify a shared attribute and build upon that original identification to form a relationship. An additional perspective is observable in a crowd because the *shared* adoration of the loved object amplifies the feeling of solidarity and permanence.

A PERSONAL EPIPHANY

I have particular sympathy with this interpretation of group formation because I can relate it directly back to my early experience of trading. I was not making money with any kind of regularity and was struggling to improve my performance. I remember clearly when the solution hit me. It felt like an epiphany. David Fuller and I were teaching the Chart Seminar for a bank in Copenhagen, and as I was waiting for my turn to speak I realised I had been treating my positions as if they were my girlfriends.

My analysis had been correct more often than not and my trades tended to do well initially. But when things started to get a bit bumpy I would hang on in the hope it would get better. I only tended to exit the position when there was no chance of the situation improving. I realised that while this might be justified when in a relationship with another person, it was stupid in the case of an investment position. I was allowing my idealised view of my position to override the clear signals presented by the market that I should exit the trade.

Everyone is different, but for me identifying this ambivalence was a major milestone in achieving a better trading record. Perhaps more importantly, I can trace my biggest losses back to occasions when I have allowed myself to regress.

I was allowing the investment to occupy the position of a loved person and I was failing to recognise imperfections in the relationship. The idealisation of the loved object contributes to a sentimental attitude between people but this is not healthy when applied to one's investments. The challenge is that while as a rational being we can differentiate between people and investments, for the unconscious mind the demarcations are much less clear. Emotionally, we want to see our investment do well. We nurture it, hold it, wish for it to do better, brag about it to our friends, imagine its future achievements and attempt to stick with it through thick and thin. All of these aspects could as easily be applied to a loving relationship as to an investment. The problem is that if you stick with an investment through thick and thin you can lose a significant amount of your money.

Delegates at a number of my seminars have related the same experience. They have no problem entering positions and often do so at favourable levels, but have much greater difficulty exiting. Part of the reason for this will be a reluctance to sell for fear of missing out on additional profit. But a greater part will often be related to a reluctance to accept that the consistency characteristics of the investment have deteriorated and the investment has become less likely to recover. The longer someone holds a position, the more reactions within the overall trend endured, the more difficult it is to sell when the trend's characteristics deteriorate. We have unconsciously built up a relationship – albeit one-sided – with the vehicle.

Both the delegates and I have been subject to the same tendency: treating the investment as if it were a person we were in love with. Anthropomorphising an animal in children's fairytales is acceptable in one sense but doing the same thing with a financial instrument is a recipe for trouble.

BEAR MARKETS AND THE JILTED LOVER

The above examination concentrates on one's relationship with an investment in a bull market. Bear markets or short positions also offer ample opportunity to observe love-based crowd formation and dispersion in action. There are some important psychological differences between bull and bear markets not least because the former is an example of group formation while the latter is an example of group dissipation. In the financial markets, as one grouping falls apart another is by definition bonding. The uniting idea of the new group is its shared antipathy towards the original investment vehicle.

A bull market is fuelled by more and more capital being dedicated to whatever the prevailing theme is. The buy and hold investor might not be trading his/her position but this means that they are withholding supply. Others will be coming in to participate in part of the move only to get out and come back in at higher levels, as the bull advances beyond their expectations, so demand is continually renewed. New buyers will be coming in all the time to drive prices higher, and momentum traders will be taking on additional leverage to enhance returns even further. All of this adds up to increasing participation and acceptance of the prevailing bull market hypothesis.

A bear market is driven by investors withdrawing cash from the system. This is initially driven by the prevailing theme losing adherents and an opposing argument gaining devotees. Buy and hold investors initially experience some profit erosion and if they fail to sell will begin to experience larger losses. Profit erosion is emotionally debilitating and the obvious emotional solution is to liquidate a position if it continues to deteriorate. This action turns once-passive supply into active selling pressure which in turn puts even greater pressure on other investors.

PANIC

Over the last decade investors have become familiar with the sensation of panic during major declines. Here is Freud on the nature of panic in the military:

> "A panic arises ... each individual is only solicitous on his own account, and without any consideration for the rest. The mutual ties have ceased to exist, and a gigantic and senseless dread [angst] is set free ... the emotional ties, which have hitherto made the danger seem small to him, have ceased to exist."

A sharp decline can be emotionally debilitating for an investor and it can be difficult to avoid falling into a panic over the difficulty with the position. The process of someone succumbing to panic is best examined by looking at what was occurring to insulate the investor from this emotion in the first place. No one panics when everything is going according to plan. However, when a position goes awry, the bonds holding the crowd together begin to fray and fail. When the sense of comradeship and fellow-feeling that held the group together disappears, and the participant emerges 'newborn' from the group morass to face the market on their own, they are often overcome by no more than the burden of individuality, responsibility and rationality that had been suppressed by being part of the crowd. Their reaction is to panic. The investor who suddenly gains independence from the bullish group has one overriding inclination and that is to sell. The important aspect from an emotional perspective is that the ties holding the crowd together have disappeared.

In a panicky environment market slippage means that stops are often ineffectual because they are triggered well below the desired level. This 'acceleration' is an ending signal because the speed of the activity together with the concentration of emotion expends available supply in a shorter period of time than might have normally been the case.

The act of selling in turn unleashes an array of powerful emotions that tend to make markets fall further. Disappointment will be a primary response, mingled with relief to be free of the stress of a losing position and to have raised relatively secure cash. The investor's emotional capital has been drained and they are less likely to jump straight back into the market, unless compelled to do so by their employer. Even then investors will tend to act more cautiously.

Relief can also quickly give way to the fear that one might have sold at the bottom. Hence the investor who has just liquidated their position becomes emotionally invested in seeing the market fall even further. They become inclined towards a bearish view because it is in line with their own response to the price action.

DEPRESSION AND SELF-RECRIMINATION

Self-recrimination is another powerful emotion which often surfaces during a bear market. A market which had at one time seemed trustworthy and reliable now appears unpredictable, capricious, arbitrary and cruel. Investors will often reflect on the reasons that brought them to such a juncture. Feelings of inadequacy and disillusionment are common. Emotional attachment promoted a sense of security with our investment. The subsequent betrayal of the trust poured into the investment contributes to the change of attitude toward it.

Melancholia is an extreme example of self-recrimination but the inclusion of revenge in the equation offers a valuable window on the attitude presented by investors who have taken a heavy loss during a market decline. The loss has crystallised the investment mistake and illustrated in no uncertain terms how wrong it was to adopt the bullish hypothesis. Here is Freud on the subject of melancholia:

> "A leading characteristic of these cases is a cruel self-depreciation of the ego combined with relentless self-criticism and bitter self reproaches. Analyses have shown that this disparagement and these reproaches apply at bottom to the object and represent the ego's revenge upon it."

People react to personal mistakes in different ways. Perhaps the healthiest way is to assess the analytical and emotional errors that caused the loss and quickly move on.

However, while rationally uncomplicated, this can be an emotionally difficult process. Some people will blame the instrument for their own mistakes, taking revenge upon it rather than reforming their own character. Where once they would have ignored the flaws of the object, now they will accentuate its weaknesses and the prevailing sentiment of the crowd will be dominated by negativity.

Clear examples of a desire for revenge are evident in just about every bear market, particularly when those who profited from being short are portrayed as predators – sharks, wolves or vultures. Notwithstanding the fact that when bull markets fail, crimes perpetrated during the boom years come to light as the supply of credit dries up, the deeply seated search for someone to blame is rooted in a communal desire for revenge upon those who profited from the demise of others. Purveyors of lousy investment vehicles dressed up as bargains bear a great deal of blame for the degree to which financial markets have lost credibility in the last decade, but investors are no less to blame for their own actions since many failed to perform even the most basic due diligence. Theories such as the 'great moderation' (reduced volatility in the business cycle evident between 1987 and 2007) and claims by some politicians that boom and bust had been eliminated have, of course, been shown to be temporary phenomena.

Following any market decline where blame is being hurled about for bad investment decisions, those seen to have profited from everyone else's misery are targeted as enemies of the system. The fact that the bears' strategy has been correct and the bullish argument that has been so wrong, at least in its latter stages, encourages even more stale bulls to liquidate positions and sentiment deteriorates even further.

CONCLUSION

The range of emotions described here is not exhaustive because no two people will have the same experience of emotional intensity. However, we all share enough common characteristics to drive major bull and bear markets. Developing an awareness of the depth of emotion these interactions create is essential if one is to successfully navigate away from the crowd as it reaches a climax of bullish emotion and to spearhead the bullish minority when a nadir of pessimism appears. At Fullermoney, we describe the process through which we first identify the emotional makeup of the market and then assess how we are interacting with it as developing emotional intelligence.

CHAPTER 6:

PSYCHOLOGICAL PERCEPTION STAGES OF BULL AND BEAR MARKETS

What we will cover in this chapter:

Major bull and bear market cycles can be broken down into the psychological perception stages of the move as price action influences investor sentiment.

Disbelief/dismissal – during a base formation, characterised by lengthy ranging following a decline, expectations of upside potential deteriorate. The received wisdom for many people will be that bull markets are gone for good and anyone expressing an optimistic opinion is considered maverick or delusional. To the extent that people have positions, they tend to be small because of the high perception of risk.

Acceptance – prices have been rising for a while and people are beginning to make money. Nothing bolsters a bullish perspective like making money, not least if it is accompanied by relative outperformance. This stage represents when a buy and hold strategy will work best, because tolerating occasional pullbacks will be rewarded with higher prices later.

Euphoria – as a bull market progresses, investor expectations of future upside potential have to increase in order to justify purchases at progressively higher prices. People have to literally buy into the idea that price appreciation is a certainty. This encourages risk-taking and position sizes tend to be large while stops tend to be loose.

The turn – as ever, more people take bigger risks and prices jump higher from an already elevated level. The reservoir of potential demand available to make additional purchases is dissipated so that a point is reached where all that are left are potential sellers. The third stage of the bull market represents the first stage of the new bear market as the ranks of those holding long positions have not considered the possibility that prices could decline.

Acceptance – fear is a much more immediate emotion than greed so prices fall faster than they rise. The emotional response is to doubt, question or stick one's head in the sand. As prices deteriorate decisions are forced on participants and leverage is squeezed out of the system. As prices drop and losses are crystallised everyone gets the message that the bull market is over.

Depression – in the instrument that represented the epicentre of risk during the decline those with short positions will be invested in prices going to zero and those who have taken losses wish that prices would go lower in order to justify their decision to sell. Perceptions of upside potential crater and investors migrate to more interesting markets. The depressed psychological state is consistent with base formation development and will last for as long as it takes for a new demand driven story to evolve.

THE VAST ARRAY OF EMOTIONS that an investor can experience while participating in bull and bear markets will differ from day to day and year to year depending on their personal circumstances. However, emotions tend to follow a reasonably well-defined evolution of steps which can be described both in terms of emotional cues and the interaction of supply with demand. This progression can be monitored by remaining alert to the signals that crowd sentiment provides us through various media channels and through the interpretation of price charts.

Price is a simple but invaluable tool in assessing where perceptions of value lie and is too often ignored by those of a more fundamental or econometric persuasion. A chart of price action distils the bullish and bearish arguments down to the raw interaction between supply and demand. The manner in which these opposing forces interact holds discrete information for those willing to examine it. Charts give the most straightforward depiction of the crowd's mood and are a graphic representation of how the forces of the bears are aligned against the bulls. I put such a high emphasis on chart reading that I believe no decision to buy or sell should be made without first looking at a chart.

David Fuller's unique description of the psychological perception stages of major bull and bear markets has been a highlight of the Chart Seminar since the early 1970s. The reason for this is simple. Too many times we are unaware of how our previous actions affect our perception of the market. How we respond to a situation will be highly dependent on what has already happened. If we form an awareness of the psychological state of the investment crowd we are immediately in a better position to measure our emotional response against it. Since price charts offer the simplest exposition of how supply and demand compete, let's plot the psychological perception stages as they might be seen in the market.

It is not unusual to observe that the biggest bull markets evolve from the lengthiest bear markets and vice versa. Nevertheless, price action is fractal and one can witness the same emotional drama unfolding on a short-term tick chart as a multi-year long-term chart. Position sizing, leverage and the stress of short-term trading amplify the emotional responses of the trader while the investor has more time to deal with the same set of emotions. For the purposes of illustration and in order to throw light on the wealth-transforming potential of major bull and bear markets, I will use medium to longer-term charts in the below examples.

(I) DISBELIEF/DISMISSAL

The first psychological perception stage of a new bull market is disbelief. The previous bear market will have been traumatic for large numbers of investors. A common reaction to such trauma is to swear off investment for a while. No one will be brazen enough to publicly predict that the old highs will ever be regained because they would be ridiculed. People tend to predict what they see, so forecasts are likely to be bearish more often than not and those who are bullish will ring-fence their modest optimism with provisos that the market can advance but only under strict conditions.

Such is the disappointment attached to the end of a bull market that there will usually be a cohort of investors who vow to never again participate in the market. Importantly, all those people who sold on the way down will have a psychological vested interest in the belief that the market will never recover because no one wants to think they sold at or near the bottom.

Following the major decline and subsequent failure to sustain a rally, the only people consistently making money from this market are those shorting rallies. Sentiment will continue to deteriorate as the prevailing attitude to the market is that it is weak or 'has no legs'. Those playing the long side will have to be very nimble to make a profit and the trading tactic will be 'if you see a profit take it' because it is probably going to disappear quickly.

Participation decreases during the ranging, choppy action characteristic of market bottoms because those representing potential demand find it much more difficult to make money. During market bottoms, the speculative component decreases and the demand side is dominated by value investors and contrarians who perceive the market to be cheap. However, those who have sold have no good reason to get back in and the most active participants are short. If participation decreases, the attention of investors is likely elsewhere and interest dissipates. There will probably be another sector or asset class that is doing far better and what is rumbling through a lengthy bear will often decline into relative obscurity.

The accepted wisdom will be that historic highs will never again be reached, and certainly not surpassed. Whatever the investment vehicle is will have been deemed to have become obsolete and investors will look back in disbelief at how they could ever have believed the bullish hype. This will no longer be a front page news story. To the extent that anyone is aware of the market, it will be as a somewhat interested observer but barely as an active party. Demand has hunkered down in the proverbial foxhole and won't come out until it has a good reason.

BASE FORMATION DEVELOPMENT

On a chart the disbelief/dismissal stage is consistent with base formation development. As with the foundation of a building, a base formation is what the subsequent uptrend is built upon and appears to emerge from.

How long the disbelief/dismissal phase takes will depend on two separate factors. The first is that the excesses of the prior bull market will have to be worked through. This can take years but will proceed for as long as it takes people who failed to sell on the way down to liquidate their inventory and accept the loss. Expectations will be low because everyone will have seen that as soon as prices get back up towards the higher side of the base they are quickly stamped back down. However, sooner or later, everyone who wanted to sell will have sold so that the overhang of potential supply above the market will have dissipated. This is a necessary condition for the next bull market to begin.

A corollary is that once everyone has sold and is sitting with their cash, this represents a potential pool of liquidity that will eventually help to fuel a new bull market in something.

The second prerequisite for a new bull market is a compelling fundamental reason to shake the demand side of the equation out of its torpor. Major bull markets in equities generally start from historically attractive P/E ratios and relatively high yields. Whatever the catalyst is, it will need to be powerful enough to act as a catalyst to stir the demand side of the market to action. In the stock market a company will need (for example) to have discovered a new way to drive efficiency, new products or a new source of demand for its existing products. If it is a bond price or a currency, the country concerned will need to have finally begun to get its economic act together. If it is a commodity, then some new technology or source of demand will be helping to sponge up available supply. The biggest bull markets have genuinely inspiring stories. In order to generate the faith in an idea necessary to propel an asset class into a secular bull market, the story has to be big. As participants investors want to feel that they are at the forefront of a new movement that will change the world.

At this stage of the new cycle, the most important factor about the new fundamental story is that the *majority* of people will be ignorant of it. If they have heard of it they will have dismissed it. Even those who have heard of it and believe are likely to underestimate the powerful effect new sources of demand can have on thin supply.

Commodities offer an excellent relatively recent example of an asset class that has rumbled through a lengthy base formation development before breaking upwards and hitting highs well beyond the expectations of even the most vociferous bulls. Although the tech bubble burst more than a decade ago, a number of technology shares continue to extend lengthy base formations. At the time of writing, the most glaring example of base formation development is in the financial sector, where some of the largest banks continue to trade at levels that would have been deemed impossible before the 2008 crash.

AN EXAMPLE OF DISBELIEF – OIL (1980–2003)

Let's take the example of commodities because they also offer the opportunity to examine the necessary change in the supply/demand dynamic that contributes to base formation completion and the dawn of a new bull market.

Historical oil prices 1962–2003

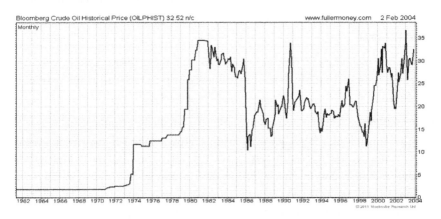

In retaliation for the USA's support of Israel during the 1973 Yom Kippur War the Organization of Arab Petroleum Exporting Countries (OAPEC) proclaimed an oil embargo. An additional cause for Arab oil producer discontent was the end of the Bretton Woods Accord in 1971 which allowed industrialised countries to float their respective currencies and resulted in the inflation-adjusted revenue from oil exports deteriorating. The effect of this action was exacerbated by the fact that USA oil production had peaked in 1970 so there was less additional supply to meet demand. The price of crude oil surged from $3 to $12 and retained an upward bias over the following years.

In 1978 striking Iranian oil workers shut down 4.5 million barrels per day of supply. In 1979 the Shah went into exile and domestic support for Ayatollah Khomeini surged. During the revolution energy infrastructure was damaged and the new regime struggled to return to previous oil production levels. At the same time Saudi Arabia and OAPEC were raising prices. In response to the Iranian hostage crisis President Carter banned imports from Iran and this drove prices even higher. Iraq's invasion of

Iran in 1980 raised the risk premium in the region. By October 1980 OAPEC was charging $32 per barrel and agreed a ceiling of $38.

The crisis fuelled massive non-OAPEC investment in additional supply. The USA developed the Prudhoe Bay field in Alaska, the USSR increased production, the North Sea, Venezuelan and Nigerian fields were all developed during this period and represented considerable additional supply. As the crisis eased, prices came back down and the panic over permanently high prices subsided as did interest in alternatives. Participation decreased as investors got used to the idea that oil spikes were not going to occur every other year and the numbers of people speculating in the market and in the sector generally collapsed relative to the peak of interest. The accepted wisdom was that prices were largely rangebound. Following the first Gulf War in 1990 when prices briefly spiked, oil prices ranged mostly between $10 and $25.

At the same time technology shares were emerging that promised new innovative ways of doing business that would change our lives forever. The productivity gains that resulted from rapidly advancing microchip technology, personal computers, the internet, mobile phones etc. inspired millions of investors to buy tech shares. This drove a phenomenal bull market and acted as a magnet for investor interest so that other sectors were largely neglected.

From the early 1980s through to the early 2000s commodities went through what many refer to as a *triple waterfall crash*. Just about everything went wrong for the industry. Demand deteriorated just as massive new supply hit the market. Inflationary pressures, which had been fuelled by the oil crises and central bank money creation, moderated as Fed Chairman Paul Volcker committed the institution to combatting inflation. He raised the Federal Funds Rate to 20%, from 11.375%, within five months of taking office in a successful attempt to squeeze inflationary pressures from the system. This policy reduced the appeal of commodities as a safe haven and secure store of value as inflationary pressures moderated. A large number of commodity producers went out of business and those that survived did so by slashing costs to the bone, engaging in aggressive hedging activities and using every rally to liquidate inventory.

WHO SURVIVES A BEAR MARKET?

When demand for what you produce declines, those that survive are not risk-takers. They have gone through a generation of disappointment. Such is the malaise that affects a sector in a prolonged bear that people simply no longer want to work in the industry. I remember chatting to another tourist at a market in Shanghai in 2007. He was an American who came to China every month for business. His company exported damaged mobile phones from the USA to China for reprocessing and repair and he now employed hundreds of people at home and thousands in China. When I asked how he got into the business, he said that he had been an oil-driller but had been fired from three different companies in a year because of various cost-cutting measures, rationalisation and consolidation. So he decided to switch careers. People simply leaving the industry because they can no longer make a living in it contribute to an inability to raise supply when demand eventually returns.

Those that survive in an industry when the business moves from being highly profitable to borderline loss-making spend their careers attempting to keep their heads above water. In the industrial resources sector they did this by mining or drilling the most difficult-to-access resources when prices were comparatively high so that they could access cheaper production when prices fell. They did not invest in new machinery, green-field exploration or other capital-intensive operations because they didn't have the cash and had been burnt by doing just that in the last cycle. People who know a suffering industry best will often be some of the slowest to believe a new bull story. There is an oft-quoted maxim that encapsulates the moribund attitude of people in an industry experiencing a bear market – 'those who know it best love it least because they have been disappointed the most'. In the early stages of a new bull market, those who make the most money are *risk-takers*. However, within the industry, people exhibiting those characteristics will have been winnowed out during the lengthy bear market, because taking risks was a quick way to lose money.

In the case of commodities, the emergence of China as a major consumer and demand-growth engine coupled with the wider global theme of the greatest urbanisation in history represented a significant new demand story from 2002. The supply side of the equation had been inelastic because the capacity had not existed to increase supply for vital commodities and those capable of increasing production were unwilling to take the risk. From 2002 onwards, David Fuller dubbed this emerging theme as *supply inelasticity meets rising demand*. Despite the fact that prices were rallying strongly and increasing numbers of industrial commodities were breaking upwards from their bases, the majority of analysts and commentators simply refused to believe that anything beyond a short-term change had occurred. The argument was that the industry is cyclical; always has been and always will be. People pointed to the available price history, which mostly covered the bear market, and said that rallies are never sustained so this one wouldn't be either.

In the latter stages of a bear market, sentiment will remain abysmal; most investors – to the extent that they are involved at all – will deny that anything important has changed. In oil's case, senior oil executives were often quoted as saying that they did not understand why prices were going up, claimed that they thought fair value was in the region of $20 and forecast prices would fall back to those levels when people came to their senses. Oil prices broke out of their base in 2004. In 2005 Lord Browne, then

CEO of BP, stated that he believed prices were "unsustainably high", a view shared by then-chairman of the Federal Reserve, Alan Greenspan.

This widespread attitude led oil executives to refuse to increase their exploration budgets, refinery capacity or modernise pipelines, all of which are highly capital-intensive projects. As prices extended their breakout, the industry had difficulty increasing supply and had little incentive to rush into such a move since profits were improving. Royalty agreements with various governments had also been structured so that more profits passed to the respective governments at higher prices. When oil companies signed those contracts they never really believed that prices would ever get that high but have since been forced to honour them.

WHEN DEMAND GETS THE UPPER HAND

We know that lengthy base formations are volatile and can fail to sustain upward breaks. Very few really believe that the asset class is ever going to move into a new bull market. So what do we look for to indicate that demand is beginning to get the upper hand?

On a chart, when the low of each successive reaction is higher than the last – what we refer to as 'a progression of higher reaction lows' – this tells us that demand is returning to dominance at progressively higher levels. This means that something has changed fundamentally to drive this imbalance between these two competing forces. It does not tell us the market is imminently going to break out from the base and soar because we do not yet know if supply above the market has been sufficiently thinned out. However, if the lows are rising, it is the first powerfully bullish signal that the investment environment is changing and that risks are now to the upside.

It is for this reason that a base formation can be regarded as an *accumulation phase* in its latter stages. If the lows are rising this is a clear indication that some important players are accumulating positions in whatever the vehicle is. Wider perceptions of what is going on might still be ignorant of the new demand story but if the lows are rising it does exist and is important.

In this context oil provides an interesting example. The market bottomed near $10 in 1998 and rallied to almost $40 by 2000, which at the time was an historically high and psychologically important level. During that time, it sustained a progression of higher reaction lows but was unable to gain enough momentum to break above $40. At least in part, this was because the tech bubble burst, interest rates rose and the USA and Europe experienced a recession. Prices fell back to less than $20 by late 2001 but didn't stay there for long and quickly re-established the progression of higher reaction lows.

Crude oil 1990–2011

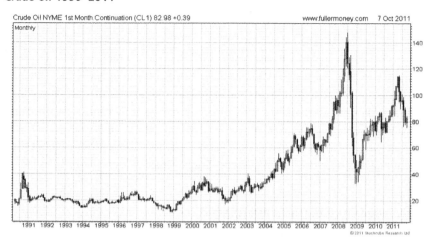

The chart above dates from 1990 and demonstrates that, apart from the spike due to the Gulf War, prices seldom rallied above $25 between 1991 and 1999. $40 was seen as the upper limit because that was where prices had peaked previously during times of crisis. However, on this occasion, while prices pulled back to below $20 for a short time they mostly ranged above $25 from late 1999 to late 2003. In the process they sustained higher prices for longer than anyone had seen in a generation. Yet very few investors paid any attention to the market at all. They were much more concerned with the aftermath of the tech bubble and whether we were going to enter another Depression.

Oil's $25–$40 range was relatively well-defined and had a psychological overhead barrier at an historic high. Its most important aspect was that it sustained the advance above the lengthy base formation for the better part of three years before successfully breaking above $40 and improving on that performance in no uncertain terms. This led more people to pay attention to the market because prices were staying elevated for longer. In Fullermoney's terminology we refer to this as the *first step above the base* and it occurs often enough that one needs to be aware of it. It is a powerful continuation pattern.

Markets would be a lot easier to deal with if they provided us with nice orderly moves that did not question our resolve. But oil's first step above the base is a real-life example. It was volatile, difficult to deal with and even broke back down into the prior base briefly – yet its defining characteristic was that prices held mostly above $25.

The first step above the base need not form after a lengthy base and will depend on the scale of the new demand story driving prices higher. However, when it does form, it is one of the most reliable continuation patterns you can see in financial markets. It signals in no uncertain terms that the bear market has ended and a new bull has begun.

Check Point Software Technologies 1997–2011 (Nasdaq)

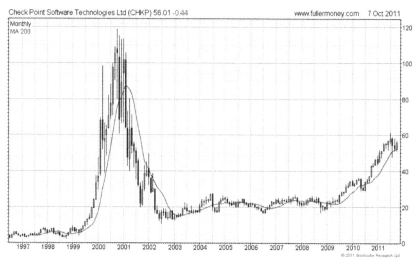

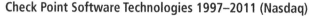

Check Point Software Technologies provides another instructive example. It formed a lengthy base formation from April 2002 to July 2009 before breaking upwards and rallying impressively. Following a 33% advance it pulled back and found support at the upper side of the base, above $28, forming a first step above the base. The fact that it sustained the breakout from the base told us the bear market for this share was over and a new bull beginning. What we didn't know and no can tell us is how long it will proceed or how much it will go up. What is evident on the chart is that the advance from mid-2009 is more consistent and rhythmic than the 1999 bubble.

When a market eventually breaks out from a multi-year base, demand overwhelms supply due to fundamental behavioural change. Prices rally faster and farther than they have in years. The instrument will often move to new multi-year highs and certainly higher than most people will remember it ever trading at. In an internationally traded vehicle or globally significant share, this will be enough to begin to spark investor interest, but they will not know if this is the beginning of a major bull market or whether this is a cyclical move which will swiftly peter out. Therefore many will simply wait to see what happens next.

Those closest to the industry in question – who have been most traumatised by the experience of surviving the lengthy bear market – will see prices at a multi-year high as a great opportunity to liquidate inventory at the best prices they have seen in a generation, anticipating that they will be able to get back in at much lower levels. A Greek delegate at the Chart Seminar in May 2008 described exactly this sentiment when, in 2003, his family sold their bulk carrier. Prices had been ranging for a generation. The accepted knowledge was that there was a ceiling on how much could be charged for shipping goods around the world and when prices fell back from the upper side of the range, the ship had to be idled because the rates available were not economic. They used the first upward break following the generational bear market to get out of the shipping business because it was just too hard to make money. However, prices subsequently more than tripled before collapsing in 2008.

Baltic Dry Index 1990–2011

An over-reliance on 'the accepted knowledge' by the majority of investors is what allows a first step above the base to form because demand has reasserted dominance but the bullish story or hypothesis is not widely accepted. Investors are not yet inspired to commit large percentages of their capital to the market.

(II) ACCEPTANCE ('I'M NOT SURE I BELIEVE IN THIS THING BUT I BETTER OWN SOME JUST IN CASE')

The climactic low or base formation marks the beginning of the new bull market. A first step above the base represents a reconfiguration of the supply/demand imbalance within the new uptrend. Given the medium-term (anything from a few months to a couple of years) nature of a first step above the base it might also be referred to as a *consolidation*. Once it has been completed with a successful upward break, the market can be deemed to be in the second psychological perception stage: with grudging acceptance eventually giving way to more wholehearted belief.

Completion of the first step above the base will be enough to spark at least some investor interest because as much as one might like to denigrate the new bullish hypothesis as yet another overhyped story, it is difficult to argue with performance. Nevertheless, the most dyed-in-the-wool bears will still be attempting to short rallies and will claim that the price action is nothing more than another bear market rally. They have been right every other time and they will refuse to see the fact that historically high prices have been sustained for a relatively lengthy period as proof that the fundamentals of the market have really changed.

The price action is clearly signalling that a major new demand story is unfolding but it will as yet be relatively poorly understood by the majority of investors. Those who are getting long and risking their reputations and money on what they see as a new secular bull market will be seen as mavericks, investing in a 'high risk' market where no one reliably makes money. The attitude to a market which has recently completed a multi-year or even decade-long base is one of caution.

This marks a clear divergence between sentiment and price activity. Price is the only reliable indicator we have of where supply and demand are actually positioned and the first step above the base means that demand *is* dominant despite the refusal of many investors to believe it. So few people have been converted to the new bullish hypothesis that once the market has sustained a breakout from the base, there is a better-than-even chance that it will come back and range about the base for a period of time. The first step above the base is important because it marks a war for dominance between supply and demand.

Those who continue to talk down the price – and there will be plenty of them – will propose all the old arguments for why the market cannot rally. But these will stand in contrast to the fact that prices are holding the breakout from the base. The 'cyclical versus secular' argument often appears at this juncture. The bears will argue that the breakout is nothing more than a cyclical rally that will end any day now. The bulls will maintain it is a new secular (as in long-term) advance that has many years left to run.

Participation on the bull side is still low but it is growing and is enough to make sure that prices hold more or less above the base. By the time the first step above the base is completed, the new bullish argument will have gained some adherents and will have moved from comparative obscurity to being occasionally mentioned in the media. However, because large numbers of investors are not yet long, the commentary on the market will still be relatively sparse.

Once the market sustains a breakout from the first step above the base, we can say with a high degree of certainty that the new bull market has entered the second psychological stage. This is *gradual acceptance*, more often referred to as the 'wall of worry'.

There will still be myriad views for why the market cannot rally but it is advancing and those who are long are making money. However, because sentiment remains so cautious, position sizes at this juncture are small relative to the size of portfolios because the perception is that the market is high-risk.

As prices continue to advance, investors will have heard more about the market and can justify having a position. However, they will remain in a 'sell the rallies' mentality because they won't trust what they are seeing. This is often the most consistent on a chart because the difference between supply and demand is relatively wide and well-defined. The wall of worry allows crowd sentiment to catch up with the bullish price action and allows more people to learn and literally 'buy into' the new story.

Every bull market has a compelling story that inspires investors to throw caution to the wind and participate – whether it is railroads opening up the Wild West, Japanese efficiency transforming the way businesses are run, the internet changing the way we live our lives, the debasement of fiat currencies by central banks spurring demand for gold or the greatest urbanisation in history lifting billions of new consumers out of poverty and into the new middle classes. However, it takes time for the crowd to get used to the idea. And nothing speeds the conversion process up faster than seeing a profit grow in one's portfolio.

At this point in the story, imagine a portfolio manager going to meet a client and feeling pretty good because they have returned 6% for the year to-date. If the market's mentality is now moving to the next phase, the client will be thinking differently. They have done their homework and figured out that if the manager had only held onto their positions in this sector, rather than closing them when they did, they would have returned closer to 8%. The client accuses the banker of churning the account to raise commissions rather than managing it in their best interests. Of course, the manager was just using the most risk-averse attitude to the market that he could while having a position. But the client just wants the returns. More to the point, the client now believes the returns are readily available. This type of activity heralds the dawn of a 'buy and hold' mentality. It means the decline of a trading strategy and indicates that more people are really starting to believe in the long-term story.

The prevailing strategy among those building positions will morph from selling the rallies to buying the dips. As long as the instrument remains in a demand-dominated environment, this will be the most successful strategy. Expressing confidence by making purchases even after a decline and being rewarded for it by a subsequent rally is a powerful reinforcement of the bullish hypothesis.

Prices will have already risen significantly from where they traded back in the base. Some of the most level-headed, least greedy, most far-sighted value investors, who were early buyers and saw the potential, will now view the market as too expensive, overextended relative to what could be justified by the fundamentals. They will often sell or reduce their positions. Their rationalisation will be that they have seen it all before. It will end in tears. They want to be far away when that happens. The problem for these people is that they are assuming that they know where the market will eventually top out. In fact, *no one knows*.

Let's take a globally significant consumer-led company like McDonald's as an example.

McDonald's (NYSE) 1992–2013

Shares in McDonald's peaked in 1999, fell to near $30 then more than halved to $13 between 2002 and early 2003. Price then entered an impressive uptrend which saw it move from relative obscurity to a position of relative strength and absolute-return leader. In a market where investors have developed newfound respect for yield, McDonald's is one of a small number of companies that have raised their dividends every year for at least 25 years. S&P compiles an index of these shares and refers to them as *Dividend Aristocrats*. In a global economy where the spending power of the new middle class is an increasingly important determinant of growth, McDonald's is ideally placed to grow, subject to governance and the continued consistency of its price action.

The share no more than paused during the credit crisis of 2008 and proved comparatively immune to the euro debt crisis of 2011. Following the interval of the 2008 crunch, it returned to a rhythmic uptrend with a succession of ranges forming a step sequence one above another. A break in this sequence would be a minimum requirement to begin to question the potential for additional upside.

(III) EUPHORIA (FANCY RATIONALISATIONS AND EXTRAVAGANT PROJECTIONS)

Ask yourself how many times a winning strategy is questioned. In any organisation, when a marketing strategy works, or a new product is hugely successful, or a methodology is productive, we don't tend to rush out and change everything. At most we will look at how to tweak it at the edges to squeeze out a bit more profit. We don't have crises of confidence and interrogate the fundamental methodology. In my experience what generally seems to occur is that those involved in whatever is helping to drive the company's revenue growth are held up as paragons of ingenuity. Their example is highlighted as something for other employees to aspire to and there is often widespread criticism of the old methods that were apparently less productive.

The financial markets are no different.

The depth of a bear market sucks demand out of an asset class but as a new bull gets moving, rising prices are hard to argue with and investors begin to cautiously accumulate positions. As this strategy is seen to work the financial rewards increase, as does the sense of self-congratulation at having the intelligence, confidence and fortitude to participate in the bull market. However, the really *big* bull markets (and these occur comparatively rarely), offer an added psychological dimension because they seem to take on a life of their own.

The idea is inspiring enough that it acts like a magnet for investor demand. An important paradox develops. The crowd is unified by the simple idea that the bull market will change the world and at the same time radically increase the wealth of everyone who is long. If people were prepared to think rationally they would accept that in order to realise this profit they will have to sell. But as long as prices continue to rise, *how* they should sell will be way down the list of most investors' priorities. Anyone who can look at the market from the outside can see that prices are becoming divorced from reality but the crowd doesn't care. As long as prices continue to head higher, nothing will have happened to question what has been a highly successful strategy. Investors will continue to add more capital to the market.

All the aspects of crowd formation, such as a lowered sense of responsibility and contagion previously discussed, are especially evident in these latter stages of a bull market. Every major bull market will share the crowd characteristics of latching on to a simple idea, accepting huge contradiction, thirsting after a dream or promise rather than fact, and wishing to listen only to those who proclaim with the loudest voice and least equivocation how bullish they are. (And exactly the same characteristics play out in reverse at the bottom.)

The reality is that an asset class in a major bull market can continue to attract more and more buyers despite its price becoming increasingly divorced from what could be described as fundamental value. Crowds can move well beyond what can be rationally justified, ignore the simple dictates of common sense and to promote ever-more elaborate justifications for why the market will always go up.

So *who*, exactly is buying at this point (and not just holding)? Those inside the crowd who are already long may be motivated by greed to buy more, get more leveraged and try to make even more money by following what has been a winning formula. Those who have not yet bought may be enticed by the fear of missing out on a chance to make life-changing profits. Bull markets are a lot of fun, capital is abundant and anything seems possible, so the perception of risk goes down. Those who are not participating are viewed as fools; at minimum they are quietly patronised.

Human beings are social animals and few of us like to be the one to question the consensus regardless of how much we strive to be contrarian. In the markets, those who are making money are right. One may be able to comfort oneself with the academic argument that the crowd is running off a cliff. But as we say at Fullermoney, "*a consistent trend is a trend in motion*". It will keep on going until it has a reason to stop. The crowd will continue on its bullish trajectory until something happens to derail it. And until that happens, the lure of potential mega profits is enough to attract ever more capital.

New buyers go through an interesting conversion process. They have to set aside the reasons that stopped them from buying previously and accept the rationale of the bull market story. They have to believe that they are not coming in at the end of a phenomenal advance but that things have much farther to run. Projections for where prices are going next must now *far exceed* whatever the current price is. For the contrary investor, this will be a signal that the bull market is nearing its end. But the new buyer and everyone who is long will put anyone making extravagant forecasts on a pedestal. It is what they want to hear.

An additional aspect of crowd psychology is its reaction to someone who seeks to lead it. Here is Freud on the subject:

> "A group is an obedient herd, which could never live without a master. It has such a thirst for obedience that it submits instinctively to anyone who appoints himself its master. Although in this way the needs of a group carry it half-way to meet the leader, yet he too must fit in with it in his personal qualities. He must himself be held in-fascination by a strong faith (in an idea) in order to awaken the group's faith. He must possess a strong and inspiring will, which the group, which has no will of its own, can accept from him."

PERSONIFICATION OF CROWD SENTIMENT

Leadership is a relatively similar concept in politics, the military or religion. In the financial markets it takes on an added subtlety. This is particularly the case in the latter stages of a bull market where individual analysts, traders, money managers, journalists, authors, commentators, TV presenters etc. are competing to attract the most attention for themselves. Every one of them wants to be the biggest possible bull. They don't show a shred of caution and will often have leveraged up to extraordinary levels in order to capture even more market share, more profit or more viewers. The fact that the so-called 'experts in their field' are demonstrating the most chronic symptoms of being under the sway of the crowd is often lost on individual investors. The whole process actually helps to further reinforce the prevailing bullish hypothesis and convert even more new buyers.

There is also substantial career risk for money managers in not participating in a major bull market. They will be finding it difficult to outperform their benchmark and will have to explain to an unsympathetic crowd why they are not long. To the extent that the crowd is aware of those holding the opposite view, it pauses only to heap derision on them. Investors tend to favour managers who understand these 'new markets', even if that means managers who are prepared to throw caution to the wind and leverage up aggressively.

At the same time as this happens, anyone who has sold early will be under enormous pressure to come back in. They saw the potential but underestimated it. If they are going to catch up with the performance of their competitors they will now need to have even larger positions. They have to admit to themselves that their decision to sell was at least ill-timed and they should have held on. So they run the risk of being even less likely to sell in future because they have been punished for doing so in the past.

There is a temptation to deify the market as a malevolent being whose sole purpose is to deprive the wary investor of their hard-earned savings by sucking them into investment bubbles. However the fact is that the crowd mentality is powerfully attractive. It exhibits characteristics many people admire. It is powerful, righteous, assumes a position of dominance over the individual and magnifies peer pressure – making it much easier to cede autonomy and allow oneself to be swept along by the feel-good factor. This is the time of maximum bullishness, when anyone who wants to be long is long, where the crowd feels most powerful and is most self-absorbed.

However, what was the strongest market in the world can turn into the weakest overnight if demand is finally satiated. Logically, once everyone has bought, all that are left are potential sellers.

DO DREAMS COME TRUE?

Prices will continue to rise for as long as there are buyers and this can go on for much longer than most people are willing to countenance. Anyone saying that gold prices could rise for ten years in 2000 would have been laughed out of the room. At the time of writing (mid-2013) the shoe is on the other foot and those who have been steadfast bulls are being presented with evidence that demand has been sated. US Treasury bond yields have trended lower from 1980 and an argument is now raging as to whether this 33-year secular bull market is over. The Japanese stock market had been in a secular bear market since peaking in 1989 and while this has been interrupted by some impressive cyclical uptrends, the general trend remained skewed towards underperformance until 2012. Prime Minister Shinzō Abe is now engaged in an all or nothing bid to break the cycle of deflation. Both secular bull and bear markets offer wonderful opportunities to profit but one also has to bear in mind, particularly when everyone else forgets, that as sure as night follows day a secular bear follows a secular bull and nothing ever goes up forever.

At some point everyone who wants to buy will have bought. Central banks moving to raise interest rates and generally making monetary conditions less accommodative are often a precursor to major tops in the stock markets. This occurs to such an extent that I believe it is no exaggeration to state that rising interest rates have killed off more bull markets than just about anything else. A major upward acceleration in the price of crude oil can have the same effect because it acts like a tax on consumption.

All of the elements discussed above – unquestioning adherence to the most bullish hypothesis, fanciful predictions, increasing supply of stock, rising short-term interest rates and high energy prices – were evident in Potash Corp of Saskatchewan as prices moved from under C$50 to almost C$250 in less than two years. The story motivating investors was that the world was running out of food. The fertilisers this company dominated the production of were indispensable in raising crop yields. Food riots were breaking out in low income/high population countries. People were starting to believe that prices for potash fertilisers could only go one way. In retrospect we can argue that farmers do not have such deep pockets that they can afford such remarkably high fertiliser prices. Surging fertiliser prices coupled with higher interest rates and high oil prices were contributing to demand destruction. However, as prices accelerated higher, the sector sucked in new money from all over the world. Investors sought a safe-haven hedge for the perceived inflationary threat gripping the global economy.

Potash Corp of Saskatchewan (TSX & NYSE) 1999–2008

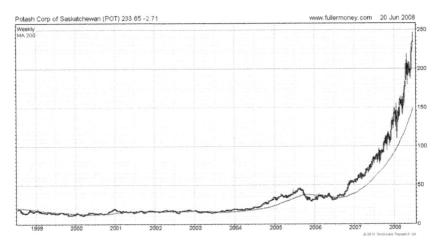

(IV) THE TURNING POINT (THOSE WHO ARE LAST SHALL BE FIRST)

Major tops and bottoms are another topic, but in terms of the psychological perception stages, the euphoria that marks the final stage of the bull market will be the first stage of the bear market. The majority of participants simply will not believe that prices can ever fall.

They have been well-rewarded for this belief, after all. Even the most rational argument for why prices cannot continue to rise will be met with the response: "Yes, but we have a few more months right?" or "Yes, but give me just one new high". And that is if such arguments are listened to at all.

Most deniers of the bull market hypothesis are treated like heretics and vilified or ridiculed. It is for this reason that religion is often used as an example of crowd psychology at work. The fervent belief of the fanatic is eminently transferrable to the financial theatre, and at least in part explains why investors can feel combative with the market when it stops going in their favour.

HEGEL'S MASTER-SLAVE DIALECTIC

Let's take a moment to think about the emotional mechanics of how a bull turns into a bear market and vice versa. There is much in the process that is analogous to Hegel's description of the master-slave dialectic which he outlined in his *Phenomenology of Spirit* in 1760. The model has been applied to many different disciplines for more than

200 years. It describes a tension between dominant and submissive parties that eventually exchange roles. Let me summarise.

Two beings compete for dominance. In order to avoid mutual destruction the loser accepts a position of subjugation while the victor assumes a master's role. Both settle into their new relationship. However, the situation does not prove to be satisfactory. Despite his mastery of the loser, the master becomes increasingly dependent on the slave for the services he provides. Without the recognition of the slave, the victor would be master of nothing. The slave's servile position is gradually improved as he moulds nature into products for the master and sees himself reflected in his creations. He gains greater control and eventual dominance as the only one with the ability to sustain himself. And thus the roles are reversed.

Hegel's resolution of the dialectic evolves to a point when both parties exist as individuals. But this cannot occur in the financial markets because for every buyer there must be a seller. This means that in markets that persist over time, a new bull market will inevitably rise phoenix-like from the ashes of the last bear. The seemingly omnipotent bull will crash and burn like Icarus who flew too high only to fall back to earth.

The perception of risk is never lower than at market tops. A strategy has been seen to win for what could be years and all the doubters have been proved wrong. However, this cannot go on forever. Despite the apparent powerlessness of the bears, their influence is in fact growing. The increasing ranks of those who are long are all potential sellers.

Very few people succeed in selling at the top. Those that make a name for being prescient once the top has been recognised by the multitude are often those who were dismissed as cranks when prices were rising. They now assume a leadership role among the nascent bears because they personify the mood of the market.

When a bull market ends most people do not want to admit to themselves that the good times are over. Just as in everyday life, people react differently to a challenging situation. Some seek to deal with it immediately and sell. These people are often either most disciplined or those least infected by the crowd's mood. Many people wish to defer the decision to sell till a later date. No one wants to liquidate a position only to see it hit and sustain new highs, so they wait in the hope that things will get better. But procrastination is a risky strategy at major topping areas. In our regular lives, how many of us put off till tomorrow what we could really do today? How many of us have waited until the last moment to write a paper or study for an exam or prepare a proposal when we had ample time to do so before action was forced on us. Or think of the person who allows a credit card debt to mount up. How many feel reluctant to open credit card bills? They know the news is probably going to be bad but until they see it written down in front of them, there remains an air of unreality about it. They know the problem of interest accrual is ramping up and yet they delay paying it off until it reaches crisis point. In much the same way procrastination in the financial markets can cost money.

Those somewhat prone to sentimentality about their investments will be slow to sell because they want to give the market the benefit of the doubt, just as they would with a loved one.

When a bull market ends even some of the people who have been most disciplined with stops and money control can fall foul of their emotions by buying back too early. They have not had a traumatic experience and got out relatively close to the top with most of their profits intact. Rather than forget about the market and hunting for new quarry they will continue to monitor it. Often when a market falls, they will look at it and see that the majority of the bullish arguments they adhered to on the way up are still valid but prices have fallen so they conclude that it must be a buying opportunity and start reinvesting. The most over-confident or cavalier will commit larger amounts of capital because they will want to make even more money than they did the first time. Often they will end up giving back most of what they earned on the way up. In terms of crowd psychology they remain strongly identified with the relevant instrument but fail to realise that the group is losing cohesion.

All of these people are disbelievers that anything has really changed. For whatever reason they have not sold, are delaying the decision or are denying compelling evidence and have concluded that this is nothing more than a temporary setback before the market soars once more.

The end of the third psychological perception stage of the bull market which is marked by overconfidence and euphoria is always the beginning of the next bear market because the latter emotions can just as easily be reinterpreted as ignorance and hubris. As a new bear market begins, the bears are making money, their hypothesis is gaining credence, a crowd of likeminded people is beginning to coalesce around them and many of the strongest adherents to the bullish hypothesis are in denial or are rationalising the price action to fit in with their pet theories.

Let's take Apple as an example:

Apple 1992–2013

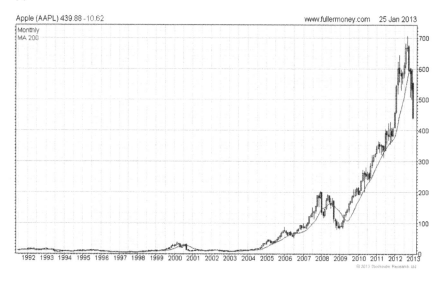

Apple (AAPL) 439.88 -10.62   www.fullermoney.com   25 Jan 2013

There has perhaps never been such an iconic share as Apple. The company under Steve Jobs revolutionised the music, mobile phone and PC markets. The growth trajectory of each new product as it came to market was beyond even the most bullish expectation of the majority of analysts. The legions of people who queued overnight at each product launch were a testament to the cachet of the brand but above all to the quality and ease of use of the iPod, iPhone, iPad and iMac. Those who invested in Apple's shares were richly rewarded as it went from relative obscurity in 2004 to the largest capitalised share in history by 2012.

I taught the Chart Seminar in San Francisco when prices in Apple shares were just pulling back from their first look at the $600 area on the way up and market pundits were proclaiming that $1,000 would be reached within the year. No one wanted to admit that prices were becoming increasingly overextended and that the likelihood of at least a reversion towards the mean was increasing. The price action was being rationalised by the strength of the company's balance sheet, the success of its products, its dominance of the phone, music and tablet markets, its substantial cash reserves.

The share trended consistently higher between 2009 and early 2012. The pattern of ranges one above another then changed to a much more aggressive uptrend. Investors were racing to own the share on the expectation that it would continue to soar. It posted its largest pullback in more than five years in April 2012 but found support by May and rallied to $700 but could not hold the gain and quickly fell back to break the progression of higher reaction lows and posted a substantially larger correction in the process.

At a minimum, technical deterioration occurred, confidence was shaken and time would be required in order to repair both.

(V) ACCEPTANCE ("SNAP BACK TO REALITY / OH THERE GOES GRAVITY … " – EMINEM)

Investment committees at pension or mutual funds don't call emergency meetings when prices are going up. They call them when they've just taken a hit. You can imagine the discussion that goes on when that happens. Some rationalise the price action: "OK, prices have gone a bit too far too fast so we'll see some consolidation before it makes new highs." Others disagree: "Actually, the fundamentals have changed, higher prices have increased supply and demand destruction is taking place so prices are going to go back down." Following such a meeting, at least some funds will stop buying until the situation becomes clearer. And when large institutions stop buying, they rob the market of a major source of new demand. That means someone else has to step in to replace them.

Retail investors can often fill that role. They tend to take longer to hear about the big investment story. They also represent a significant cohort who may never have invested in a major bull market before and are therefore less likely to be early in selling. Nevertheless, when large players stop buying and begin to reduce their positions, the likelihood of prices being able to continue to hit and hold new highs beyond the short term is severely limited.

The first big fall shakes confidence among the bulls and raises the profile of the bears who are suddenly starting to make money. However, most people who built up a long position over a period of time during the bull market will still have fairly decent paper profits. The experience of the sharp decline will be akin to hitting an unexpected speed bump. The jolt will shake them a bit but permanent damage is unlikely. When prices were advancing day after day or week after week, or when we find that we are making money from our investment portfolio faster than from our regular job many people, myself included, start to dream about how they are going to spend the money. Maybe it will be on a new car, or a new boat or even a second home in sunnier climes. However, the first big hit to the portfolio begins to raise questions about whether these dreams are realisable. Investors might not be ready to give up on them right away but enough people will be more cautious so that it changes the group dynamic from expansion to attrition.

There will still be plenty of people who are not willing to acknowledge that anything has changed and will continue buying. However, if the market has in fact topped out they will not succeed in pushing the market to significant new highs. Once prices begin to deteriorate, the bears' profile is raised as the bulls begin to experience profit erosion. Investors begin to think not of when they are going to buy the next gadget but how to protect the principle. Profit erosion is unpleasant, to put it mildly, and has a debilitating effect on investor sentiment. Someone might be able to sit with a position for a while if it is still profitable, but as the profit is chipped away by successive days or weeks to the downside the urgency of the situation becomes more pressing. Profit erosion is the kind of thing that can keep you up at night. This is the kind of scenario where investors feel like the market has gone 'crazy'. (Notice that the market only ever seems to go crazy when it goes against us.) Emotions such as powerlessness, confusion and intimidation come to the fore. The market seems to be ganging up on us. The simple solution when the pressure becomes too much is to abandon the old bullish hypothesis, adopt the new bearish credo and sell. But selling for emotional rather than technical reasons is a risky strategy.

As the market deteriorates, those who are long will be experiencing a wide variety of emotions ranging from fear to hope. Confidence takes a severe beating as optimism that prices will recover so the position can be liquidated at a favourable level goes unrewarded. Fear multiplies as one's base level of capital is jeopardised. Each of us has what can be referred to as a store of *emotional capital* which helps us to deal with the stresses involved in investing, particularly leveraged trading. When things are going well, the confidence we have in our abilities grows, sometimes to the extent that we take risks we really shouldn't. When profit erosion sets in, our store of emotional capital is steadily siphoned off. Our strategy has been proved to be flat-out wrong. The bears will be keen to point out in detail why anyone bullish is a fool. The likelihood that we will have the emotional, not to mind financial wherewithal, to establish new positions once the market eventually shows signs of bottoming decreases because we know what happened to us last time.

CRIMINALITY AND CROWD SENTIMENT

"You don't know who's been swimming naked until the tide goes out."

– Warren Buffett

The end of most bull markets leads to crimes being unearthed, where we later wonder how we could ever have missed them. Enron, Bernie Madoff and a host of financial institutions all offer examples of a model played out in just about every major bear market. The prospective criminal invariably uses the availability of loose credit and a reduced sense of fiduciary responsibility to create a skein of respectability to hide their nefarious business dealings. Warren Buffett's above quote is invariably true when a bull market ends. Those who relied on easy access to credit and light-touch regulation will inevitably suffer when credit conditions tighten and investors begin to look around for someone to blame for their financial trauma. If you look hard enough you will unearth evidence of financial crimes coming to light after just about every bull market because the conditions to make crime pay, at least for a while, are present in *every* bull market and prove too tempting for some.

When crimes are brought to light, the news can have a material impact on crowd sentiment. The bears will be self-satisfied and will point to the criminal and ask how anyone could have been foolish enough to believe his lies. Those still long are presented with clear evidence that the bullish hypothesis had major holes. The pervasive fear is that even more crimes will be unearthed, which would further damage their investment position, and they will thus have an additional reason to sell.

THE PACE OF BEARS

Markets often fall faster than they rise. From the perspective of crowd psychology, this is because it takes time to gather more and more adherents to an investment theme, but the growth of the crowd depends on the stream of new believers continuing. When it stops, it quickly reverses because the idea that acted as a gel to hold the participants together is no longer credible. There are a number of sayings to illustrate this fact such as 'trust grows like an oak but falls like an acorn' or 'it takes 20 years to build a reputation and five minutes to ruin it'. Falling prices, profit erosion, the realisation that one's utopian view of the future was wrong, the revelation that some of the paragons of the bull market were in fact lying criminals, the one-time crank turned media darling combined with disillusionment, fear, stress and hopelessness all combine to increase the numbers of sellers. The second psychological perception stage of the bear market sees the bull crowd diminish as the bear crowd grows and becomes more confident.

As prices deteriorate sentiment becomes increasingly bearish. The media will seek to find money managers and commentators who can explain the price action, so they naturally drift towards those who are most bearish. These people then have a vested interest in painting the most apocalyptic picture possible because they are often making money from the decline and want to continue to do so. The bearish camp continues to accumulate new devotees. Those who are short are leveraging up and those who have sold and now hold cash are often inactive because the perceived risks are too high. Those holding cash are therefore withholding demand from the market and in the process contributing to the dominance of the bearish perspective.

Those who are attempting to pick or anticipate the bottom do so very carefully. The 'catching a falling knife' analogy is often used to describe this situation. With the perceived sense of risk increasing, investors are much more likely to use stops than when prices are rising, because they fear being thrown out of a potential profit. When one thinks a situation is high-risk, position sizes are then commensurate with the perceived risk – so even when buyers do participate, they keep purchases small. This attitude allows the market to contract even further as speculative interest dries up and leverage is squeezed out of the system. By the time the second psychological perception stage of the decline has runs its course everyone gets the message that the market is weak.

AN 'ORDERLY DECLINE'

AstraZeneca is an example of a market which deteriorated in a relatively steady fashion, rather than the 'falling off a cliff' decline experienced by many financial shares during the 2008 credit crisis. This was at least in part because of its steady cash flows and reliable yield.

AstraZeneca (LSE, NYSE, SSE) 2003–2008

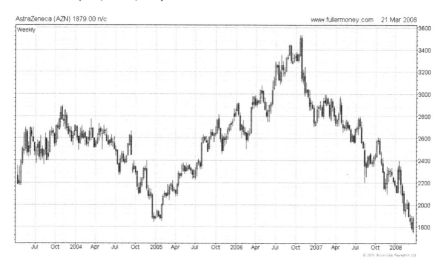

Prices pulled back sharply from the 3500p peak and fell to around 2800p in a very short period of time at the end of 2007 but steadied for the better part of six months near those levels. This was by far the largest reaction in the course of the 20-month uptrend. It was a clear warning that the dominance of demand in the market had eroded and would have triggered a large number of stops. Many of those who bought during the 20-month uptrend would have been taken out of the market with a high percentage of their profits intact and even those who took a loss on an unleveraged position would have been unlikely to have sustained meaningful damage to their principle investment capital.

As the market ranged for almost six months, those seeking to buy on the dips or those who were waiting for an opportunity to pick up a position on a significant pullback may have been tempted back in on the assumption that the share had stabilised. However, while this was a winning strategy throughout the course of the uptrend, the relationship between the opposing forces of supply and demand had changed. Sellers were now in the ascendancy and gathering adherents to their cause.

From December 2006, prices were not able to sustain a breakout from the range as they had on every other advance in the course of the uptrend. The breakdown from the six-month range in May 2007 helped to confirm the bearish hypothesis. Those still holding long positions were either enduring the negativity associated with profit erosion or nursing losses. As more investors decided enough was enough and sold, and as short sellers increased their positions, the pace of the decline picked up. More and more people accepted that the situation had definitely changed and for the worse.

AstraZeneca is a major pharmaceutical and healthcare company and its steady stream of cash flows lends it defensive characteristics, particularly during a crisis focused on a dearth of credit. This helps to explain at least in part why its decline was relatively orderly compared to companies which had a greater reliance on access to cheap credit to fuel their business model. It also contributed to its subsequent rebound from 2009 onwards.

AN ABRUPT DECLINE

Xstrata offers an example of a company which had relied on cheap credit to fuel expansion.

Xstrata (LSE, HSE) 2004–2009

The company had benefitted enormously by engaging in rapid expansion through numerous acquisitions fuelled by access to cheap credit. This allowed it to amass an impressive portfolio of assets, particularly in the coal and zinc sectors, and the share price rallied from near 500p in 2005 to a peak near 2500p by mid-2008. However, as the credit upon which the company relied to sustain its business model dried up, major questions began to be asked about its ability to hold onto its various acquisitions. Prices quickly deteriorated.

Xstrata offers an example of a disorderly disintegration of the bullish crowd that had coalesced around a plucky management team that seemed capable of defying the odds. The company went from relative obscurity to being the world's fifth biggest miner in a comparatively short time. As prices fell through 2000p and continued to deteriorate, the speed of the decline forced people to make up their minds quickly. The realisation that the company was in trouble happened faster than with AstraZeneca. By the time it bottomed from late 2008, the question of survival was to the fore, with many doubting whether recovery was even possible. This meant that the second psychological perception stage proved to be quite short, as people moved from being relatively sanguine to depressed in a very short period of time.

(VI) DEPRESSION ('I JUST CAN'T TAKE IT ANYMORE')

Depression sets in as investors crystallise losses and realise that they have fallen victim to the powerful influence of the crowd and made a succession of bad investment decisions. They may have bought too much on the way up, failed to sell on the way down, ignored the warnings of more cautious pundits who are now glorified in the press or just generally given in to the crowd's siren song. Some people will accept the blame for their actions and work on their strategy in an effort to avoid the same mistakes again. Others will blame the market and either swear off investing altogether or join the ranks of those talking the market lower out of a vindictive wish to see the market punished for exacting such a heavy toll on the 'innocent' investor.

Following the October 2008 lows I received a number of emails from subscribers to **Fullermoney.com** who said that while they could accept the market was close to a bottom, the pressure was just too great and they had to sell. In behavioural terms this is referred to as *capitulation* because the final hold-outs are starting to throw in the towel and are liquidating long positions. The intensity of losing a large percentage of one's investment capital is traumatic. People will often choose to sell at an unfavourable level rather than hold out even longer because the stress of accepting additional potential losses outweighs what seems to be a tenuous promise that the blow might at least be lessened by waiting. A signal that a market is bottoming therefore lies in the extinction of hope among those who hold 'stale bull' inventory. Those who held on through much of the decline, even as others were selling around them, finally give up hope that the market will ever recover. The other side of the equation, of course, is that there are value investors and contrarians who are initiating long positions and accumulating positions which helps to bring supply and demand back into balance close to the bottom.

CHICKEN LITTLES AND PRICE ACTION

Sellers will not be alone in their attitude. Because the market has deteriorated so devastatingly, many people who were long and failed to sell will be feeling exactly the same. Those who did sell on the way down will be psychologically invested in the idea that the market will never recover. They seek to comfort themselves with the idea that they at least got out at a reasonable level. The bears will be triumphant and heralding the end of the financial markets as we know them.

There is always someone who luxuriates in anticipating the worst possible outcome. In the words of the musician Wouter de Backer, "You can get addicted to a certain kind of sadness". For them the optimism so characteristic of bull markets is an alien concept. When a clear bear environment becomes evident they are now in their element and jump to say "I told you so" as prices deteriorate. They will be receiving a great deal of press coverage because they are seen to have been right and more in tune with the reality now provided by the market.

The pervading mood will exemplify the contradiction that most people believe (or at least act as if they believe) that the market will go to zero, when they know this is a physical impossibility for most markets. Everyone has heard prognostications such as "buy when there is blood on the streets, even when the blood is your own" or Warren Buffett's "We simply attempt to be fearful when others are greedy and to be greedy only when others are fearful". In a cool, rational environment buy-low-sell-high is a pretty simple way of doing things. But when a market is bottoming and emotions are running riot it is not so easy. Every fibre of our being will be telling us it's a bad decision but history tells us that buying at extremes of bearishness proves to be a good long-term decision more often than not.

At market bottoms we are looking for clear evidence that sentiment and price action are diverging. When sentiment among the bears continues to discount ever-more-aggressive downside targets, but prices have actually stopped deteriorating, we are given a clear signal that the bearish crowd – although increasingly vocal – is in fact running out of steam. This is what contrarians are looking for in order to begin initiating long positions. It offers clear evidence the supply side is being exhausted, leaving nothing but potential buyers on the sidelines. Those who will need to eventually cover short positions also represent a potent source of potential demand.

THE WRONG LESSONS

We try to learn from our mistakes. Following a major financial market decline where we have taken a loss, the first thing we resolve to do is not to get caught out like that again. Many people therefore approach market bottoms and the early stages of a bull market by doing what they wished they had done in the last market cycle. Someone who has taken a loss following a significant decline will wish that they had stopped buying when crowd sentiment reached a pinnacle of bullishness, or that they had implemented a disciplined series of stops to protect their profits. And they often refuse point-blank to buy back in on the first rally after the peak.

However, at the bottom, this means that one adopts an overly cautious stance towards the market. Such investors have too small a position, or place stops too close to the where the market is trading and sell as soon as the market begins to rally. As a result, having learned the lesson of how not to get hurt in a declining market, they do everything wrong when it comes to an advancing market. Many people employ investing tactics that are simply incommensurate with the actual risk profile of the new market environment. Part of learning lessons is knowing *when* to employ them.

THE SHAPE OF RECOVERY

Following a major bear market decline, the shape of the subsequent recovery will depend on a large number of factors. Monetary policy, economic stimulus and demand for the product concerned whether in the equity, bond, commodity or currency markets are all legitimate concerns. Base formation development will take as long as is needed for supply above the market to be expended, for valuations to become attractive once more and for a new bull market theme capable of inspiring investors to manifest itself. However, the process whereby the crowd moves from dismissal, through acceptance to overestimation and from underestimation through acceptance to depression plays out in every market cycle. The processes are readily observable using price charts.

Prior to the 2008 crash, Citigroup was considered by many investors as the bluest of blue-chip shares. For years prior to 2007 it yielded a competitive 3% to 4% and for a brief period from 2003 it outperformed the S&P500. It was deemed to be a stolid but secure investment one could rely on for the long run. Behind the scenes the company was gorging on cheap credit, while becoming heavily leveraged to the real estate market where it was earning fat fees from arranging suspect mortgages, securitising and selling them to investors in a financial perversion of the old children's party favourite 'pass the parcel'. Former Citigroup CEO Chuck Prince was quoted in the *Financial Times* on 10 July 2007 as saying:

> "When the music stops, in terms of liquidity, things will be complicated. But as long as the music is playing, you've got to get up and dance. We're still dancing."

Well, the music stopped in 2008 and without government intervention and funds from the Troubled Asset Relief Program (TARP) the company would have disappeared and taken a good part of the US economy with it.

Citigroup (NYSE) 2003–2013

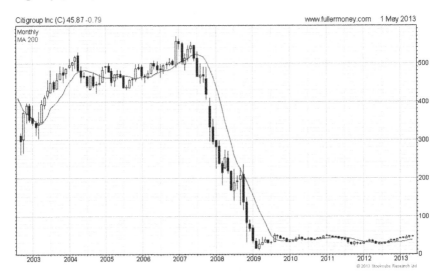

By the time the share began to bottom from early 2009, bearish pundits were predicting a Depression more extreme than the 1930s. For investors in Citigroup who had ridden the trend all the way to the bottom it must have felt like it. However, TARP also identified Citigroup as systemically important. It was unlikely to be allowed to disappear. In fact, you could reasonably anticipate that it would persist for some time to come. However, such has been the depth of the decline that no one believes the highs near $50 are ever going to be revisited. I have talked with a number of people who argue that the history of the share should be reset because the reality the company is dealing with today bears no relation to that which prevailed before the crisis struck.

From a visual perspective, it is probably now more appropriate to view such shares on a logarithmic scale rather than an arithmetic scale. This depiction offers a better reflection of the volatility in percentage terms since the 2009 lows.

Citigroup (NYSE) 2003–2013 in logarithmic scale

Investors were tempted back in as prices rallied from $1 in March 2009 and a small number of people made decent profits on the short covering rally. They were traders, most of them would not have bought for the long-term, and they would have been looking for an opportunity to realise their profits rather than run them. Investor confidence in the suitability of a buy-and-hold strategy for Citigroup had been broken. There are plenty of people holding large chunks of stock that would welcome an opportunity to sell on a rally and those who are most active are traders. If one wanted to express a truly bullish view on the prospects for the US economy and the banking sector there are probably better opportunities than Citigroup, which means that interest is likely to decrease as the base extends and participation will dissipate.

CONCLUSION

The psychological perception stages of major bull and bear market moves give us a window through which we can interpret the actions of investors and how the emotional condition of the crowd affects decisions and aspirations.

Equipped with this knowledge we can build our investment strategy so that we are initiating long positions when almost everyone else is concentrating on other markets, running a trend-running tactic as the crowd comes around to our way of thinking, and maintain discipline when exuberance captures the imagination of the crowd.

As the market deteriorates, the psychological perception stages highlight just how important discipline is as one major trend gives way to its antithesis, how likely short positions are to be profitable and when to realise that despite extremely bearish sentiment very few instruments go to zero.

CHAPTER 7:

HOW PAST SUPPORT BECOMES FUTURE RESISTANCE (AND VICE VERSA)

What we will cover in this chapter:

- In simple terms, prices are always either trending or ranging. While trending phases tend to be exciting, it is worth spending time to consider what goes on to create the range and the effect this has on sentiment.

- Since ranges are boring relative to trending phases, expectations of breakout potential deteriorate the longer a market remains in the congestion area.

- Five emotions are commonly associated with every breakdown from a range. These are: fear, anger, self-recrimination, hope and shock.

- How past support becomes future resistance and vice versa.

FOR A MAJOR BULL OR BEAR MARKET to develop there must be an imbalance between perceptions which create or alter the supply and demand factors. This imbalance often occurs in response to a fundamental economic change which then drives the bull or bear market. However, even markets in multi-year trends spend a good deal of time ranging. Such episodes signify when supply and demand have come, temporarily, back into balance. Ranges will continue for as long as it takes the conditions necessary to create a breakout to reform. In between, the duration, volatility and amplitude of ranges force investors to refocus on the short term. The longer they persist, the greater the effect they have on perceptions (and on animal spirits).

Given the propensity of markets to range, it makes sense to spend at least some time thinking about what is going on to lock prices into a broadly lateral trajectory – both in terms of investor actions and psychology. At this juncture it is worth highlighting the difference between a ranging step within an overall trend, and a rangebound market of considerable duration which may reflect a lack of interest and is generally consistent with lengthy base formation development.

Within an overall trending market the trajectory of prices will be punctuated by occasional ranges where supply and demand come temporarily back into balance. The consistency in size, duration and volatility of these ranges is a key component in addressing the consistency of the overall trend, which is the basis upon which we build our analytical framework.

This is not at all the same as a base formation where lack of interest, a compelling theme or fundamental basis and ample overhead supply can combine prices to a range for a lengthy period of time – often years and possibly decades.

Over the years David Fuller reasoned his way through examples of what happens to supply and demand and investor psychology to form the range. The following example has featured as part of the Chart Seminar for over 40 years, and while bereft of the group dynamic's drama I am happy to relate it below.

FORMING THE RANGE

To get the most out of this example, think of it as if the trade involves your own money. You may come from any walk of life or manage money for a living, but there is nothing more personal than your own money. Our individual successes and failures are distinctly personal experiences and help to shape our psychology. When we make money no one shares the credit, and when we lose our own money the blame rests squarely on our shoulders.

You have some money to invest when you receive a call from a trusted broker who recommends that you buy 'X'. To cement the view he regales you with an investment story. The premise sounds as compelling as anything else you have heard lately.

I know when my money is on the line I need to overcome a certain amount of sales resistance and even suspicion. So while the story sounds attractive, you need more information. But once you have finally accepted the investment thesis, the most important question is: what's the price?

The broker tells you that the price is at level A. You decide to buy at level A ... and the price begins to edge lower.

You are now running a loss. Of greatest importance to the behavioural analytical process is how you feel about it. Everyone is going to feel at least a bit disappointed by the initial outcome of this trade. If you don't feel just a little bad about it you are probably reading the wrong book! You might think 'I should never follow a tip ... they never work out'.

However, prices begin to rally and reach level B.

How do you feel about it now?

Better? Perhaps a little self-congratulatory?

Obviously better. But then you receive another call from your broker. He thinks you should sell.

The stress level immediately increases: you are now being asked to make a decision. No one likes change. We all want the good news to go on. When we are asked to make a decision, we are forced to reweigh the reasons for our participation. A common response is to delay or avoid the decision altogether.

In this case you might question the broker's motives: Why does the broker think I should sell? Maybe he is trying to churn the account? He couldn't possibly be right twice in a row, could he? Maybe I should buy more? Should I simply accept the sell suggestion?

Stress levels at this point will be dictated by your past experience but also by how large the position is, how much leverage you are using, or how important, generally, this trade is to your financial wellbeing.

Your most recent experience will play a vital role. If the broader market environment has been characterised by generally firm trading conditions, and you have made money on most of your trades, you will be more inclined to let the profit run. However, if the environment has been whippy, where the buy and hold mantra has been questioned and profits have been ephemeral, you will be more inclined to realise the gain before it slips away.

An excellent quote from George Eliot's *Middlemarch* encapsulates this tendency: "*Our deeds still travel with us from afar, and what we have been makes us what we are.*"

Ultimately you decide that, since you followed the broker in, you'll follow him out. You sell at level B.

Do you forget about it?

I've found myself in a similar situation on a number of occasions, particularly when I've had leveraged positions prior to going on holiday. I'll make sure to check prices regardless of where I am or what the time difference is because I need to know if a price has fallen back or if I've just sold the buy-and-hold of the year!

George Eliot is again useful here: "*Anger and jealousy can no more bear to lose sight of their objects than love.*"

Your investment in X has been good to you. In the markets this means one thing – you made money from it. So you don't forget about it. While you are no longer financially invested, you remain emotionally attached.

Prices start to fall back from B. As they approach level A, the broker calls to say that he has some buy orders and asks if you would like to participate. Your previous resistance to purchasing has diminished because you know what happened last time.

What about the other market participants? Ask yourself how many short-sellers will be increasing their positions the first time this instrument looks at level A? Not many. They know what happened last time. As others begin to purchase near this level and the market bounces, even more participants are tempted in because it offers a second bite at the proverbial cherry.

The next time X looks at level B the opposition to selling will have decreased. The learning procedure has now become relatively well-advanced. *To make money we can buy at level A and sell at level B.*

Typical commentary supporting this type of trading environment is that "It's just a big trading range" or "Take your profits when you see them". Some traders might be thinking of getting short as X gets back to level B. Those with long positions will also be starting to become wary as prices approach level B.

The next time X looks at level A you'll be calling the broker rather than him calling you. You might even be increasing the size of the position to harvest this range. Prices find support in the region of level A and trend back towards level B where you decide to sell and open a short position.

This conditioning process is practically Pavlovian. Your actions have been seen to generate the desired result and are demonstrably repeatable. As prices fall back towards level A for the third time you are covering the short. The expectation that it will find support and rally has increased considerably. You may feel like you have discovered a reliable money-making formula. Some people might even allow themselves the vanity that they are 'getting a feel for this market' or that they 'only like to trade in this market because they really understand it'.

As confidence increases so, generally, does the size of your position. You might even be using the profits from our short sale to leverage up the size of our next long. The fourth time X tests level A you are leveraging up heavily. The market is pausing for somewhat longer near level A but that won't worry us. The prevailing opinion will be that it is only a matter of time before the market starts to rally. But …

The market has just fallen abruptly. *How do you feel about it now?* The answer to this question is important because you have just experienced trauma. How you deal with that emotionally will have a strong influence on how you respond with your market position.

There are five different emotions we go through when something like this happens …

THE FIVE EMOTIONS OF MAJOR MARKET DECLINES

Following such a decline, gut-wrenching **fear** is the primary emotion we experience. Fear for our investments, fear for our career, fear for the result our actions might have on our family's wellbeing. Our dreams for how we were going to spend the money have evaporated with our paper gains and we are now running a loss. A leveraged loss can turn into a nasty blow very quickly.

Denial is perhaps the most primitive of defence mechanisms. It reflects the at-least-temporary inability to deal with the magnitude of the change. However, in the financial markets, denying a swiftly evolving reality can be dangerous to your wealth. For leveraged traders denial is a luxury they cannot afford because margins will be called in and action will be forced upon them.

Anger is an almost guaranteed response. We feel anger at the end of what had been a previously reliable trading strategy, anger at the market for lulling us into a false state of security, anger at the broker for suggesting the instrument in the first place or anger at ourselves for allowing our emotions to control our actions. Anger tends to get sprayed around. Of course, it is most appropriately directed at ourselves rather than our colleagues, spouse or pets. Anger at the apparent stupidity of our actions is virtually a given.

Self-recrimination is a natural by-product of this fall. Our confidence has taken a hit and we have no choice but to question our methods. The reserve of emotional capital we draw on to support our participation in the markets has also been depleted. It will take time to rebuild our confidence.

Despite the negativity of the fear, anger and self-recrimination, **hope** is an important part of this emotional rollercoaster. We've seen examples of sharp pullbacks before. Some have extended their declines, others have recovered. Maybe, just maybe, the market can rally from here. It is said that there are no atheists in a foxhole but this is equally true in troubled financial markets. Most investors and traders can empathise with the prayer, "Please God give me ten more points in the market and I'll never do it again".

The **shock** of this event can be paralysing. We would never have been leveraging up at level A if we had ever in our wildest dreams thought that a fall to A-10 was possible. Surprise will always be a part of this experience.

When I teach The Chart Seminar, it is interesting that the emotional state most voiced by the delegates bears a strong correlation to how the stock market in that country has recently been trading. Following a sharp pullback, negative emotions are always expressed first. But when the market has been generally firm, hope for a recovery is dominant. This emphasises just how much we are affected by recent experiences. A disciplined approach, focusing on facts rather than emotion is essential.

One might reasonably argue that you could have had a stop on the position. That would certainly have been a smart thing to have done in this scenario, but it also means being wise after the fact. Whether investors place stops or not is most often dictated by how much confidence they have in a vehicle's potential performance. In this example we believed that X was going to remain in its range and that we could continue to harvest profits from the status quo. After all, you would only have a stop if you thought the price wasn't going to trade in a range. And if it wasn't going to trade in a range, you would hardly have taken up the positions that you did.

Back in our example, for one reason or another the market begins to rally back up towards level A. Following the emotional trauma of A-10 – plus the fact that you are still long – your brain will be smoking with activity. Lots of small questions start bombarding you. What about the management? What about monetary policy? What about the dollar/euro/pound/yen/yuan? What about the deficit? What about earnings?

However, one big question looms above all others.

Will I get out even?

Very few will want to be the first to buy at level A because they know what happened last time. You decide you will certainly not be increasing your long position; you already have plenty of inventory at that level. This means that it only takes a few relatively aggressive short sellers or one large fund to decide enough is enough: the market can encounter resistance near level A and begin to fall back towards the new first area of potential support at A-10.

EXAMPLE 1: THE THAILAND SET INDEX IN 1997

The devaluation of the Thai baht was the spark that ignited the Asian financial crisis in 1997 and it fell from ฿25 to ฿55 against the US dollar between June and December 1997. As the domestic economy collapsed the Thai stock market index trended lower for much of the year in an orderly step sequence downtrend before accelerating lower as sentiment reached apocalyptically bearish levels.

On the following chart we observe a series of ranges where the behavioural dynamics described here will have played out over a number of weeks or even months before an individual range is resolved to the downside. As the trend progresses, participants get the message that the market is weak and a swifter deterioration is evident from May onwards. The market more than halved in the subsequent year but this period offers the most consistent portion of the trend.

Thailand SET Index 1997

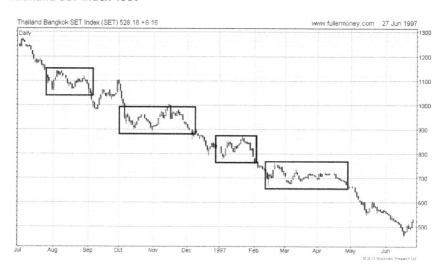

PAST RESISTANCE OFTEN BECOMES FUTURE SUPPORT

This process works exactly the same in reverse. Past resistance often becomes future support. The upper side of a well-defined range can represent the perception that prices will never successfully break upwards. However, once penetrated, the old area of resistance becomes the first area of potential support in a reversal of the process that occurred in the first example.

EXAMPLE 2: MONDELĒZ INTERNATIONAL

Mondelēz International (NYSE) 2008–2013

Kraft changed its name to Mondelēz International in October 2012 and spun off its US operations in to Kraft Food Group. The share now represents just the company's international operations. Despite the overall bullish environment, the psychological conditioning process that goes into the formation of a range is exemplified in each of the consolidations posted between 2010 and 2012.

EXAMPLE 3: THE DOW JONES INDUSTRIALS AVERAGE FROM 1975 TO 1985

While the previous examples of a range forming, and the response of investors to a breakout, is characterised in terms of a short to medium-term move, the exact same pattern of supply and demand is evident over the very long term. This illustrates the fractal nature of market actions. In other words, the exact same patterns are just as observable over very short time periods as over very long ones.

The Dow Jones Industrials Average offers an excellent example. Throughout the 1970s and early 1980s this index went through a generation-long process of valuation contraction and rising dividend yields. A 'glass ceiling' at 1000 was perceived to exist. Once successfully penetrated, prices found support above it and embarked on a new bull market.

The Dow Jones Industrials Average from 1975 to 1985

The tendency of past support to become future resistance and past resistance to become future support is readily observable in the markets. Understanding the psychological processes and the interaction between supply and demand that occur to create these conditions is a necessary step to appreciating the actions of the crowd on price action.

CHAPTER 8:

HOW DOES A BREAKOUT OCCUR?

What we will cover in this chapter:

- Ranges might be boring compared to the trending phases but we will see how every range is an explosion waiting to happen.

- Ranges are decision-making processes which create vacuums of supply above, and demand below, the ranges. When prices eventually move into these vacuums, they surge until supply and demand come back into balance.

- Failed breaks indicate that the vacuum of supply above or demand below the range has not yet formed.

- The dynamic nature of the failed break will give us clues as to how emphatic the counter-trend move is likely to be.

- Base-formation completion is the most important example of where a lengthy range is completed with an emphatic breakout, the size of which often takes participants by surprise.

- A breakout from a range does not change the fundamentals of the market but it does change the perception of those fundamentals.

- When a market ranges for a prolonged period, expectations of future potential, both up and down, deteriorate.

WHEN A MARKET IS MOVING SIDEWAYS there will inevitably be other sectors or assets that are performing better. Speculative interest migrates to those instruments. This in turn shifts the focus of attention from the ranging market. Fund managers, for instance, will make a relative value comparison and some will conclude that upside potential in other vehicles exceeds that of the ranging market. They will rotate out of the ranging market accordingly.

As long as the market is ranging, those who continue to participate are forced to accept the reality of a loss of momentum. In the course of a medium-term trend, ranging is boring compared to the trending phases. And when we are bored our motivation is reined in.

The ranging process conditions us to expect less. However, we know that every market is either ranging or trending. Therefore, regardless of how long a range persists for and how low expectations are, *every* range will eventually be followed by a trending phase. *Every* range will be completed by an emphatic breakout either up or down. David Fuller has long defined ranges as *"explosions waiting to happen"*.

In the previous chapter we considered the psychological conditioning and investor and trader actions that go into forming a range. It is also worth considering what has to happen in order for a breakout to occur.

SUPPLY AND DEMAND

By definition supply and demand come back into at least temporary equilibrium during the congestion area trading range. The market activity is boring compared to the trending phases and expectations deteriorate the longer the market ranges. Looking at the thought process of participants, there will be potential buyers below the market, potential sellers above the market and those who are participating within the range. Over time, those who want to own this instrument have to make a decision. They have a number of choices.

1. They can decide that the market has formed a well-defined range and is unlikely to fall to their desired level and therefore raise their bids up into the range.

2. They can refuse to raise their bids, deciding that the instrument is not worth the higher price and they will only pay the level they want, leaving their bids unchanged.

3. They can decide that it has already moved too far ahead; they no longer see value so they desert the market completely.

As the range persists, those interested in owning the instrument choose one of these options. Another way to describe a range is as a *decision-making process*. Over time, as participants choose to move their bids up, remove them or hold steady, this series of actions serves to thin out demand below the market. This creates a vacuum of demand beneath the range.

On the supply side there will be potential sellers above the market. Prices have been ranging, the market is comparatively boring and expectations have gone down. A decision-making process is occurring here as well, with a similar set of choices:

1. They can decide that the market has formed a top and is unlikely to rally to their desired level, so they lower their offers down into the range.

2. They can maintain their current stance and refuse to lower their offers, believing that they will be able to sell at their desired level in future.

3. They can turn into 'born-again bulls' by deciding that they underestimated the upside potential and remove their offer entirely in the hope of substantially higher prices.

As the range persists, this decision-making process thins out supply above the market. This creates a vacuum of supply above the range.

The congestion area trading range will continue for as long as supply and demand remain in balance. However, the decision-making process that characterises every congestion area eventually creates vacuums of supply above and demand below the range. Once prices move into these vacuums, explosive moves occur which prompt new sources of demand (in the bullish case) or supply (in the bearish case).

THE BULLISH CASE

Once the vacuum of supply has formed, whatever offers exist above the range are easily overcome by demand and the market surges higher following what might have been only a modest initial breakout. In an internationally traded, liquid vehicle, this move will attract at least four new sources of demand.

1. Buyers who had been waiting for lower levels. They will need to rush to buy now if they want to avoid paying even higher prices.

2. Momentum buyers who will see the breakout and conclude "Here we go again".

3. Shorts being covered. There will have been a cohort who were trading the range and shorting near the upper side. If they had stops, the most likely place for them to have been was above the previous high. And they have just been triggered.

4. Supply above the market raising offers. In a rising market, sellers have the luxury of being able to choose how to sell their inventory. Now that a powerful new breakout is in motion they may not be so keen to sell their entire position and will raise their offers.

THE BEARISH CASE

Once the vacuum of demand has formed, a small move to a new low is often all that is needed for prices to plunge lower as the vacuum of bids is hit. Prices will fall until supply and demand come back into balance again. If this is an internationally traded, liquid vehicle, this move will also attract at least four new sources of supply into the market.

1. Many of those wishing to sell above the market will now be forced to sell at this lower level if they want to get out.

2. Momentum sellers will see the plunge and seek to short into the weakness.

3. Those who were buying within the range and those who were buying at the lower side of the range will most often have their stops below the most recent low. Those stops are now being hit, adding to supply.

4. Those who were thinking of buying below the market may now be reconsidering. They have the opportunity to wait for better prices and will lower their bids or desert the market entirely.

In either case, the breakout will persist until supply and demand come back into a new equilibrium. At that point another congestion area trading range is likely to form.

Every range is an explosion waiting to happen and this is as true of a range within a multi-year bull or bear market as it is for an intraday chart. The emotions and actions market participants go through are the same regardless of the time frame. The difference is one of *compression*. An unleveraged long-term investor will go through the same range of emotions as a short-term market maker, but while for one the experience will unfold over a number of years, for the other it can happen multiple times in one day.

FAILED BREAKOUTS

Every trading range will eventually be completed by a powerful and sustained breakout, but some follow a more torturous route to that fulfilment than others.

Buying or selling breakouts works often enough as a strategy for large numbers of investors to watch for these conditions. However, not all breakouts are equal and some fail utterly. Let's take a moment to examine what is happening to supply and demand and by extension sentiment in such a scenario.

When a market has been ranging for a while, one would normally assume that the thinning out of supply above and demand below the market has been completed when the breakout occurs. But what if, instead of attracting the typical new sources of demand, prices fall back into the range?

How this can occur is important. Here are two examples:

EXAMPLE 1

In this example the market breaks upwards, and then *eases* back to test the upper side of the range. It has dipped back into the range but the process has been relatively gentle and those who bought the breakout will not have been panicked by the experience. There remains a good chance that this market will be able to find support, rally and sustain the upward break because the psychological impact of the failed break has been relatively muted.

EXAMPLE 2

The market breaks upwards but encounters overwhelming supply above the market. This is a clear indication that the assumed thinning out of supply above the market has not occurred. The price will have fallen back into the range in a dynamic fashion. Those who bought the breakout have just had a sharp reality check. Short-term market makers are likely to take the attitude that if it can't go up it will go down and may get short. The psychological impact for participants in this market has been immediate and traumatic. In this case, the chances of prices being able to find support, rally back to the upper side of the range and breakout again are less than for Example 1.

Hence one of David Fuller's rules of thumb, which has been a feature of the Chart Seminar for decades, is:

> "If the dynamic of the failure is larger than the dynamic of the breakout, the chance that the market will at least go back and test the other side of the range has greatly increased."

When a market returns to test the opposite side of the trading range following a failed break, the question then is whether the vacuum of supply or demand has formed at that side of the range. I have observed on more than a few occasions that a failed breakout at one side of a range can result in a breakout at the other side. Therefore failed breakouts are a potential cause of concern to the prevailing trend.

Magnit is Russia's largest supermarket chain and offers examples of both a breakdown from a well-defined trading range and a step sequence uptrend which is characterised by a series of ranges posted one above another.

Magnit (LSE & MCX) 2010 to 2013

1. Failed upside and downside breaks

For much of 2011 Magnit ranged mostly between $26 and $32. It failed to sustain the upward break in April and returned to test the lower side of the range. It failed to sustain a downward break at the lower side in May and rallied back to test the $32 area, where it failed again. This succession of failed breaks both to the upside and the downside showed a war going on between supply and demand, and that the vacuums of supply above and demand below had not yet formed.

On the decline from $32 in July 2011, the price did not rally from the $26 area and broke emphatically lower, falling to a low near $16.80 by October. The range was resolved to the downside, not least because the succession of failed upside and downside breaks forced an increasing number of participants to conclude that it was not worth the wait.

2. A step sequence uptrend

A step sequence uptrend is characterised by a market rallying for a time before supply and demand come back into balance for a time. A range forms where market participants adjust to the reality of higher prices. This allows vacuums of supply above and demand below the market to form again and creates the conditions for the next successful breakout to occur.

From a trend-running perspective, this type of market environment demonstrates a medium-term pattern of demand dominance which is comparatively easy to monitor. The upside can be given the benefit of the doubt in such circumstances, provided each successive range is resolved to the upside.

BREAKOUT FROM A BASE

If we return to the premise that a range is an explosion waiting to happen, then the longer a range persists, the more powerful the ensuing breakout is likely to be. It is for this reason that a breakout from a lengthy base can be regarded as a reliable continuation pattern. This assumption forms the basis for the strategy where participants initiate long positions when a market hits a new high following a lengthy range. They believe that the breakout will be sustained and improved upon. In terms of supply and demand, a breakout from a well-defined range that is sustained tells us that the equilibrium that constituted the range has been altered. The breakout, then, is evidence of a return to *demand dominance*.

Woolworths (ASX) 2003–2013

Australian-listed Woolworths offers some interesting examples of these phenomena. The share accelerated to a peak near A$35 in 2007 and pulled back sharply, giving up approximately 35% of its value in the next six months. It then spent the next five years ranging mostly between A$25 and A$30. Prices deteriorated for most of 2011 and even broke below A$25 for a time, before forming a failed downside break. Prices then turned around, rallied back to the upper side of the range breakout, before rallying to post new all-time highs. The five-year range reflected the decision-making process, where weak holders gave way to those with more conviction and the vacuum of supply above the market created the conditions for a powerful breakout.

DOES A BREAKOUT CHANGE THE FUNDAMENTALS OF A MARKET?

How often do a company's fundamentals really change? Earnings reports are at best quarterly and new product lines are relatively rare events, but prices move a lot. For a currency there is considerable debate about what even constitutes fundamentals, but GDP changes are comparatively slow when compared to the action of the currency markets. The fundamentals of the bond market are another case of where the movements of the underlying economy or company move relatively infrequently but prices move a lot. The fundamentals of commodities such as gold or oil are relatively staid compared to the action of the underlying price. (Soft commodities such as grains or other foodstuffs are susceptible to weather events which can have immediate effects on fundamentals so these markets are somewhat different.)

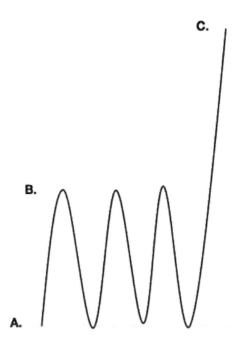

The move from B to C in the graphic opposite will not change the fundamentals of the market but it will change the *perceptions* of that market's potential.

As previously demonstrated, a successful upward break attracts four primary sources of new demand to the market. During the range, expectations decreased but interest is reignited as prices improve. The media, seeing the breakout, feel compelled to comment on this market precisely because interest has been reignited. On financial TV channels, interviewees will be asked for their opinions and those who are long will be given more air time because they have more things to say about this market. Following an upward break, bulls will be able to list any number of reasons why this instrument has just broken upwards to new high ground and the more attention-seeking fund managers will be very happy to talk about how they bought it well in advance of the breakout.

Journalists will need to write a story for their respective publication and will tap their contacts in the financial industry until they find a bull and quote him or her in an effort to explain the action. In the financial industry, the fundamental analyst will be expected to issue a report and unless he has a very strongly held view that the market is running counter to common sense, the self-survival instinct is to slant the interpretation of the underlying fundamentals to the bullish hypothesis. What else is he supposed to do when the price action is clearly supportive of the bullish view?

Those who do not understand the intricacies of macro behavioural technical analysis and who have not gone to the trouble of finding someone knowledgeable about the market, may attribute the breakout to 'technical buying', 'black box buying' or the ubiquitous 'high frequency traders'. However, all that has happened is that the range has created the conditions for the breakout by thinning out demand below and supply above the market. In an overall demand-dominated environment, the price has hit a vacuum or empty pocket of supply on the breakout, and this is helping to drive the rally.

The breakout does not change the fundamentals. It changes the *perception* of those fundamentals. On an upward break, the bullish case is proffered because it supports the price action. Investors are understandably more interested in the bullish view, because it helps to plausibly explain the price action. Perceptions of the crowd towards the market improve.

The bearish case will now have fewer adherents but will also not have been materially changed by the breakout.

Of course, the reverse of all this would happen in the case of a downward break. Those who are short will have a long list of reasons why prices can continue to deteriorate. An equity commentary will question the integrity of the board, growth projections, market share etc. In a bond or currency, the price action might be attributed to a country running into economic trouble. If it is a commodity, perhaps supply has surged or demand fell. Journalists and analysts will tend to focus on the bearish argument because it reflects the price action but the explanation based on supply and demand is that the price has hit a vacuum of demand below the range.

WHEN FUNDAMENTALS DO CHANGE

While an individual breakout will not change the fundamentals of a market, a multi-year bull or bear market trend *will*.

Really big moves in financial markets are driven by investment themes that change the world. These stories really do change the fundamentals of underlying markets. When prices have been rallying for a prolonged period of time, it prompts a supply response. In the equity markets, more private companies seek a listing in an effort to source capital. When yields are historically low companies and governments rush out to lock in a low cost of capital. When a currency has been too strong for too long, competitiveness deteriorates and increases the incentive to print more money. When commodity prices have been rallying for a prolonged period of time, companies invest in new supply. In each case, long-term trends actually change the fundamentals of the market, and this can eventually lead to reversal.

CONCLUSION

Once we understand the interactions of supply and demand that form the range and the psychological machinations that create the conditions which allow the range to be completed we have the foundation on which to base a trend-running strategy. The rhythm with which a trend forms, ranges and successfully breaks out is the basis for the consistency characteristics that are the cornerstone of macro behavioural technical analysis.

CHAPTER 9:

CONSISTENCY CHARACTERISTICS

What we will cover in this chapter:

- The most consistent trends develop where the greatest imbalance between supply and demand exist.

- Classic mistakes people make with charts

  (i) Myopia

  (ii) There are three things you can see on a chart: what you want to see, what you think you will see and what is really there.

- Your first impression is almost always your best.

- We can see what is really there by following a disciplined approach. This means asking the right questions:

  1. Is the market in a major bull or bear market phase?

  2. Is it trending or ranging?

  3. Is the trend consistent or inconsistent?

  4. If the trend is consistent, what are the consistency characteristics?

- Example 1: Gold

- Example 2: S&P500

- Example 3: US Treasuries

IF WE BREAK TRENDS DOWN INTO their constituent parts, they are made up of a series of ranges which are completed by successful breakouts that progress somewhat before another range is formed. In Chapter 7, we examined how supply and demand shape behavioural factors to form ranging consolidations and distributions. In Chapter 8, we examined how supply above and demand below ranges are thinned out, creating the conditions for breakouts to occur. We also began to look into how a breakout can alter investor perceptions of how a market might perform. In this chapter we will develop a methodology that will allow us to identify the consistency characteristics of any trend.

A thorough understanding of the consistency of a trend provides us with the foundation on which to build a strategy for investing in that market. No two trends will be the same, just as no two pieces of music are the same. However, we can recognise a rhythm when we hear it. And with some practice we can identify a consistent trend when we see one.

The consistency of a trend tells us a great deal about how supply and demand are interacting. If prices are trending powerfully, the chart is likely to be very consistent because there will be a large imbalance between supply and demand. In such cases, consistency characteristics will be easy to identify, a trend-running tactic can be employed, where to place stops will be easier to judge, position-sizing can be managed with less difficulty and we will be able to script what an ending might look like.

Uranium 2005–2009

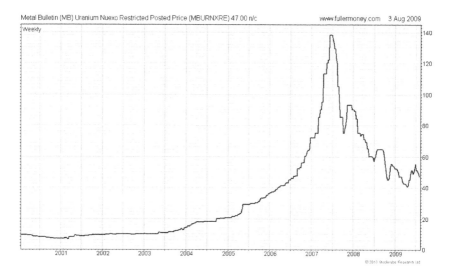

Metal Bulletin (MB) Uranium Nuexo Restricted Posted Price (MBURNXRE) 47.00 n/c   www.fullermoney.com   3 Aug 2009

From 2005 through to early 2007, uranium provided a price chart unparalleled for its consistency characteristics. Prices only went up. There were no reactions. Prices were neutral to higher for more than two years. The obvious tactic was to get long and stay long until the primary consistency characteristic faltered. When this happened in 2007, following an impressive acceleration, we could assume with a high degree of confidence that the bull run was over for at least the medium-term. The imbalance between supply and demand that had motivated the market for more than two years had clearly changed.

Uranium is an extreme example but succeeds in conveying the fact that the most consistent charts are found among the biggest movers. Advances and declines of this magnitude are not unheard of and a diligent monitoring of the trend's consistency characteristics will give us cues for how to develop our trading or investment strategy.

If prices are trending weakly or ranging in a volatile fashion, the relationship between supply and demand will be more in-balance and the trend is likely to be less consistent. We then need to make a judgement as to whether we want to invest in this market at all (or, if we have a long position, whether we are justified in increasing it or should be exiting). Our tactics need to be tailored to that particular situation.

Prolonged volatile, ranging phases often occur at major tops and bottoms because a war between supply and demand is underway. At major bottoms, the consistency of the prior downtrend has deteriorated considerably. One has to reach for consistency characteristics rather than them being immediately obvious. In such circumstances we must also remember that if a previously consistent downtrend is becoming less consistent it tells us that the supply dominated environment is changing. After-all, large bases are the seedbeds for the next bull market.

Rather the opposite is happening at major ranging, volatile tops. A war is also underway here between buyers and sellers, but in this case supply is gaining the upper hand. The consistency of the prior uptrend has been lost one step at a time and the seeds are being sown for the next major decline.

In each of these scenarios a thorough understanding and subsequent diligent monitoring of the consistency characteristics will stand us in good stead when it comes to making decisions on whether to initiate, increase, hold, decrease or exit a position.

CLASSIC MISTAKES PEOPLE MAKE WHEN LOOKING AT CHARTS

Macro behavioural technical analysis is, above all, an aesthetic discipline. All of us carry a certain amount of emotional baggage. This must be taken into account as we prepare to analyse any situation – market-related or otherwise.

There are a number of common mistakes that we should be aware of before we begin to analyse charts. Once we are aware of these, we will be in a better mindset to identify consistency characteristics.

1. TRIPLE VISION

There are at least three different things we can see when we look at a chart:

A. We can see what we want to see. As soon as we initiate a position our objectivity is immediately compromised. There is no way to avoid this. Therefore we need to have the discipline to recognise when we are interpreting the available facts from an emotional rather than rational perspective. When we have a long position, we all have a natural desire to make the best possible interpretation of the price action (and vice versa if we are short). A simple focus on chart *facts* is the only way to avoid imposing our own pet interpretation, which may not fit what is really going on.

B. We can see what we expect to see. Many less-experienced analysts and investors fall into this trap. They may have heard in the media or from a respected commentator that the instrument is in a major bull or bear market. For whatever reason, they do not have the courage of their convictions and superimpose what they think should be the case onto their interpretation. The only way to avoid this temptation is to address the market from the perspective of someone gathering facts and ignoring the market noise.

C. We can see what is actually there. In order to ensure that we see what is actually there, it is usually advisable to trust one's first instinct. Psychoanalytic 'free association' invites us to verbalise whatever comes into our minds and not to censor our thoughts. In chart analysis, our attitude should approximate this initial approach: *trusting our first instinct*. To do otherwise is to risk talking ourselves out of a sound initial analysis by overlaying our personal preconceptions towards that market.

2. MYOPIA

When we are interested in an investment vehicle there is a temptation to believe the most recent data is by far the most important. When we have a leveraged position, relatively small moves can have a big effect on our profit and loss (P&L) so we tend to focus on short-term data. When familiar with an instrument, we can allow ourselves the vanity that we know what the longer-term picture looks like so we can afford to focus on the shorter-term data. All these scenarios lead to us looking at condensed scales and exaggerating the importance of short-term data relative to the big picture. Beginning any analysis by looking at the longest possible time frame is a simple solution to this issue and takes but a moment with charting software.

Myopia can also be a problem outside of chart reading. When the bulk of our investments are in one sector or in one asset class we tend to focus our attention on that subject to the detriment of our appreciation of what is going on in others. I have occasionally been guilty of this tendency in my own analysis and it has had an opportunity cost. In early 2008, my personal trading was focused on commodities and as a result my writing focused on that sector. I was bearish on the banking sector in the USA and Europe generally, but I did not have positions in the sector and so gave it less attention than it deserved.

Additionally, what I have referred to as 'model myopia' contributed to some of the worst failures prior to and during the 2008 credit crisis. Common sense was relegated to the sidelines as a focus on financial modelling took precedence. Securitisation models were used to package and repackage dodgy credit. During the panic selling that followed the Lehman Brothers and AIG bankruptcies, an over-reliance on narrow credit models centring on credit default swaps led to an increased perception of default risk than might have existed.

Myopia in our analysis and indeed in our personal lives is a characteristic we need to be constantly vigilant against. Taking time to look at the big picture will always be time well spent.

ASKING THE RIGHT QUESTIONS

Once we appreciate what the most common mistakes in chart reading are, we need to make sure we are asking the correct questions in order to avoid them.

Most people tend to rush in when they begin their analysis. The first question usually asked is "Where is it going?" or "What's your target?" However, instead of being the first question, this should be the last – as we attempt to script how the trend will continue or end.

No two trends are the same, but they all share a number of characteristics which we can monitor for clues to any change in the broad relationship between supply and demand. In the following examples let us imagine that we are describing the consistency of the chart to a blind person who is asking us questions.

EXAMPLE 1: GOLD

Spot gold 1992–2013 logarithmic scale

Spot gold 1992–2013 arithmetic scale

London Spot Gold (GOLDS) 1286.2 +26.42   www.fullermoney.com   11 Jul 2013

Blind Questioner: Is the market in a major bull or bear market cycle?

Factual Interpreter: It went through a major bear market between 1982 and 2000 but a bull market was evident from 2003 until 2011 and it experienced a deep pullback in 2013.

Blind Questioner: Is it trending or ranging?

Factual Interpreter: It has been susceptible to some lengthy ranging periods, but when it breaks out, it really accelerates. This is the case during both upward breaks and downward breaks.

Blind Questioner: Is it consistent or inconsistent?

Factual Interpreter: It was very consistent on the upside between 2008 and early 2011 and has since become less consistent. In fact it has trended downwards since September 2012.

Blind Questioner: Can you explain that a bit better?

Factual Interpreter: A progression of higher major reaction lows is evident from 2001. These are at $330, $410, $545, $682, $1,044, $1,308 and $1,462. $1,532 represented the lower side of the range from late 2011. The last four lows occurred from late 2008 while the first three occurred between 2003 and 2008. The pace of gold's advance picked up between 2009 and September 2011, making the chart action more consistent.

From September 2011, gold moved into another lengthy consolidation where it held onto the majority of its gain but spent more time ranging than any time since 2008. It broke downwards in April 2013.

Blind Questioner: Can you tell me more about the reactions you describe?

Factual Interpreter: Gold rallied to more than $400 by early 2004 and ranged mostly above that level until Q3 2005. It then broke upwards in September and accelerated to approximately $730 by May 2006.

The subsequent reaction found support above the previous range in June 2006 and gold moved into another lengthy range. It broke upwards again in September 2007 and rallied to just over $1,000 by March 2008.

The following reaction found support in the region of the previous high near $730 but did dip below that level briefly. It then rallied quickly back to test the high, broke upwards in September 2009 and rallied to a peak just above $1200 by December 2009.

This pattern of approximately 18-month consolidations followed by successful breakouts in Septembers of uneven years sped up in 2010.

Gold broke out in May 2010 after a comparatively short consolidation. It formed a range, with an amplitude of $108, mostly above $1,200 until September 2010 then rallied persistently to $1,400.

The next reaction had an amplitude of $121 and lasted for six months. Gold broke upwards in March, consolidated for a month above $1,400 and subsequently rallied to $1,541 by May 2011.

It then pulled back and ranged with an amplitude of $115 before breaking upwards in July 2011 and accelerating to a peak of $1,921.50.

Prices then pulled back sharply, posting the largest reaction since 2008, and found support in the region of the 200-day MA near $1,530.

All of these reactions have occurred one above another, creating a step sequence ten-year uptrend.

However, gold held a progression of lower rally highs from October 2012 and accelerated down out of the 19-month range in April 2013.

Blind Questioner: Can you tell me anything about the advances?

Factual Interpreter: Until 2010 each ranging consolidation had been completed by an emphatic upward break and was followed by an acceleration higher. The late 2005 and early 2006 breakout was of approximately $275. The late 2007 and early 2008 breakout was of approximately $320. The advance from September 2009 was $226. From 2010, gold tended to pause in the region of the previous peak before accelerating higher. Measuring from the initial breakout, rallies since mid-2010 have been $220, $143 and $335. Over the last decade, it has not been unusual for gold to have a somewhat larger and lengthier pause following an acceleration.

Blind Questioner: How has gold performed relative to a trend mean such as the 200-day moving average?

Factual Interpreter: Gold found support in the region of the 200-day MA more often than not until 2012. Until then, the only aberration was during the financial crisis of 2008 when it spent five months below the trend mean. During that time it held the consistency of the step sequence uptrend described above. From early 2009, the 200-day MA was a useful touchstone in terms of identifying potential areas of support.

Gold became wildly overextended relative to the MA on a number of occasions. For ease of comparison let me quote the overextensions in percentage terms. These were 28% in 2006, 29% in 2008 and 26.8% in 2011. Previous large overextensions relative to the MA have been closed, often rather swiftly, and been followed by quite lengthy periods of support building.

In 2012, gold spent three months trading below the 200-day MA. It then broke back above it and rallied before encountering resistance at $1,800. It then dropped back below the MA before extending its decline by dropping below the lows near $1,532 and falling to $1,321.

Blind Questioner: Let me summarise the consistency characteristics.

- Gold exhibited a progression of higher major reaction lows until 2013.

- A progression of higher highs until 2012.

- It previously posted a series of 18-month consolidations but the duration of consolidations shortened from 2009 until 2011 as the consistency of the trend improved. The 19-month range that followed was an inconsistency relative to the 2009–2011 period.

- Overextensions of more than 25% relative to the 200-day MA generally represent rarefied territory for gold prices.

- The large pullback from the September 2011 represented an inconsistency relative to the prior 30-month portion of the secular uptrend not least because of the size of the decline. The breakdown from the 19-month range represents significant deterioration in the trend's consistency.

Does anything in this list suggest that the multi-year dominance of demand over supply has changed?

Factual Interpreter: Taking a long-term view, possibly. The progression of higher reaction lows has been broken. In the absence of a rally back above the 200-day MA and a break in the progression of lower rally highs that has been evident since September 2012, the only conclusion based on trend consistency is that the ten-year bull market is over.

EXAMPLE 2: 10-YR US TREASURY YIELDS

US Treasury yields 1963–2013 arithmetic scale

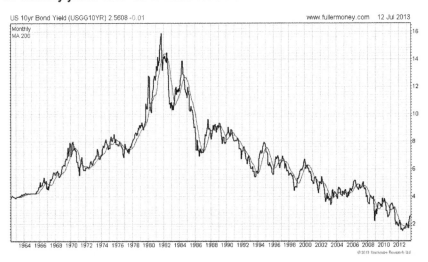

US Treasury yields 1963–2013 logarithmic scale

Merrill Lynch 10yr+ US Treasury Futures Total Return Index 1983–2013

Blind Questioner: Is the market in a major bull or bear market phase?

Factual Interpreter: The last major bull market in yields (bear market in prices) ended in 1981 and yields have been in a secular bear market since (bull market in prices).

Blind Questioner: Is it trending or ranging?

Factual Interpreter: Yields collapsed from the peak between 1981 and 1986 and entered a rangy downtrend over the last 26 years. When we look at the log scale chart we see that the decline accelerated in 2008 and again in 2011. The yield halved on both occasions. This introduced more volatility than seen in the course of the prior 25 years. In tandem with this war between supply and demand, real interest rates were negative for much of the time from 2011 until mid 2013.

Blind Questioner: Since we are examining an interest-bearing instrument would it not be more appropriate to deal with a total return index in order to get a more complete idea of what has motivated investors over such a long period?

Factual Interpreter: I agree, a total return index should offer some additional insights. If we examine the Merrill Lynch 10yr+ US Treasury Total Return Index we are presented with a well-defined view of the almost 30-year demand dominated environment for US Treasuries.

Blind Questioner: Is this chart trending or ranging?

Factual Interpreter: The index has been trending higher since its inception in 1983.

Blind Questioner: Is the trend consistent or inconsistent?

Factual Interpreter: It has mostly been consistent. There has been a series of quite lengthy ranges over the last 28 years but the broad upward bias remained intact until June 2013.

Blind Questioner: What are the consistency characteristics?

Factual Interpreter: There was an unbroken progression of higher major reaction lows over the course of the 28-year uptrend, which was broken in June 2013.

A series of higher rally highs is also evident.

The index has found support in the region of the 200-day MA on successive occasions but has dropped further below it at the time of writing than at any time in the course of the overall advance.

Almost all of the major ranges have been posted one above another.

Blind Questioner: Tell me more about the ranges.

Factual Interpreter: There has been a rhythm to the way this trend has unfolded. An almost unbroken succession of medium-term ranges, one above another, is evident since 1983.

Without going into the minutiae of each of the ranges, what is now apparent is that the ranges are persisting for longer than 'normal'.

Relative to the previous 25 years this is an inconsistency.

Blind Questioner: How has the index performed relative to a trend mean such as the 200-day MA?

Merrill Lynch 10yr+ US Treasury Futures Total Return Index 2008–2013

Factual Interpreter: Overextensions of approximately 10% relative to the MA have been quite common over the course of the uptrend. Price often overshoots on reversions towards the mean. It would therefore be accurate to say that prices have tended to find support in the region of the MA rather than at the MA. The pullback posted in June and July of 2013 represents the largest overshoot of the MA in the history of the index and as such can be considered a major trend inconsistency.

Blind Questioner: I now have a clear picture of the index's long-term consistency characteristics. Can you tell me more about the size of the ranges?

Factual Interpreter: During Q3 2008, the index had been ranging in the region of the 200-day MA. In October 2008 it accelerated higher, reached a peak near 1,660 and mostly ranged, which allowed it to unwind the overbought condition relative to the MA.

It then broke upwards again in May 2010 and rallied to a peak near 1,800. The subsequent unwinding of the overextension relative to the MA was quite sharp but prices again found support in the region of the 200-day MA.

It broke upwards again in July 2011 and lost momentum from September in the region of 1,900. This range was shallower than the previous two and was characterised by another ranging consolidation. It found support in the region of the 200-day MA in March 2012 and rallied to test the 2,000 area by April. It ranged in the region of 2,000 for more than a year and broke downwards in June 2013.

The index failed to sustain an upward break in April 2013, then dropped back and broke down from the more than year-long range, and at the time of writing was falling into the underlying trading range. These represent major inconsistencies in what has previously been a very consistent trend.

Blind Questioner: On a commonality basis, if we return to the price action of the underlying bond futures, how is the US 10-year Treasury future performing relative to other sovereign benchmarks?

Factual Interpreter: A bull market was also evident in the government bonds of Japan, the UK, Germany, Switzerland, Canada and Australia, so there is a high degree of commonality in the sector.

Blind Questioner: Let me summarise. The primary consistency characteristics are that the market has been in a secular bull for the last 30 years. Yields have been declining but not in a particularly consistent fashion and two separate accelerations have occurred in the last few years. The total return index reflects a much clearer representation of the bull market but this previously consistent trend is deteriorating and may have already topped.

What can we now conclude?

Factual Interpreter: If the secular bull market in bonds is to be sustained, the minimum requirement is that the total return index hold a rally back above the 200-day MA. In the absence of such a move we can only conclude that the secular bull market in Treasuries is over.

EXAMPLE 3: THE S&P500

S&P500 Index 1963–2013 logarithmic scale

S&P500 Index 1963–2013 arithmetic scale

S&P 500 Index (SPX) 1675.02 +22.40   www.fullermoney.com   11 Jul 2013

Blind Questioner: Is it in a major bull or bear market phase?

Factual Interpreter: The market experienced a phenomenal bull market following a breakout from a lengthy base in 1980 but peaked in 2000 and has been largely rangebound since. Therefore in terms of the long-term trend the last 13 years could be described as a lengthy range. This stagnation could also be described as a generational long process of P/E ratio contraction and rising dividend yields similar to that which occurred between 1965 and 1980.

Blind Questioner: Can you tell me more about the decade-long range since 2000?

Factual Interpreter: The range persisted for 13 years from 2000 and posted new all-time highs in April 2013.

Within this very broad pattern, there have been a number of cyclical bull and bear markets which have posted impressive percentage gains and declines. The index has halved twice and the subsequent multi-year rallies have seen the index almost double.

Blind Questioner: What can you tell me about the various trending phases?

Factual Interpreter: The downtrend from the 2000 peak to the October 2002 low had a number of ranges which tended to dip into one another but the defining characteristic was the progression of lower rally highs and resistance encountered in the region of the 200-day MA. The decline ended in a Type-2 bottom with failed downside breaks and a massive reaction against the prevailing downtrend.

111

The uptrend from 2002 to October 2007 was relatively consistent with a series of ranges mostly one above another. The index found support in the region of the trend mean on successive occasions. The pace of the advance picked up as the 2000 peak was approached, the reactions became larger and it failed to sustain the breakout to new highs. The index completed a Type-2 top in January 2008. The index ranged below the MA in a first step below the top until July and accelerated lower from September 2008.

It accelerated lower in a Type-1 bottoming characteristic until early November 2008, then lost momentum and completed another Type-2 bottom from May 2009.

The uptrend from early 2009 until early 2012 has been considerably more volatile and less consistent than the advance between 2002 and 2007. A progression of higher major reaction lows is evident but the reactions have become successively larger. The pattern has been characterised by impressively persistent advances which gave way to sharp, swift, deep pullbacks in April 2010 and April 2011, and the index encountered resistance near 1,400 from April 2012. The index posted another powerfully persistent advance from November 2012 and posted new all-time highs in April 2013.

Blind Questioner: Is there any evidence of Type-1, Type-2 or Type-3 trend-ending characteristics?

Factual Interpreter: The index may be in the process of completing a Type-3 13-year base formation. If this assumption is correct the index will continue to find support in the region of the 200-day MA on occasional pullbacks and will sustain the majority of upward break posted in April 2013.

Blind Questioner: What would your tactic be?

Factual Interpreter: At the present moment we have no way of knowing whether the breakout to new highs will hold or not. There is potential that a reversion towards the mean may take place before additional higher prices can be sustained.

Considering the depth of disagreement among investors, if prices hold the majority of the breakout, a first step above the base could form. The potential for this to occur would be heightened by the removal of extraordinary monetary accommodation.

If the 13-year range is to persist, the breakout will fail to hold and prices will sustain a move below the 200-day MA.

Considering these options, the risk-adjusted way to approach the market would be to hold long positions and resist the temptation to chase the market higher, at least until there is evidence that a new secular bull market has been established.

CHAPTER 10:

ANTICIPATING PRICE ACTION

What we will cover in this chapter:

- In order to participate effectively we cannot afford to be reactive, we need to develop a methodology for anticipating in what way price action is likely to evolve.

- A consistent trend is the most reliable continuation pattern. "*A consistent trend is a trend in motion.*"

- Commonality – no financial instrument exists in a vacuum, therefore the performance of one instrument can give us clues to how related instruments will perform.

- Relative strength and the importance of leadership – leaders lead for a reason. Leaders tend to lead in both directions.

- Banking sector leadership – as liquidity providers banks should respond well in any environment where demand for liquidity is increasing. When they are not performing in line with the market, there is usually an important reason for it.

- Dynamics – moves forceful enough to make the crowd sit up and pay attention serve to either confirm a move or to check sentiment.

IN THE DIGITAL ERA IT IS ALL TOO EASY to become overawed by the mass of information one is presented with. We have never before been confronted by so much information, opinion and conjecture. Learning to synthesise this constant flow of data is a skill in itself, but as we spend more time processing information there is a risk that we become reactive rather than anticipatory in our actions. If we are to form a reliable investment process, we need to attempt to anticipate what may happen so that we can frame our response ahead of time.

A consistent trend is a trend in motion. As long as the rhythm of the market is not interrupted, the benefit of the doubt can be given to the direction of the trend. A consistent trend is therefore the most reliable of continuation patterns because it can be expected to unfold as it has been doing. Once we grasp the primary consistency characteristics of the trend, we can then move on to script what an ending might look like. When the rhythm of the trend changes or is interrupted, it signals that how supply and demand have been interacting has been altered. This necessitates action or at least a change of emphasis in our analysis.

Let's begin by looking at a range:

Typical range

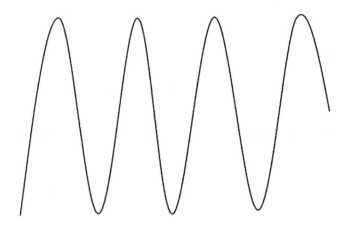

As previously discussed, a range can be defined as an explosion waiting to happen. Since the process that causes a range to form also thins out supply above and demand below the market, how are we to anticipate in what direction the eventual breakout will occur?

There is nothing on this chart to indicate in which direction the eventual breakout is likely to occur. We need more information.

In order to avoid myopia, we need to first look at as much back history as possible so that we have an idea of where we are in the overall cycle. Are we in a secular bull or bear market? Are we in a cyclical bull or bear move within the larger secular trend? Here is the same chart with more back history on a somewhat more condensed scale:

Series of ranging consolidations one above another

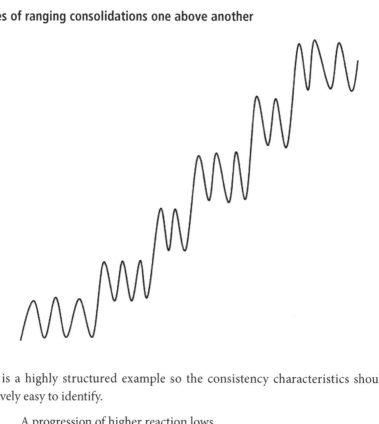

This is a highly structured example so the consistency characteristics should be relatively easy to identify.

- A progression of higher reaction lows.
- A progression of higher rally highs.
- Each of the congestion area trading ranges is relatively similar-sized.
- The trading ranges go on for approximately the same amount of time.
- The 'steps' formed one above another.

Nothing has happened to the relationship between supply and demand to indicate that anything has changed. People involved in this market are comparatively sanguine and nothing has happened to shake them out of their bullish complacency. Sentiment will invariably be improving in such a scenario. Therefore this is a trend in motion and will continue to advance provided the consistency characteristics remain intact.

Each of the ranges is completed with a successful upward break. Given our previous examination of failed breakouts we might ask how we are to know if a breakout will be successful or not. There is no way to know, but we can tailor our tactics to both possible outcomes. On the one hand if the trend is to remain consistent it will sustain the upward break. In the context of a consistent rhythmic trend in motion, David Fuller developed a rule of thumb which is appropriate to this situation. *"If the market has further to go NOW, it will sustain the upward break."*

If on the other hand the upward break is not sustained, it tells us that for the first time in the course of the uptrend, the vacuum of supply above the market has not formed. This might be considered a yellow warning light for the bullish hypothesis that was supported by a previously consistent trend. Since a failed upside break will often see prices fall back to test the lower side of the range, the importance of support being found above or in the region of the lower side of the range becomes more pressing. If the uptrend is to be reasserted, prices would have to break out to new highs and hold the advance.

When the rhythm of a previously consistent trend is interrupted by inconsistency, it is indicative of a change in the relationship between supply and demand. However, the momentum of the crowd can often be such that inconsistencies are tolerated at least for a time. Another observation David Fuller has long maintained is that *"consistent trends will often lose their consistency at the penultimate high or low"*. Let's examine why this might occur.

As long as the market continues to trend consistently, by definition nothing has happened to shake the complacency of those with positions in line with the trend. However, if the instrument then posts a larger pullback, enters a prolonged ranging phase or accelerates, we have a signal that the imbalance between supply and demand that helped drive the trend has changed.

An inconsistency, particularly following a consistent trend, can mark the penultimate high or low because while the behavioural analyst will identify the change to the consistency characteristics, the investment crowd will still be enamoured with the prevailing story. Some will use a larger pullback or extended range to increase positions and will often succeed in pushing the market to new highs. However, the event that led to the inconsistency of the trend will have shaken the resolve of enough investors that the imbalance between supply and demand will have changed. The inconsistency often signals that the dominance of demand over supply (or vice versa) is beginning to be exhausted following the consistent move. As a result the impetus to fuel a sustained additional extension of the trend will be reduced.

EXAMPLE 1: THE FTSE-100

The FTSE-100 trended consistently higher from its 2003 lows until the first half of 2006 when the consistency of the uptrend began to fray. Let us first identify what the consistency of the uptrend had been:

(i) A progression of higher major reaction lows is evident.

(ii) A sequence of higher rally highs is evident.

(iii) Each upward break from a well-defined trading range is sustained.

(iv) Each of the trading ranges formed above the previous one so that a step sequence uptrend is evident.

(v) Each of the trading ranges was relatively similar sized.

(vi) Prices found support in the region of the 200-day MA on successive occasions.

The FTSE-100 2005–2009

The **first** inconsistency was the larger reaction. Prior to April 2006, each reaction was less than 350 points but from April to mid-June 2006 the market pulled back by more than 600 points. While this would have been a nervous time for those with long positions, the index found support in the region of the upper side of the previous range and the region of the 200-day MA which would have been viewed as an entry point by enough participants to provoke a rally.

The **second** inconsistency occurred between the end of 2006 and early 2007. This trading range did not form above the previous one and dipped back below the previous high. This was the first time that two successive reactions had overlapped in the course of this multi-year uptrend. Since the market found support at the psychological 6,000 level and the progression of rising lows remained intact, this did not cause most people to exit their long positions.

The **third** inconsistency was represented by the emphatic failure of the first move above 6,500 in 2007. The index pulled back so sharply that it tested the lower side of the previous range, but it found support in the region of the 200-day MA.

By this stage, the index had posted larger reactions than seen previously, those reactions had started to dip into one another and it was posting failed upside breaks.

The primary consistency characteristics were reduced to a progression of higher reaction lows, progressively higher highs and finding support in the region of the 200-day MA.

The **fourth** inconsistency occurred following the failure to sustain the move above 6,500. Prices fell, to post the first lower reaction low in the course of the multi-year uptrend. The market then ranged below the 200-day MA for two months before rallying back to test – but not exceed – the previous peak. In this four-month period the remaining consistency characteristics were all violated.

The period of increased volatility where each of the trend's consistency characteristics were challenged and dismissed resulted in the market spending most of 2007 in a range. Broadening following a consistent advance is seldom a reliable continuation pattern. Why might this be?

At this point, supply and demand have come back into equilibrium. Increased volatility following an already mature advance is indicative of a war between supply and demand. In terms of the structure of the market, one does not have to be an engineer to see that the chart is beginning to look top-heavy. That does not mean prices can't successfully breakout again, reaffirm the uptrend and continue to move to new highs. However, if that is going to happen, it will first have to at least sustain an upward break.

Within such a lengthy range, this one went on for more than a year; anyone who wanted to buy had probably already done so. Unsatiated demand, those who could normally be expected to have had bids below the market, will probably be less enthusiastic about the instrument than during the trending phase because they have had more than a year to think about their strategy without being forced to make a decision. Rather than waiting for a pullback an increasing number will remove bids and wait to see a breakout in order to confirm the bullish hypothesis rather than give it the benefit of the doubt.

For those already long, the ranging phase is boring compared to the trending phase. They have done well from the uptrend and will want to be in a position to benefit from its reassertion, but they will also want to make sure they protect their paper profits. The logical step is to introduce stops. Most people place their stops underneath the last reaction low.

Since the market is ranging, supply is now at least equal to demand. For everyone who wanted to buy there is at least one more who wants to sell. What had been a demand-dominated environment is being challenged. The bearish case will be beginning to gain some credence, though relatively few wholehearted adherents at this point.

Stops have been introduced, buyers are waiting, people shorting rallies are making money, and the hope that the market will break upwards once more represents a good deal of what is helping support the market at this stage. The lower high posted in December 2007, then lower low posted in early 2008, were the first consistency characteristics of the new downtrend. As the market failed in the region of the 200-day MA from May 2008, the new downtrend was affirmed.

A loss of downtrend consistency then becomes evident close to the 2009 bottom. The index's value collapsed in 2008, with the accelerated decline being the most consistent portion of the drop. The index lost momentum from October 2008, volatility increased and it posted a failed downside break in March 2009 which marked the low. The subsequent rally tested the upper side of the overhead range, posted a higher reaction low and sustained an upward break in July, beginning a new uptrend.

COMMONALITY

Nothing exists in isolation. David Fuller proposed more than 40 years ago that if we wish to examine one instrument we should compare it to similar instruments so that we can gain additional perspective. Commonality forms one of the most useful tools in the arsenal of the macro behavioural technical analyst because it helps to reveal additional information we might not otherwise have been privy to. It is not an exaggeration to claim that some of my best calls in the market have been based on analysis where commonality highlighted a new investment theme.

For instance, in a mostly rangebound stock market environment we can look at a wide number of national indices. If downward breaks are mostly failing but an increasing number are sustaining upward breaks we can deduce that demand is beginning to exceed supply.

When looking for evidence of market bottoms we are often tempted to focus on the epicentre of the problem. However this would be to submit to myopia. We would be better served by surveying a wide number of markets for evidence of upside leadership. The first movers in such a scenario give us clues to recovery potential and are much more important than focusing on laggards. We are looking for a transition from supply to demand dominance. Markets that break upwards first demonstrate greater sensitivity to the new bullish hypothesis that is likely to animate wider investor interest later.

This approach is equally applicable to the bearish case. For example, if stock market indices are mostly ranging and an increasing number are breaking downwards we can deduce that supply is beginning to exceed demand. The performance of downside leaders, when looking for evidence of market tops, is more important than the performance of late-in-the-cycle movers. Here again we are looking for evidence of a transition of dominance from one group of market participants to the other.

Another adage David Fuller has long propounded is that "*In a bear market, investment vehicles are taken out one by one and shot*". The reason for this is that when we consider a range of markets, they do not all rise and fall at exactly the same time. However, as bearish sentiment takes hold, investors become progressively less inclined to give the upside the benefit of the doubt. More investors introduce stops. As these are triggered, sentiment towards other markets also deteriorates. This can set off a chain reaction. A similar process was particularly evident in the aftermath of the Bear Stearns bankruptcy, where market participants began to ask who was next.

Commonality is equally applicable to other asset classes. With sovereign bonds we will look at not only the bonds of one country but similar maturities across a wide range of countries. In corporate bonds, we will want to look at the credits of companies of the same rating or the same sector across international boundaries. For currencies, we will want to look at our base currency versus a large number of other currencies. In stock markets we can compare the performance of multiple different indices. On a sector level, we can compare sector indices across countries and geographical regions, or we can compare the price charts of individual shares within a sector to each other and with those in other countries.

With precious metals, we can compare gold, silver, platinum and palladium. With industrial metals we can compare copper, aluminium, nickel, zinc, lead and tin. We can additionally look at some of the minor metals such as ferro-chrome, indium, manganese, molybdenum etc. In the energy sector we can compare the charts for crude oil listed on various exchanges. We can also compare crude oil with heating oil, gasoline, coal and to a lesser extent natural gas.

In the agricultural sector, the approach is a little more complicated. In grains we can compare corn, soybeans, wheat, oats, rough rice, canola/rapeseed to each other. However, in the coffee market there are only two types: robusta and arabica. Cocoa, sugar, orange juice, cotton, lumber, rubber and others are individual markets largely governed by their own fundamentals. Nevertheless, commonality can also be applied across the soft commodity sector because when we see that they are all rising or falling at the same time, we have a clue as to how broad-based commodity index funds or commodity market trackers are acting.

Here is an example of a commonality-based analysis I presented on 6 September 2010 relating to cloud computing:

> "I performed a search of Nasdaq-100 companies on 5 March looking at 20-year charts in an effort to find shares that were close to completing long-term bases. In retrospect, while technology was a major theme in the results it is now becoming clear that there was also a high degree of commonality in the results with Citrix Systems, Check Point Software Technologies, Cognizant Technology Solutions, Juniper Networks and Oracle all sharing a connection to next generation data storage … "

> " … In conclusion while a great deal of time has been spent worrying about the future since April, companies such as those listed above have been busy advancing technological solutions that could make all the difference to the USA's technological edge. Their relative strength, particularly over the last month, clearly signals investors are betting these shares offer medium to long-term growth potential."

In this example, commonality was used to identify a group of shares that were just beginning to exhibit base formation completion and relative outperformance. A considerable number of such shares subsequently rallied spectacularly.

Commonality is an invaluable tool in our analysis. It forms at least part of the decision-making process in just about every major market call I make. I firmly believe that time spent examining related markets is seldom wasted. Commonality is a key tenet of macro behavioural technical analysis.

RELATIVE STRENGTH AND THE IMPORTANCE OF LEADERSHIP

Relative strength and leadership are two important topics in macro behavioural technical analysis. To differentiate between the two I characterise relative strength as a performance metric, while leadership is about timing. Therefore while an instrument can be a leader and show relative strength at the same time, there are important differences between the titles.

Relative strength is observed in an instrument which is outperforming either its sector or wider asset class. Relative weakness is observed in an instrument that is underperforming its market or asset class during a decline.

Leadership is a timing designation. Upside leaders find support first, break upwards first and importantly often top out ahead of the wider sector or market. Downside leaders peak early, complete top formations first and will often bottom ahead of the wider market.

Leaders in a major bull or bear market will often also show considerable relative strength by outperforming to the upside or downside respectively. They will regularly post their greatest outperformance in the early stages of a bull or bear market because they have been comparatively less affected by whatever caused the prior advance or decline and so look more appealing to counter trend investors. However, as a major trend develops, other sectors or instruments begin to play catch-up and this means that it would be unusual for an early leader to hold an unchallenged position of relative strength for an entire bull market. The strongest likelihood is that while the temporal leadership is likely to be sustained for most of the bull market, the early leader will go through phases of outperformance and underperformance compared to other sectors and asset classes during the course of a medium-term bull or bear market.

EXAMPLE 1: MICROSOFT (NASDAQ) COMPARED TO THE NASDAQ-100 1994–2013

Microsoft / Nasdaq-100 Index 1994–2013

Microsoft peaked three months before the wider market in absolute terms. It also bottomed more than three years before the Nasdaq.

Microsoft / Nasdaq-100 Index 1990–2013

The above ratio of Microsoft / Nasdaq-100 clearly illustrates Microsoft's relative strength compared to the wider market for the vast majority of the tech bubble. It went through minor phases of underperformance but the general trend was towards outperformance for the better part of a decade. It hit an important relative peak in April 1999 and while it moved to a positive position of relative strength from September 2000, this was more a factor of Nasdaq-100 weakness rather than strength in Microsoft. The underperformance of the share in the period from 2010 to early 2013 reflects the company's failure to compete in an environment where operating systems for handheld devices have largely bypassed the company.

EXAMPLE 2: S&P500 BANKS INDEX WITH THE S&P500

S&P500 Banks overlayed with S&P500 1994–2013

This chart of the S&P500 Banks Index is a slightly different comparison because it overlays a sector to a very broad market. The previous example was of a technology share to a technology-led index.

In the decade to 2007, banks went from being a mid-sized to a major weighting in the S&P500. The overlay chart demonstrates that in the late 1990s, the banking sector peaked almost two years ahead of the wider market. Banks were particularly amenable to the Fed's liquidity infusion in the aftermath of the tech bust and were already rallying before the wider market peaked in 2000.

The S&P500 Banks sector was finding support at progressively higher levels by the time the S&P500 bottomed in 2002 and showed considerable early relative strength. In absolute terms, the Sector topped out six months ahead of the wider market in 2007 and deteriorated much faster than the wider market subsequently.

S&P500 Banks Index / S&P500 Index

The above chart of the S&P500 Banks Index / S&P500 illustrates the participation of banks in the majority of the 1990s bull market. The sector underperformed from April 1998 to March 2000 but was subsequently one of the best performing sectors until August 2002. It began to trend lower against the wider market from 2004 and accelerated lower from 2006 on a relative basis.

THE IMPORTANCE OF BANK LEADERSHIP

Major bull and bear markets are driven by the development and subsequent failure of a theme powerful enough to harness the interest of investors for a number of years. The opening up of the USA's west coast drove a bull market concentrating on railroads. Renewal following the world wars drove a bull market in the 1950s. The export-led manufacturing model pursued by the four Asian Tigers and Japan in the 1980s drove major bull markets in stocks and property in those economies. Technology and the internet drove a huge bull market in the Nasdaq and the USA in the 1990s and rise of the global consumer driven by the economic emergence of the world's population centres is likely to be the most popular theme of the next decade.

Bull markets need a major theme capable of capturing the imaginations of investors but a theme is not enough on its own. Capital markets need to be deep enough to absorb the weight of money a major international bull market can generate. No bull market can develop without credit being made available to fuel the animal spirits of investors. This is why the banking sector is an integral part of any bull market. As we saw with the example of the S&P500 banks sector and the S&P above, it does not have to lead. However, it does need to perform at least in line with the wider market.

This is a common-sense point. The basic role of banks is to be liquidity providers. In any major bull market, banks should have numerous money-making opportunities, whether from lending to new businesses, arranging IPOs, M&A activity, new issuance of debt, investing against their own balance sheets, etc. If the banking sector is not performing in line with the wider market and is in fact going in the opposite direction, then we have to ask important questions about why that might be.

Looked at the other way around, in an environment where banks have been the leading sector in a bull market, their subsequent collapse initiates a withdrawal of credit, the business models they used to make money no longer work and their convalescence has a knock-on effect for the wider market. It is not until the banking sector actually bottoms that the headwind for the wider market is removed.

For these reasons, close attention should be paid to the performance of bank sectors because they are often a good bellwether for the wider market. We looked at the case of the USA where the banking sector peaked well in advance of the wider market – representing the epicentre of risk and leading the decline. Let's now take a look at the bull market example of Japanese banks and the Nikkei in 2003:

Nikkei-225 Index overlaid with the Topix Banks Index 1995–2007

Here is what David Fuller had to say on leadership back in 2003:

> "No significant stock market rallies occur from bear market lows without good
> relative performance by bank shares. Having fallen to 7% of market
> capitalisation, compared to over 20% in most other markets, Japan's banks have
> begun to reverse their lengthy period of underperformance over the last
> fortnight."

The Japanese banking sector had been a serial underperformer throughout 2000, 2001
and 2002. However, in early 2003 it rallied to break the progression of lower rally highs
and clearly outperformed the wider market. It also topped out well ahead of the wider
market from early 2006.

Fast forward to 2013 and Japanese banks gave up the entire advance and more
following the 2006 peak but began to outperform the wider market once more from
2011. At the time of writing they continue to represent both leadership and relative
strength. As long as Japanese banks are performing at least in line with the wider
market, the outlook for Japan's recovery will likely remain positive.

Topix Banks Index / Japan Topix Index 1992–2013

DYNAMICS

A *dynamic* is a move that is immediately obvious on a chart both for its size and the dramatic impact it has on the prevailing psychology of a market.

BULLISH SCENARIO

An upward dynamic indicates bullish sentiment. In an uptrend, they are most often seen in breakouts from trading ranges as prices hit a vacuum of supply and surge higher. Following a persistent advance, if that market then begins to post upward dynamics, they can be an ending signal because upside potential is being fulfilled all at once and demand is being exhausted. In a downtrend, when the market posts a counter-trend upward dynamic, it can signal that demand is beginning to regain dominance and is at least a warning that the prevailing bearish psychology is being questioned.

BEARISH SCENARIO

A downward dynamic indicates bearish sentiment. In a downtrend, they are most often seen in breakdowns from trading ranges as prices hit a vacuum of demand and plunge lower. Following a persistent decline, if that market then begins to post downward dynamics they can be an ending signal because downside potential is being fulfilled all at once and supply is being exhausted. In an uptrend, when the market posts a clear counter-trend downward dynamic, it can be a signal that supply is beginning to regain dominance and is at least a warning that the prevailing bullish psychology is being questioned.

In a trading range, we can observe both upward and downward dynamics as either supply or demand attains temporary dominance. A rule of thumb David Fuller has long espoused is: "*We can give the benefit of the doubt to the most recent dynamic until or unless it is countermanded.*"

Bullish trampolining occurs in a trading range when we observe that prices are rallying sharply or in a dynamic fashion from the lower side of the range but fall back more slowly from the upper side. This indicates that buyers are accumulating on setbacks and are letting out less of their inventory on the rallies within the range. In terms of anticipating in which direction the market is going to breakout, bullish trampolining usually indicates an upward break.

The following chart of the Dow Jones Industrial Average (2009–2013) is replete with examples of dynamic moves.

Dow Jones Industrial Average (2009–2013)

Dow Jones Ind Avg (INDU) 14547.5 +10.37   www.fullermoney.com   19 Apr 2013

1. The massive downward acceleration in October 2008 was the most consistent part of the decline because it went straight down and exhausted supply for at least five months. While this climactic downward dynamic did not mark the absolute low, it did signal that the endgame for the overall decline was underway.

2. The succession of four consecutive downward dynamics in February 2009 exhausted supply and the early March countertrend upward dynamic signalled that a low of at least short-term and ultimately medium-term significance had been reached as shorts began to be put under pressure.

3. The upward dynamic following the pullback from 9000 occurred from the lower side of the short-term range and is a good example of bullish trampolining. It also helped to confirm the return of demand in the region of the 200-day MA and signalled that the medium-term progression of lower rally highs was about to be broken.

4. In August 2011, the index posted a large downward dynamic to break downwards from a six-month range. It stabilised mostly above 10,500 where the internal dynamics of the congestion area were volatile, up one week down the next, suggesting a war between supply and demand. The failed downside break in October was confirmed with an upward dynamic the week after. The index subsequently found support above 11,000, again in a dynamic fashion, and price action became progressively more consistent afterward.

CONCLUSION

The financial markets are inherently uncertain. The speed with which prices move on occasion can force people to be reactive. However, if we remain aware of the methods discussed in this chapter – consistency, commonality, relative strength, leadership and dynamic moves – we can gain an edge in attempting to anticipate how prices will evolve.

CHAPTER 11:

MOVING AVERAGES

What we will cover in this chapter:

- Moving averages can be defined as *"trend-smoothing devices that lag by definition"*.

- A 200-day moving average is best thought of as a trend mean.

- The closest thing we have to a natural law of physics in the markets is that when prices diverge from the mean they will eventually revert back to it.

- The moving average also offers a crude indication of trend direction.

DAVID FULLER HAS OFTEN DESCRIBED mean reversion as "*the closest thing we get to a natural law of physics in the social science of investor sentiment*". As market sentiment ebbs and flows within a trend, we invariably see prices become divorced from a mean before eventually reverting back towards it. This often occurs in a rhythmic fashion which forms part of the consistency of that market move. As long as we are sensitive to the inevitability of this movement we are in a position to profit from it.

It might seem unusual in a book devoted largely to the analysis of price action that there is only one chapter devoted to technical indicators. However, I think it is relevant to point out that the proportion of this book devoted to technical indicators is roughly approximate to the percentage of time I spend looking at them in the course of my own analysis on a daily basis. In fact the only indicator I use with any kind of regularity is a 200-day moving average because it approximates a trend mean.

Many investors have their own cherished set of indicators that they use successfully in the course of their analysis. Most successful traders and investors form tactics that are appropriate to their temperament. My aim is not to proselytise or trample on someone's pet indicator but to simply outline my approach to the use of these tools.

I taught seminars all over Europe when I worked at Bloomberg. However, when someone first asked me why an indicator worked, my instinct was to say because this line crossed that line, or the level was above a certain percentage. But this was a hollow approach. The reality was that I had been accepting at face value the results of indicators that worked on some occasions and not on others. I began to winnow out indicators from my repertoire that I could not explain in clear common sense terms. As a result of this process, Elliott Wave, Gann and most of DeMark went by the wayside because they all tended to either rely on subjective interpretation or had rules I simply could not explain to an uninitiated observer. What I was left with were a small number of indicators that I could explain. Some worked in ranging markets, others in trending markets but none worked all of the time. My belief in the discipline of technical analysis was flagging and I was beginning to become disillusioned.

I was lucky enough to be transferred to the Dutch sales team in 2003 and on my first trip to Amsterdam was privileged to sit in on a talk given by David Fuller. His approach of focusing on chart *facts* rather than theory – recognising that everything we need to know about the price action is there on the chart if we are prepared to see it – resonated with me and considerably accelerated my analytical development.

I realised that if I could approach price action without attempting to impose my own preconceptions of what I might see or what I thought should be there, I had a better chance of successfully identifying the aspects of the trend that would signal when it was ending. Adding trend lines or other technical overlays did not appear to be providing me with a great deal of additional value but were proving to be a hindrance. I began to see that my previous reliance on indicators was a crutch I relied on because I was not prepared to analyse the data available without the aid of another tool. I decided to throw that crutch away and now seldom use indicators. However, moving averages are worthy of some further investigation.

MOVING AVERAGES

If a trend line is defined as a line that is used to connect two or more pivot points on a chart, then a moving average can be considered a curved trend line that connects multiple points. David Fuller defines moving averages as "*trending-smoothing devices that lag by definition*". Since moving averages are trend-smoothing devices they tend to be most useful in trending markets and least useful in ranging volatile markets.

Since macro behavioural technical analysis is a social discipline, there are no absolute answers to the following questions: every market and every investor's aims are different. There is also considerable academic debate centring on the use of moving averages which I am loath to get mired in. This section will discuss the use of moving averages in so far as they are useful to the disciplines of behavioural technical analysis and little more.

Before we advance to a more detailed exposition of the use of moving averages there are some common questions we need to deal with first.

1. What kind of moving average should we use?
2. Which period moving average should we use?
3. How many moving averages should we use?

WHAT KIND OF MOVING AVERAGE SHOULD ONE USE?

There are multiple different types of moving averages. One can create a simple average or a weighted average. A weighted average gives greater importance to more recent data. An exponentially weighted moving average (exponential MA) applies weights to data that decrease exponentially from newer to older data points. Personally and from an academic perspective, I favour exponential moving averages because I believe the most recent data should be given more importance. Whenever you see a moving average in an illustration in this book it will be an exponential MA. There is also anecdotal evidence that exponential MAs are also used more by the creators of program-trading platforms so they may have more psychological significance.

WHICH PERIOD MOVING AVERAGE SHOULD ONE USE?

The most common moving averages, and the most psychologically important, are five-day (one week), 20-day (one month), 50-day (one quarter) and 200-day (one year). Depending on the software used to calculate the average if one is looking at a weekly chart, the above values may need to be adjusted for weekly moving averages – so 5, 20, 50 and 200 will become 1, 5, 10 and 40-week moving averages. In any case the shape of the resulting indicator will be the same.

In the FT-Money Chart Library, where each of the charts in this book originate, all of the moving averages are calculated on a daily basis – so a 200-period moving average will always be a 200-day moving average irrespective of whether one is looking at a daily, weekly, monthly or quarterly chart.

The answer to the above question will differ considerably depending on the aims of the market participant. Some people spend a great deal of time back-testing various sets of data in order to ascertain what the best set of moving averages might have been for a particular instrument. However, this is to assume that history will be repeated. In a trend-running situation this is a possibility, but it ignores the fact that the most consistent trends will eventually end, often in spectacular style, and a moving average will lag by definition.

Moving averages are at their most useful in powerfully trending markets and in my opinion are best applied over reasonably long periods such as a few years and upwards. If short-term traders are using indicators, they generally tend to stick to the myriad oscillators available which help to identify short-term overbought and oversold conditions. For trend-runners, a longer-term moving average is more appropriate.

I tend to use a 200-day (40-week) moving average because it is widely used and therefore has psychological value. It represents the approximate average of one-year's trading history and as such can be described as the mean when considering the potential for reversion from an overextended position. A 200-day moving average also strikes a comfortable balance for a relatively long-term trend-runner. It is sensitive enough to indicate when a trend has reversed and detached enough so that only major moves will violate it.

HOW MANY MOVING AVERAGES SHOULD ONE USE?

For the purposes of my analysis I only use one moving average: the 200-day exponential moving average. I am aware that a number of other systems use more than one but I believe these to be too mechanistic and out of character with the consistency characteristics upon which behavioural technical analysis is based.

OVEREXTENSION, REVERSION AND TREND DIRECTION

OVEREXTENSION

A 200-day moving average is representative of the mean for the available data. If we take a simple standard deviation bell curve, the greatest amount of time is spent within relatively close proximity of the mean value. By definition, if the present value is not in close proximity with the mean it is either becoming more or less overextended. At extreme values relative to the moving average, we know for a mathematical fact that prices will not stay at such an overextended condition indefinitely and that it is only a matter of time before a process of reversion towards the mean unfolds.

Statistical bell curve

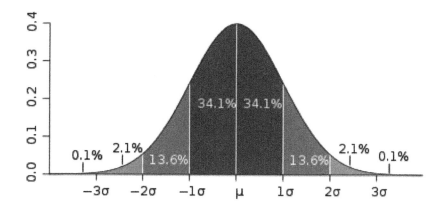

Overextension relative to a moving average can be compared to stretching an elastic band. The more pressure it is put under the greater the likelihood of a snap back in the other direction once the pressure is removed. Periods of extreme overextension relative to the moving average, both above and below, are important from a behavioural perspective because they coincide with extremes of sentiment.

For prices to become so overextended relative to the mean, something will have occurred to push the supply/demand imbalance to an extreme. In a bull market it will often be in response to the weight of money moving into the market as the bullish hypothesis gains wider appeal. In a bear market it will most often be because supply is overarching and the very integrity of the market is being questioned.

In October 2008 the S&P500 collapsed so rapidly that it developed an extreme overextension relative to the 200-day MA.

S&P500 Index 2006 to 2008

In order to demonstrate just how extreme this overextension was, I created the below indicator by subtracting the value of the MA from the index's price. The October 2008 extension was greater than any it has posted previously.

200-day overextension oscillator for the S&P500 1970–2008

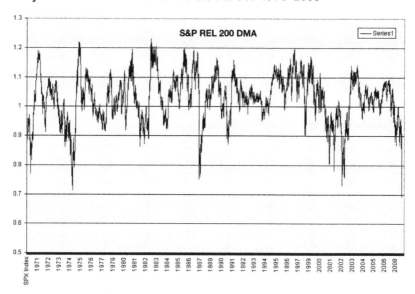

This is part of what I wrote at the time:

> "The S&P has never been so overextended relative to its 200-day moving average. Previous occasions when it got close in 1973, 1987 and 2002 all marked significant lows for the market. We have no evidence yet that the S&P has found support, but the more overextended it becomes, the sharper the covering rally is likely to be when the tide of sentiment begins to turn."

This historic overextension did not tell us that the S&P500 had bottomed, but it did suggest that it was close to a bottom because the swift decline had already pressured a large number of investors to exit the market and short sellers were becoming increasingly aggressive. In assessing the consistency of the decline, the acceleration was an ending signal both because of its size and the apparent dominance of supply. Such overarching dominance is unsustainable beyond the short term.

When a market becomes so remarkably overextended relative to its trend mean, we know that the situation cannot continue indefinitely. The overstretched condition in this example does not tell us that we have seen the ultimate low for the downtrend, but it does infer we are at an extreme price, that the risk of a reversionary rally is high and likely to be forceful given the relative overextension. At the very least, we need to be aware that following the crowd into a bearish extreme at such a juncture is contrary to the risk/reward profile presented by the market, i.e. the risk of a reversionary rally greatly outweighs scope for additional declines even though sentiment is saying exactly the opposite.

By simply adding a 200-day moving average to a chart one can quickly see if a market is becoming more or less overextended relative to the mean. Nothing more is needed to draw the necessary conclusions about the relationship between supply and demand.

REVERSION

An overextension relative to the mean is a signal to become cautious about following the prevailing market sentiment beyond the short term. Such conditions can be expected to develop at least once and possibly several times in a medium-term uptrend. The opposite process, reversion, is also worth monitoring from the perspective of providing viable entry points. If reversion morphs into trend-reversal it will invariably have been preceded by one of the three primary trend-ending signals (discussed later) but nevertheless offers categorical proof that a trend has ended.

Mathematically, the more overextended prices become relative to the trend mean, the more likely they are to revert back towards the mean. However, while it is important to be aware of this process, it is just as important to remember that behavioural analysis is a social rather than exclusively mathematical discipline. Moving averages do not offer sacrosanct levels of support and resistance. Prices can and often do overshoot on reversionary moves and a doctrinaire attitude to assessing where a market 'must' find support or encounter resistance will prove unhelpful to one's analysis.

Reversions can occur in a variety of ways:

1. Prices range, allowing the moving average to catch up.
2. Prices revert quickly back to a relatively static mean.
3. Some combination of the two occurs.

In a relatively consistent uptrend one can witness all three of these types of reversion but more important than the form of the reversion is the fact that prices find support in the region of the 200-day in the later stages of the reaction. Let's take the Brazilian market from 2005 to 2010 as an example.

Brazil Bovespa Index 2004 - 2008

Brazil Bovespa Index (IBOV) 72592.50 +794.96   www.fullermoney.com   30 May 2008

1. The reversion between January and March 2007 was largely characterised by ranging, and the progression of higher reaction lows remained intact throughout the process. It corresponds to the ranging consolidation that characterises the first type of reversion.

2. Following the upward acceleration in mid-2007, the index pulled back sharply and was completed in less than four weeks. The speed of the reversion and the fact that the moving average barely moved in those four weeks characterises this reversion as the second type.

3. The reversion that occurred between November 2007 and January 2008 held the majority of the advance and ranged for three months, allowing the ascending moving average to at least partially catch up. It subsequently fell sharply to the January low, completing the reversionary process. This reversion corresponds to the third type.

It will not have escaped your attention that reversions in this trend had a tendency to dip back below the moving average. This would have been psychologically wearing on market participants because there would have been niggling doubts about the integrity of the uptrend. However, fortitude was rewarded. Evidence that the index was finding support in the region of the moving average and that falls below it were not sustained offered close-to-optimal buying opportunities for trend-running investors.

There are no hard and fast rules about the shape of a reversion and some will be more emotionally difficult to deal with than others. If prices simply range, allowing the mean to play catch-up, very little profit erosion takes place and the associated emotions are likely to be skewed towards impatience or boredom. However, if the reversion takes place in a swifter, more abrupt manner, fear and self-doubt are much more likely to dominate.

The decision to buy on a reversionary decline towards an ascending mean in an uptrend or selling on a reversionary rally towards a descending mean in a downtrend is important in terms of market timing and should only be made once other factors have been taken into account, i.e. does the overall chart pattern remain consistent, does commonality support your market view or whether trend ending characteristics are evident.

TREND DIRECTION

The direction of the moving average offers an additional analytic clue, particularly as trends are beginning and ending. Big market tops and bottoms tend to be characterised by wars between supply and demand. As a result there will be extreme views held by both camps. As a new uptrend begins, the demand camp will be heralding a new bull market while supply will be calling it a bear market rally. Alternatively, as a new downtrend is beginning, demand will continue to hope that a rally to new highs will be achieved while supply will be claiming the bull was nothing more than a house of cards.

Such debates can continue for months and, depending on the top or bottoming activity, even years. Arguments in these scenarios generally tend to centre on issues unrelated to the reality presented by the price action.

However, at the dawn of a new uptrend, even though the moving average will have lagged the actual bottom, if it subsequently turns upwards it offers one categorical fact: prices are, on average, rising. At the beginning of a downtrend, bullish sentiment might be looking for buying opportunities on the pullback, refusing to accept technical evidence to the contrary. However, if the moving average turns downwards, if offers the indisputable fact that prices are, on average, declining.

Therefore, the direction of the moving average can be a reality check, albeit lagging, of a change in trend.

CONCLUSION

Moving averages may lag price action but they offer an invaluable reality check particularly when prices are rallying strongly in either direction. Provided we retain our emotional equilibrium we will be well placed to profit once we recognise that no trend persists forever.

CHAPTER 12:

TARGETS, CONTRARY INDICATORS, ROUNDOPHOBIA AND PSYCHOLOGICAL LEVELS

What we will cover in this chapter:

- No one knows with certainty where the market is likely to trade tomorrow, next week, next month or next year.

- We have no control over where the market is likely to trade, regardless of how strongly we feel about it.

- Provided we accept these limitations we can gain clues as to potential moves by looking at how much confidence other people express in their forecasts.

- This is generally a better indication of how they have invested their own money rather than where prices are most likely to go.

- *Roundophobia* refers to the tendency of markets to at least pause in the region of round numbers. These areas represent psychological levels investors often unconsciously target.

NO ONE KNOWS WHERE A MARKET WILL CLOSE TODAY, tomorrow, next week, next month or next year. We know for an objective fact that it is impossible to tell the future and yet analysts, fund managers, traders, pundits, journalists and other investors spend an inordinate amount of time attempting to guess where markets will trade over any given time frame. This could at least be justified if people were generally good at such predictions. But academic studies suggest that this is not the case. In fact, the opposite is true.

Here's what Gustaf Törngren and Henry Montgomery found, writing for the *Journal of Behavioral Finance* in 2004:

> "Studies assessing financial analyst predictions often give a rather gloomy picture of their validity. As early as the 1930s, Cowles [1933] showed how stocks recommended by a number of financial services in the years between 1928 and 1932 were outperformed by the average common stock. This trend continues today. De Bondt [1991] analyzed the results of a longitudinal study (1952–1987), and found that the experts could have improved their results by using historical means instead of specific evaluations. Similarly, Malkiel [1999] found that, from 1988 to 1998, the average equity mutual fund in the U.S. had a 3.3% lower average annual return than the Standard & Poor's index during the same period."

This study illustrates that human beings are generally bad at making predictions but, as if to add insult to injury, also tend to be undeservingly overconfident about their ability to make such predictions.

How we view the prospects for a market is directly linked with our past experience. If our most recent investment activity has resulted in positive outcomes we are likely to be predisposed to thinking that the outlook for the market is more bullish. Consequently, if we were asked to set a target for the market, it is probably going to be more enthusiastic than if our most recent experience was negative. In behavioural terms, this can be related back to psychological anchoring.

Anchoring can be defined as a way of describing how people intuitively assess probabilities. This example of anchoring has been offered by Dan Ariely of MIT:

> "An audience is first asked to write the last two digits of their social security number, and, second, to submit mock bids on items such as wine and chocolate.

The half of the audience with higher two-digit numbers would submit bids that were between 60 per cent and 120 percent higher than those of the other half, far higher than a chance outcome; the simple act of thinking of the first number strongly influences the second, even though there is no relevant connection between them."

We need to take a view on the market before we ever take a position, but it is important to understand that our hopes, expectations, desires and confidence are nothing more than conjecture. The price action is reality and we have no control over where it goes. The challenge is to tailor our tactics so that we benefit when the market moves in our favour and lose less when it doesn't.

If we accept that we are starting from a psychological disadvantage in predicting where a market will find support or encounter resistance, and take into account the limits of what is in fact possible, then there are behavioural factors that can add a considerable amount of value to the discipline of making judgement calls on where a market is likely to trade.

CONTRARY INDICATORS

Since it is a fact that individuals are bad at predicting both the direction a market is likely to move in and how far it is likely to move, we can look on extremes of crowd sentiment as *contrary indicators*. This is an essential skill for the aspiring contrary investor and it is important to also appreciate the limits of such knowledge.

When extremes of sentiment develop following big moves in the market, when people are loudly proclaiming their confidence that prices are going to move even higher or lower, this is usually an indication of what participants have done rather than what they are going to do.

Following a big decline, sentiment will be apocalyptic because investors are taking losses, shorts will be trumpeting the news of how bad the instrument is and those who sold higher up have an emotionally vested interest in seeing the market fall further. This tells us that a large number of those interested in the vehicle have already sold. Those seeking to set targets for the market will be extrapolating the price action and predicting even further declines. However, potential supply of the instrument is quickly being exhausted and only a small rally is needed to begin to pressure the shorts, which can lead to short covering and potential reversal.

Following a big upside move, sentiment will be euphoric because investors are making money fast. Those with long positions will be trumpeting the new paradigm. They will have both a financial and emotional interest in seeing the market move higher. New buyers will also need to buy into the idea that prices will continue to advance to justify buying now. If sentiment is at such a bullish extreme, it tells us that large numbers of investors are already long so potential demand is being exhausted, at least in the short term, and a relatively small decline can begin to hit the stops of leveraged traders.

Armed with the knowledge that extremes of crowd sentiment are seldom reliable continuation patterns, together with our appraisal of the consistency characteristics of the trend, we have valuable tools in assessing market potential and protecting profits.

There are limits to such analysis. From time to time stories are spread by those seeking to draw attention to their pet sector or asset class. The internet and social media allow such stories to receive more attention than they might deserve. Highly plausible investment themes can become the flavour of the month and if they are well-funded can gain popularity among the political class. In the last decade we have had genuine bull markets in commodities and emerging markets. However, along the way, a wide number of minor themes have garnered attention and a great deal of media coverage but failed to provide the outsized profits promised by the marketers.

No bull market can get started without the necessary credit expansion, a story powerful enough to inspire investors and fundamentals that justify optimism. We use the four pillars to macro behavioural technical analysis in our attempt to decipher which are going to turn into the big bull markets and which are going to peter out. But one simple filter is that the chart action must support the spiel. If the story is wonderful but the shares are going nowhere, then it is failing to animate investor interest at that time. This does not mean it can't succeed at a later stage but if the chart action does not look like it can support a major bull market now, then it probably can't. The chart action check is also important when a bull market is in full swing because we can identify euphoria as it develops. We also run the risk of exiting too early if we do not continue to structure our strategy around the price action.

THE FALLACY OF CONTROL

In addition to overconfidence in predicative power, the fallacy of control is an additional hindrance. I give regular TV interviews and one of the first questions in any interview is invariably "What's your target?"

This is an interesting question because it assumes from a behavioural perspective that the market participant has a degree of control, not only in what direction a market will trade but how far it will move. In the real world targets are for marksmen. They have control of a gun which can propel a bullet with great force at a desired target. The expert marksman taking into account distance, wind and recoil can hit a target regularly. However, investing simply does not work like that.

Behavioural technical analysis will not tell you where an instrument is going to trade over any given timeframe. Nothing else will either. However, if we equip ourselves with a frank assessment of a trend's consistency characteristics we can draw conclusions about how a trend is most likely to unfold.

Newton's First Law of Motion states: "*A body persists in a state of uniform motion or of rest unless acted upon by an external force.*"

David Fuller states: "*A consistent trend is a trend in motion*", which means that the relationship between supply and demand will continue to unfold in an orderly relatively predictable manner until some external force acts upon it. Therefore, as long as a trend remains consistent, we can expect the status quo to remain in place and the rhythm of the move to persist.

In practical terms, if a market has been trending consistently with a clearly defined set of relatively equal-sized ranges one above another then we can expect the situation to continue until something changes.

In a ranging environment, if a market has found support at the lower side of the range on previous occasions it will hardly be surprising if the crowd defer to that level again on a subsequent pullback.

ROUNDOPHOBIA

David Fuller defined roundophobia as "*the tendency of markets to at least pause in the region of round numbers*".

Most relatively experienced investors can remember a time when a market they were interested in was approaching a big round number. The Dow Jones Industrials at 10,000, gold at $1,000, crude oil at $100, the Canadian dollar / US Dollar at $1 or UK gilts at 4% are all examples of where markets have either paused or reversed at psychologically significant round numbers. Just why individuals and crowds attach significance to such levels has a common-sense explanation.

Let's consider the psychological machinations behind such tendencies. When the price of an internationally traded financial vehicle is moving higher, people naturally begin to think about how far it will go, if for no other reason than they are thinking about potentially participating. If asked for their target they are more likely to give the next round number because most of us are not so pedantic as to speak in fractions. We are more likely to say $1,000 than $982, 10,000 than 9,941. And when lots of people do this, the greater the likelihood a market will pause at a round number.

West Texas Intermediate Crude Oil offered a good example of prices pausing in the region of a round number from 2007.

West Texas Intermediate Crude Oil 2006–2008

Prices found support at the round $50 in early 2007 and began to rally. Each of the steps within the trend was represented by increments close to $10. As prices appreciated, the natural question was where was it going next? $100 was seen as a major psychological level. Prices trended consistently higher for most of 2007 but encountered resistance just beneath $100 and ranged below that level for nearly six months before subsequently breaking upwards. $100 then became an area of support. The next target became $150 and prices peaked at $147 in 2008.

In the uncertain environment of the financial markets, round numbers offer anchor points upon which investors tend to base their targets. Therefore, the behavioural analyst needs to be aware that these areas can give pause to trends both up and down and are also potential reversal points.

OTHER PSYCHOLOGICAL LEVELS

Round numbers offer areas of support and resistance because the crowd attaches significance to these levels. However, the same process is also evident at other points of interest. Investors participating in any given instrument become accustomed to the levels at which they made or lost money or have had decisions forced upon them by market action.

At a London venue for the Chart Seminar a few years ago, an investor mentioned that they had bought nickel a few years ago by buying near $10,000, and seeing the price near there again had followed the same action. This example illustrates both the psychological importance of the round number and the positive reinforcement of having made money by buying near such a memorable level.

Likewise, as an instrument rallies back towards a previous peak, the obvious question among those who are long, particularly if they were also long the last time the instrument peaked, is "Will it be able to sustain an upward break this time?" This is a powerful enough question to stop investors from increasing their positions as an old high is approached, which raises the potential for the market to pause in close proximity of an old high.

On the other hand, as a market falls towards a previous low, investors begin to ask whether it will find support at that level again. The simple asking of that question can contribute to short sellers lowering stops and not increasing their position.

The UK's FTSE-100 offers a clear example of just such action taking place at both previous highs and lows.

FTSE-100 1992–2013

A previous high or low will have more psychological impact if the people trading the vehicle now have experience of a level being a pivot point in the past because it will be more likely to influence their actions. The further one moves from a previous high or low, the less meaningful it is likely to be because the number of people who remember it will decrease over time.

CONCLUSION

David Fuller has long advised that *"we need to foster the humility necessary to allow the market to unfold as it will"*. Once we release ourselves from the fallacy that we have any control over price action, we allow ourselves to become sensitive to the conviction others have in the integrity of their targets. When the crowd is unwilling to accept any form of equivocation it is usually an indication that sentiment has reached an extreme and may be close to reversal.

CHAPTER 13:

STOPS AND MONEY CONTROL DISCIPLINE

What we will cover in this chapter:

- The perception of risk tends to be greatest at the bottom because the memory of having accepted a loss will be fresh in people's minds. They tend to be highly disciplined with stops and as a result they are much more likely to be taken out of the position.

- The longer an uptrend persists, the greater the accumulated profits and the greater the expectation of future appreciation. This contributes to a lower perception of risk. Investors tend to tinker with their stops for fear they will inadvertently sell a market which they believe still has considerable upside potential.

- A stop strategy needs to be tailored to the individual consistency characteristics of the instrument concerned.

- Potential sequence of stops:

  1. Stop loss – initial stage of an investment.

  2. Break-even stops – getting a free ride.

  3. Mid-point danger line – middle to late phase of an investment's life.

  4. Trailing stop – in an accelerating or overextended market.

- Position sizing – positions should be sized to allow for what might be considered a 'normal' reaction for that trend, rather than how much money we would like to make from the investment.

- Cost-averaging – the simplest maxim, yet one of the most difficult to follow, is to buy low and sell high. Cost-averaging is a relatively simple discipline that ensures we buy more when prices are low and less as they appreciate.

THE QUESTION OF HOW, WHERE AND WHEN to place stops is often controversial – it is a subjective discipline. How we are inclined to approach it will at least in part be dictated by our most recent experience of the market and where we are in the market cycle.

Many novice traders despair of ever getting a stop strategy correct because they are often unaware of the emotional pitfalls that can upset a nascent investment before it ever begins to develop into the profit initially envisaged.

There are many different strategies for implementing stops which can be successful but first we need to address the issue of when it is advisable to place a stop on a position. As with almost everything related to macro behavioural technical analysis we will relate the subject of stops to the consistency or otherwise of a particular trend.

RISK PERCEPTION

The greatest perception of risk is usually experienced following a major decline or perhaps more accurately when participants have experienced profit erosion or taken losses. However, if large numbers of people have already sold, the likelihood that base formation can take place increases. Therefore a frank assessment of the consistency of the downtrend is necessary before any type of stop can be considered.

Due to an increased sense of risk, influenced by bearish sentiment expressed via the media, investors are more likely to have tight stops at the bottom of the market. Their most recent experience has been of a sharp decline and they are wary of living through another such experience while holding a long position. However, by definition, if a market has entered a base-building phase, the potential downside is likely to be limited to the region of the lower side of the base. This means that from the perspective of the investor, perceived risk of taking a loss and the reality provided by the market are at odds.

Base formation occurs when supply and demand come back into balance following a sharp decline. A war then proceeds for dominance which can be lengthy, but crucially from the perspective of placing a stop on a long position, bases are *volatile*. Conditions where prices are likely to jump around a lot require a swing-trading strategy, and imply that the use of stops will be counterproductive because the chances of the stop being triggered at a loss relative to the entry price are high. Given this reality one then needs to make a judgement call as to whether it is worth tolerating volatility at the risk of prices declining further or waiting for evidence of demand dominance but accepting that the entry price will be higher.

The fact that the perception of risk in a base is high relative to the actual risk of loss means that those who place tight stops on initial positions are likely to lose money. This will have the secondary effect of galvanising the perception of high risk with experiential evidence and detracts from the investor's store of emotional capital. In such a situation, if one is investing at all, a tolerance to sit out comparatively large swings is needed and if a stop is used it needs to be wide enough to take the potential volatility into account. This usually means that it needs to be placed below the lowest point of the base. The logical corollary is that positions need to be sized taking the potential for volatility into account rather than the hoped for return on investment.

The perception of risk is at its lowest when prices have been appreciating for some time. However, when the trend begins to lose consistency, particularly following a major advance, it may be topping out. The perception of risk will be low because the bull market hypothesis has been reinforced with positive investment outcomes and bullish sentiment is reflected back to the crowd through the media. As human beings, we don't like change. We want the good news to continue and in the absence of profit erosion, have enormous capacity to ignore evidence contrary to our prevailing mood. This contributes to stops being most loose close to the top, if they are present at all. The fear of not taking part in whatever further upside might occur overrides the perception of downside risk.

A top forms when supply and demand come back into balance. In future chapters we will look at how markets top and bottom, but for now let's focus on the perception of risk which will invariably be lower than it was at the bottom. Therefore, some form of stop is most appropriate when a potential top may be forming. This will have to be tailored to each individual instrument.

Logically, if a market has been trending more or less in one direction for a prolonged period, it is closer to a major reversal than it was at the beginning of the move. However, emotionally, we tend to believe the opposite. Armed with an appreciation of the difference between apparent versus actual risk we can attempt to implement a strategy which will allow us to protect paper profits while availing us of further positive developments in the trend.

Whole books have been written on this subject and while I am only devoting a chapter to the topic, my goal is to simplify the process by relating the techniques involved back to the consistency characteristics which form the central tenets of macro behavioural technical analysis.

Let us first consider where most people place their stops, because we wish to avoid their strategy.

I have often heard of investors promoting the use of a 10% stop. However, while I can understand that this will help to preserve capital and would require a relatively large pullback to trigger, it is only realistically appropriate for a market where reactions of greater than 10% are unusual.

Even larger groups of people will put a stop under the most recent reaction low when initiating a long position or above the most recent rally high when implementing a short. This is at least grounded in the consistency characteristics of the trend but its success will depend both on where in the market cycle this is initiated and how big one's position is.

An appreciation of where we are in the market cycle can be ascertained from looking at a long-term chart of the instrument's price history. Due to the different relationships between supply and demand at the bottom, trending phase and top, different stop strategies are appropriate for different parts of the market cycle and these can be implemented in a sequence.

SEQUENCE OF STOPS

1. Stop loss – initial stage of an investment.
2. Break-even stops – getting a free ride.
3. Mid-point danger line – middle to late phase of an investment's life.
4. Trailing stop – latter stages of an investment's life.

1. STOP LOSS

No position in the financial markets is taken without the investor first forming a view as to the future direction of the market concerned. However, since none of us are infallible and we often have to kiss a few frogs before we find our prince, there is need of a strategy to limit the loss on an initial investment so that one's starting capital is not depleted while we wait for a rhythmic trend to unfold.

If the position is a prospective entry into a market which has been ranging for a period of time, one will either seek to initiate the position inside the range or wait for confirmation by initiating the position after a breakout.

Initiating the position inside the range has much less chance of slippage because you are anticipating the market, but it is psychologically much more difficult to accomplish for the same reason. A stop in such a scenario needs to be below the low of the range for a long position or above the high for a short.

Waiting for the breakout is less psychologically pressurised because you have market action to rely on and are moving in line with the crowd. However, the risk of slippage is greater because you have intentionally exchanged a better initial price for peace of mind. In this case a mid-point danger line (MDL) stop would be appropriate (see point three).

Since these are initial positions, we will have ample opportunity to increase the position, provided our thesis is correct and the trend unfolds as we expect. If we are wrong then we will have received a rap on the knuckles but will not have sustained a crushing loss and can reassess our analysis before moving onto the next opportunity.

2. BREAK-EVEN OR IN-THE-MONEY STOPS

Once a position moves into a net profit and the technical background supports the view that it can continue to move in the desired direction, we will want to move the stop up to at least the initial opening price. This is the ideal situation because we are no longer risking our own money and have a proverbial 'free ride'.

If the trend continues in our favour we have the luxury of a number of decisions. We can either let the position run or incrementally move the stop upwards, protecting more of our profit. If the trend develops as we hoped, we can think about further purchases and whether these are justified by the consistency of the move; taking into account how much profit we are willing to risk and whether the increase in the average price of the trade can be protected by a technically justifiable stop.

3. MID-POINT DANGER LINE

Consistent, rhythmic, orderly trends provide us with some of the best money-making opportunities in return for taking an acceptable risk. Doesn't common sense therefore dictate that if we have a low risk/high reward strategy for a certain set of conditions that our time would be best spent finding those conditions and applying a trend-running strategy, rather than limiting our opportunities to a relatively small number of instruments and tailoring our strategy to the conditions provided? After all, it is easier to make money in a bull market.

David Fuller's mid-point danger line (MDL) stop is appropriate for consistent step sequence uptrends as discussed in previous chapters. It is also appropriate on new positions initiated following a breakout. It will keep a trend-running investor in their position for as long as the trend remains consistent, and should help preserve the bulk of any non-leveraged profits which have been built up. If the trend ends in acceleration, an MDL stop will no longer be appropriate and one would move to a trailing stop (see below), while if the trend ends by rolling over, the MDL will take us out relatively close to the top.

So how does it work?

When we think about where to put a stop it is perhaps instructive to think about where everyone else has put their stops. If a market is topping out, the last thing we want is to have a stop at an obvious level – if a falling market hits a pocket of supply it will often gap straight through an unguaranteed stop and a sell order will end up being filled well below the desired level. From the opposite perspective, short covering rallies can be equally abrupt, so we need to avoid having our stop on a short position in an obvious region.

Let's consider a bull market example of a step sequence uptrend which will be characterised by an obvious progression of ranges one above another. In such a scenario most people will have their stop close to the lower side of the most recent range. The reason for this is because they will want to avoid being stopped out if the market moves into another range but taken out if it breaks down. This is a perfectly reasonable motivation for the trend-running investor. However, this tactic runs the risk of failing because large numbers of investors are all thinking the same way. So we need to employ an alternative strategy.

We have identified the consistency characteristics for the trend. These are a step sequence uptrend, with each well-defined trading range one above another. If this is a trend in motion then it should sustain upward breaks. We do not want to have a stop that is so close to where the market is trading that we run the risk of being stopped out if it simply dips briefly back into the range before reasserting the uptrend once more. However, if the breakout fails (see Chapter 13 for more on failed breakouts) then we have an incontrovertible inconsistency. This signals a change in the supply/demand dynamics which have supported the uptrend and is at least a warning that greater caution is warranted.

David Fuller's rule of thumb with regard to failed breakouts is:

> "If the dynamic of the failure is larger than the dynamic of the breakout, the chances that the market will at least go back and test the other side of the range have greatly increased."

In a rhythmic uptrend we know that there is a good chance that most of the stops are just below the lower side of the most recent range. The failed break suggests that at least a test of that area is likely, so the risk of a long position being stopped out is high. In such circumstances having a stop in the middle of the range will ensure that if the breakout is sustained the long position will remain intact. If the breakout dips slightly back into range, the long position will remain intact but if the breakout fails dramatically, the stop will be triggered and this will occur well before the vast majority of other stops are threatened.

4. TRAILING STOP

If one is fortunate enough to have a position in an instrument whose price is accelerating in the desired direction, then a trailing stop is the most desirable method to protect profits while availing of the opportunity for them to continue to increase.

In an uptrend this is a stop which is trailed upwards behind the advancing price with the aim of protecting the maximum amount of profit while maintaining the long position and leaving open the potential that prices will continue to advance.

In a downtrend, a trailing stop will be trailed downwards behind the price with the aim of protecting the maximum amount of profit from a short position, giving the position room for prices to deteriorate further while holding the short.

The immediate question is how far away from the price should a trailing stop be?

If we return to the aims of the strategy, we want to avail of further profit potential as long as the acceleration lasts but would like to be taken out on the first larger reaction against the prevailing trend, thus preserving as much profit as possible.

Let's look at oil's upwards acceleration in 2008.

West Texas Intermediate Crude Oil 2006–2008

In order to ascertain what a 'normal' reaction looks like we need to assess the chart action with particular focus on the last two or three congestion area trading ranges.

With oil, let us assume that we wished to protect a long position following the initial break above $100. The last two reactions were of $12 and $14 respectively. These constituted how much of a pullback had occurred before demand reasserted itself in the relatively recent past. If the accelerating price reacted by a similar amount then we would want to stay with the prevailing trend. We might even consider increasing our position because we know what happened last time. Therefore if we are trailing a stop up behind the price it needs to be somewhat larger than a 'normal' reaction if our position is to survive intact.

A somewhat larger reaction, particularly following an acceleration in prices, would be an inconsistency. It would signal that the trend's impetus has been exhausted for at least the short term and possibly the medium to long term; depending on where in the market cycle it takes place. With oil, a trailing stop of approximately $15 or $16 would have protected a long position until July 2008, when a larger reaction followed a failed upside break and subsequently broke the progression of higher reaction lows – all of which constituted major trend inconsistencies.

IMPLEMENTATION OF STOPS

In an ideal situation these stops would be introduced sequentially, but in the real world one would tailor the stop strategy to the trend as it unfolds. If in the latter part of a trending stage the distance between congestion area trading ranges grows to a level where an MDL is no longer appropriate, one would switch to a trailing stop. If it moves back to another range and breaks out again, we could reintroduce an MDL.

Aggreko offers a good example of where a tailored stop strategy would have been appropriate:

Aggreko Plc 2007–2012

Aggreko PLC (AGK) 2181 -17.00   www.fullermoney.com   8 Jun 2012
Weekly
MA 200

1. One step above another, equal-sized ranges from 2009 until mid-2010. Prices had become overextended relative to the 200-day MA by August 2010 and the first larger reaction would have triggered an MDL stop. This event reflected a change to the trend's broad consistency.

2. The steps are dipping into one another, have become much larger and the primary trend consistency has become finding support in the region of the 200-day MA.

The share lost momentum from October 2008 and rallied impressively from early 2009 in a massive reaction against the prevailing downtrend, to form a type-2 bottom. It subsequently pulled back to test the upper side of the base and the 200-day MA before embarking on an impressively consistent uptrend.

A mid-point danger line stop would have been appropriate from mid-2009 since each range was relatively similar sized and upward breaks were sustained.

From early 2010, as the pace of the advance picked up, a trailing stop would have been appropriate. The largest reaction in the course of the advance had been 150p, so a trailing stop on an unleveraged position of greater than that would have been appropriate as prices accelerated higher.

As each successive range was completed by an emphatic upward break, an MDL could have been introduced and switched to a trailing stop as it rallied well away from the latest range. This strategy would have worked well until August 2010, when a considerably larger reaction would have triggered an MDL stop as price dropped back into the previous range.

That first larger reaction, following an impressive advance and from quite an overextended condition relative to the 200-day MA suggested a pause of medium-term significance was unfolding. From Q3 2010 the consistency of the trend changed. The supply/demand imbalance is less consistent. This has repercussions both for how one places stops and how large a position can be justified given the drawdown risks associated with the price action.

POSITION-SIZING AND MONEY CONTROL DISCIPLINE

Each of us wants to see our investments do well. We never initiate a position without thinking it will make us money. Logically the following query is how much? However, that is an unanswerable question. Therefore when we decide to initiate a position, we should think not of how much money we wish to make but of how much we are prepared to lose before we admit we were wrong in our investment hypothesis. The more appropriate question is whether one should tailor the size of the position to the stop or the stop to the position size? This cuts to the heart of whether one should use technical stops or financial stops on investment/trading positions.

Let's examine two scenarios …

SCENARIO 1: THE FINANCIAL STOP

An investor has a paper profit they wish to protect with a stop. On the assumption that they are long, up to this point they have been buying intermittently over the course of an uptrend and have a relatively large profit. The investor's confidence is high and purchases have been bunched in the relatively recent past rather than spaced out over the course of the uptrend because he believes prices are likely to accelerate higher. However, due to the recent slew of purchases, made in the hope of benefiting from further upside potential, the average buy price for the total position is relatively close to the current price. In this circumstance, if he wants to protect the profit, a stop will have to be placed relatively close to the current price because to have it anywhere else would result in too much profit erosion and potentially the total position turning into a loss. In this scenario, the risk of the entire position being stopped out is high on what might be a minor pullback relative to the overall uptrend.

In the investment world you pay for your lessons, so let me share an example of one of my mistakes in the hope that you might avoid it. In 2005 I was trading gold quite actively and carelessly allowed myself to get into a position where I was forced to introduce a financial stop: my analysis had led me to believe that gold was about to break upwards and run significantly higher. I had built up a large position (for me) prior to the breakout and had bunched my purchases close to the upper side of the range in anticipation of a major upside move. I had a five-figure paper profit which I was using to increase my position but this meant that the break-even stop I needed to protect myself was too close to where the market was trading to be justified from a technical appreciation of the market. In any event, gold pulled back approximately $13, hit my stop and broke upwards a few days later. On that occasion, I was left nursing a wounded ego, lost paper profits and had to chase gold higher, ending up with a considerably smaller profit from the move than if I had remained disciplined in my purchases.

SCENARIO 2: THE TECHNICAL STOP

An investor has a paper profit they wish to protect with a stop. In the course of monitoring the uptrend, they have identified the consistency characteristics of the trend and will be familiar with what is constituted by a 'normal' correction. This will equip the investor with a realistic appraisal of where a stop would have to be in order to ensure that a 'minor' pullback does not shake him out. Purchases can be tailored to the rhythm of the trend (following reversions toward the mean) taking into account the ramifications on the average purchase price (or sale price for a short position). Provided this money control discipline is adhered to, the position will remain intact as long as the trend remains consistent. If the consistency changes, the position will be stopped out and most of the profit retained.

Here is another example from my personal experience. I was trading the Hang Seng Index as it broke upwards following a nine-month consolidation in the region of its 2004 high. I bought just prior to the breakout and was fortunate that prices simply rose from there on. I initiated a number of positions on the way up, keeping an eye on my average buy price and ran break-even or in-the-money stops on each successive position. The total position was stopped out on the first larger pullback, preserving almost the entire profit. That trade paid for my wife's engagement ring and our wedding.

This example illustrates that not only is a technical stop useful in taking us out of a position in an instrument whose price is losing consistency but it also contributes to sustaining money control discipline. I know that, when I started trading, the main mistake I made was that I believed all I had to do to make money was get the analysis correct. I was quickly disabused of this fallacy through losing money or being stopped out only to see the price rally immediately afterward. I quickly came to realise that if I was going to make money I needed to develop the mental acuity to put together a money control strategy and the discipline to stick with it.

Developing such a strategy, as we have seen, is not academically difficult. But sticking with the decision once it has been made can be emotionally draining. Remembering why we placed the stop where we did and resisting the temptation to tinker with it (without a sound technical reason to so do) is hard. I do not believe it is an exaggeration to state that my most successful investments have resulted from getting the analysis correct, maintaining disciplined position sizing and employing a technical stop.

Building a position from first principles using the consistency characteristics of the trend and implementing technical stops to preserve profits before increasing the position is a sound strategy for leveraged traders who have margin and funding considerations to bear in mind. However, the methodology employed is just as valid for an unleveraged long-term investor.

Here is a section by David Fuller from **Fullermoney.com**'s Comment of the Day on 17 April 2009:

> "Investing is less difficult than trading, which is not to say that it is easy. The analytical skills for investing are the same as for trading. The main differences are leverage and the trader's need for short-term timing. For instance, without leverage investors can cost-average. For me, the essence of investing is a common-sense, buy-low-sell-high approach. Extremes of crowd sentiment are contrary indicators."

COST-AVERAGING

Major market bottoms are defined by supply and demand coming back into balance and as a result can be volatile and above all inconsistent. These conditions are not ideal for the use of stops and are particularly challenging if one is employing leverage.

In such a situation if an *unleveraged* investor has formed an opinion that the market is bottoming, then a cost-averaging series of purchases is a sound, low-risk method of building a position on a buy-low-sell-high basis.

The logic behind the method is relatively straightforward. If an unleveraged investor decides he wants to allocate $100,000 to an investment, he has a number of choices in how his money is allocated. He can make one large purchase which requires pinpoint timing skills and a good deal of luck. Alternatively he can decide to space the purchases out on the basis that in a base formation prices tend to bounce around. This also allows the investor the chance to change his mind if the investment is not panning out as he had hoped.

Let's take the S&P500 mini contract as an example. Following the downward acceleration in 2008, one might have concluded that the market was beginning to bottom out but since supporting evidence was still tentative and the price action unusually volatile, a cost-averaging approach may have been implemented. Ten equal purchases of $10,000 from November 2008, rolling the remainder from one month into the next, would have looked like this:

S&P500 2008–2010

As price declines, more shares are purchased, as prices increase fewer are bought; contributing to the lower average cost of the overall position. This money-control tactic can easily be followed in conjunction with a frank appraisal of the trend's consistency characteristics and technically justifiable stops can then be introduced.

There are two primary dangers when implementing any purchase programme. The first is that we are plain wrong about the instrument's prospects and the decline continues unabated. In this case the fact that a cost-averaging strategy spaces out purchases allows us to reassess the strategy from a dispassionate perspective at any time. The second danger is that the market call is correct but that we deviate from the strategy. This might happen for a number of reasons but is most likely when prices are moving upwards and greed or impatience replace discipline. The allure of instant gratification is a threat to a cost-averaging strategy. The desire to see the fruits of one's labour immediately rather than wait for the market to unfold can often be powerful and leads to missteps.

As discussed previously, a cost-averaging purchase will often be entered into because the perception of risk is high. As one's initial decision to go long is proved correct and one sees paper profits accumulate, the temptation is to deviate from the assigned strategy to increase the position. This needs to be seen for what it is: a change from investing to gambling. The initial strategy is rooted in a buy-low-sell-high mantra. Changing to buy-high-sell-higher is a major deviation. The upward pressure this can put on the average buy price greatly increases the risk factor and could have serious consequences on the subsequent need to place a financial rather than technical stop.

Therefore the lesson here is *stick to the strategy that works*. Whether one is building a leveraged position behind stops or an unleveraged position using cost-averaging, deviating from a strategy that works is not analytically justifiable even if it is emotionally satisfying in the short term.

CONCLUSION

Once we identify a promising market, we need to tailor our strategy to fit in with the reality provided by that market. Irrespective of how strongly we feel about the market an objective appraisal of the consistency characteristics must form the basis for our subsequent interaction with that market. Provided we formulate our strategy of a technical rather than emotional basis we are in a much better position to not only profit from the market but to hold onto those profits.

CHAPTER 14:

TREND ENDING #1 –
ACCELERATION AND KEY REVERSALS

What we will cover in this chapter:

"Acceleration is always an ending but of undetermined duration."

– David Fuller

- Acceleration is always a trend ending, but of undetermined duration because the crowd's emotions are intensifying and liquidity available to fuel the move at that time is quickly being expended.

- An acceleration which follows an already well-developed trend is an ending characteristic. It should not be confused with an acceleration out of a lengthy trading range because a range is an explosion waiting to happen and we expect an outsized move to occur once it is completed.

- It is important to distinguish between these two types of acceleration because the first is an ending and the second is likely to represent a medium-term continuation pattern.

- When is it right to sell? This is the most important question to ask during an upward acceleration because the emotional temptation will be to buy more. However, we know for a fact that even though an accelerating market exudes an aura of strength, it is being set up for a period of weakness. Therefore, a trailing stop on at least part of the position is appropriate as prices accelerate.

- Key day reversals – *"the key to the key is size"*. They occur often enough at major peaks and troughs, particularly following accelerations, and they are a useful tool in the kit of the macro behavioural technical analyst.

FROM TIME TO TIME PRICES MOVE almost uninterrupted in one direction for minutes, hours, days, weeks and in the most extreme cases even months at a time. For as long as it lasts *acceleration* is by far the most consistent feature of any trend. However, by virtue of that fact, it is out of character with the trend's previous consistency characteristics and can therefore be considered an initial inconsistency.

During an upward acceleration those already holding long positions make money faster than at any other time. This type of situation is also what many momentum investors wait for and they attempt to profit even more by using leverage. If we are to hold onto the profits so quickly accrued it is imperative to understand what is going on in terms of the crowd psychology driving the move and how the opposing forces of supply and demand are interacting.

One might reasonably question the conditional nature of the 'but of undetermined duration' rider attached to the above proposition. Yet if one takes the time to think about the fractal characteristics of markets, we can readily accept that acceleration is always an ending but that we have no way of knowing for how long prices will reverse once the trajectory of the move changes.

At any given time there will be a limited number of potential buyers below the market and potential sellers above. This is as true of intraday trading as it is of multi-year trends. Therefore the same interactions between supply and demand occur over a short, highly pressurised timescale for intraday traders as for unleveraged investors over a considerably longer time frame. Acceleration is evident over every time scale and is always an ending because it represents times when the prevailing crowd sentiment temporarily intensifies.

In an uptrend, once all the buyers willing to purchase at that time have filled their orders, those who remain in the market represent supply and prices will fall until new buyers are attracted back and sellers begin to withdraw offers. In a downtrend, the same intensification of emotion occurs and because fear is a much more immediate emotion than greed, downtrends often accelerate dramatically towards their nadir.

Accelerations offer a powerful opportunity for momentum traders wishing to ride the coattails of a crowd moving to an extreme of bullishness or bearishness. Accelerations occur quickly, have a reinforcing influence on the prevailing crowd sentiment and are when a disciplined approach to position sizing and stops is most important. While accelerations are usually the time we make money fastest, they also signal that a market is at least temporarily overheating and as such represent an ending signal.

Accelerations, both up and down, reflect extremes of crowd sentiment and will only last for as long as the emotions driving the crowd continue to intensify. Accelerations sustain their velocity by attracting new adherents at an increasingly rapid pace. While acceleration is not a necessary condition during a move, when it occurs it always reflects a magnification of emotion. It is this concentration of the dominant emotion that sows the seeds for the approaching reversal.

In an uptrend new buyers are converted to the bullish hypothesis as prices make new highs, those bidding below the market are forced to pay the market rate for fear of being left behind and potential sellers withdraw offers and become born-again bulls. As prices accelerate higher, new buyers flood in, but as the rally continues the number of participants willing to pay ever-higher prices thins out. When a level is reached where no one is left who is willing to pay a higher price at that moment, only those willing to sell at that level are left – and a reversal occurs. This same process is repeated during every advance but the speed of an acceleration amplifies the emotional impact of the move. As a result, sentiment leading up to the tipping point becomes increasingly bullish rather than more cautious.

Any investor deciding to commit fresh capital to an accelerating market does so with the deep-seated knowledge that prices cannot continue to advance at such a prodigious rate indefinitely. However, in order to initiate a long position, any anxiety that may exist has to be swept aside and the bullish hypothesis wholeheartedly adopted. If someone is expressing worry about how elevated prices are, they would not be buying. To do otherwise would be schizophrenic. Therefore if new capital is to be committed to the market it must be because one believes that prices are going to go higher. Some might rationalise this as the bigger fool theory (i.e. I might be silly for buying now but I'll be able to sell later to an even bigger fool) but the effect is the same.

It is at this stage that one often observes extravagant forecasts for where prices are headed. It comes back to a point Freud makes about how to influence a crowd:

> "Anyone who wishes to produce an effect upon it [the crowd] needs no logical adjustment in his arguments; he must paint in the most forcible colours, he must exaggerate, and he must repeat the same thing again and again."

Analysts seeking fame or notoriety will identify a major bull or bear market and attempt to personify the sentiment of the crowd. Watch the commentary on any market that is accelerating either up or down and observe how analysts compete with one another to produce the most ambitious forecast. This is often with the exclusive aim of attracting the most customers or acolytes to their particular brand of analysis.

The crowd better than meets them halfway. New buyers have no interest in reasonable, conservative forecasts. Instead they seek out the most impressive forecast because it helps to reconfirm their own feeling towards the instrument. Anyone buying into an accelerating market will be downright hostile towards those who might question their decision. New converts to the bullish hypothesis often adopt the fervour of a zealot.

They can least afford to be wrong because they have such a small cushion of profit built up to fall back on. They have to throw themselves completely into the bullish camp. They comfort themselves with the views of the 'authorities' on the subject, who forecast prices rising for years and even decades to come. Attempting to put a present value on events that will not occur for a very long time, intensification of emotion and a rapid appreciation in prices are all characteristics of an acceleration.

It is often the case that analysts who are vilified as cranks in the bull market are heralded as prophets following a major decline. They personify the bear market as their apparently prescient forecasts of doom are seen to be correct. However, it is exceedingly rare for high-profile analysts who become media personalities to successfully call a bottom having long-heralded the peak. Their success has been formed out of personifying a bearish sentiment and they would lose their notoriety if they were to reverse course. The same is true of those who personify the bull market when attempting to predict the bear.

Therefore one will see that a prophetic bear has the most to lose in terms of prestige from reversing a long-held opinion. Exactly the same happens at major tops. In any market where those who personify the dominant theme are getting increasing airtime, it is not so much an indication of where prices are going but of what investors have already done. When prices accelerate following an already well-defined trend, and this coincides with dramatic intensification of the prevailing sentiment, the chance that an important turning point is being approached greatly increases.

One might reasonably ask how to identify an acceleration. There is a simple answer. Acceleration should be readily observable on a price chart. If one has to question whether a market is accelerating or not, it probably isn't. On a chart an acceleration will look like a parabolic advance.

Cisco Systems (Nasdaq) 1996–2000

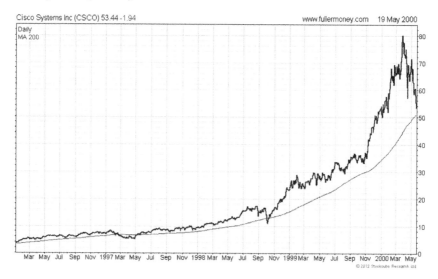

In 1999/2000 Cisco clearly accelerated as investors panicked in. No one wanted to be left behind by the bull market and there was a real sensation that if you did not buy immediately you would have to pay more later. Anyone who failed to own technology shares was seen as a dullard. The speed with which prices advanced seemed to reinforce the veracity of the bullish argument. However, the pool of potential buyers was being rapidly exhausted. Once everyone interested in buying have enough, then all that remain are potential sellers.

In a downtrend, those wishing to sell above the market watch as prices move further and further away from where they would like to sell. The only solution as prices deteriorate is to lower offers into the market or wait it out. As investors become increasing antipathetic towards the bullish case, the pressure of severe profit erosion or of enduring an increasingly large loss leads more and more active investors to liquidate their holdings. As sellers predominate, those willing to buy reduce their bids and prices fall further.

Sentiment deteriorates as those who have already sold have an emotional interest in prices going lower to validate their decision. Cheerleaders for the bearish hypothesis, who are those most likely to have short positions, will be triumphalist and predicting the demise of the financial markets. Such situations are scary times for investors and those seeking to buy turn cautious. Prices fall into this vacuum of demand. As they accelerate lower and sentiment turns ever more apocalyptic, the simple reality that very few actually go to zero will be at the back of potential buyers' minds.

The faster prices fall, the quicker wavering bulls are converted to the bearish view, which contributes to the acceleration. However, as prices fall, the number of people willing to sell at progressively lower levels dries up. Those short will be leveraging up and justifying their actions by claiming prices are going to zero. They will also have stops on their positions to protect profits just in case. Eventually, prices will fall to a level where there is no one left to sell at that moment, in which case the number of people holding cash has increased considerably, potential buyers are presented with a vacuum of supply overhead, fundamental valuations will have improved considerably and there will be ranks of short stops above the market ready to be triggered.

Citigroup (NYSE) 2006–2010

Citigroup offers an excellent example of a share that accelerated at the beginning of the downtrend and at the end. Citigroup had been ranging mostly between $42.50 and $56 from 2004 to late 2007 in a type-3 top formation. We have previously defined a range as an explosion waiting to happen and in this case the explosion was downwards.

It is important to differentiate between a powerful breakout from a well-defined range and an acceleration following an already well-developed move. Citigroup offers us an example of both. The initial decline saw prices drop quickly out of the range when they hit a vacuum of demand below the market. This acceleration was not a trend ending. Instead, such a powerful breakdown can be considered confirmation of the beginning of a new downtrend, and is exactly what we expect to see in a breakout.

Price broke downwards in October 2007 and quickly fell to $30, where it steadied for six weeks. This was an abrupt decline and shattered investor confidence. Most of those who were bearish in mid-2007 did not expect the subsequent collapse, probably because the problems besetting the company were still not fully understood. However, as prices continued to deteriorate, those holding short positions were incentivised to ferret out the reasons for the decline. More coherent bearish arguments emerged. By October 2008, the subprime loans debacle was a front page story globally and there were concerns that the company was going to go bust and take the whole financial sector with it. In the seven weeks starting 2 October 2008 prices fell from $22 to $3. The speed of the decline forced the Fed into action, which made sure the company did not go bust. While prices did not bottom until March 2009, the final acceleration and peak of bearish sentiment proved climactic and signalled that the bottoming-out process had begun.

Both Cisco Systems and Citigroup illustrate major trend endings, but the indefinite duration of an accelerated ending means that an acceleration may simply indicate that a cyclical peak or trough is being approached within an overall secular, as in long-term, bull or bear market.

Spot Silver 1992–2013

Due to its high beta relationship to gold, silver is prone to accelerations both up and down. Over the last decade it has tended to range extensively before breaking out and surging in the direction of the breakout. Investors have come to expect massive accelerations following these breakouts and extreme overextensions relative to the 200-day MA have been witnessed in 2004, 2006, 2008, 2010 and 2013. As much as these accelerations remain wonderful money-making opportunities, they have been followed by equally dramatic accelerated reversions to the mean. In such circumstances one has to tailor position sizes to the volatility. A disciplined attitude to stops once a position moves into profit is the only way to ensure that once a tipping point is reached we get out with most of the profit intact.

WHEN IS IT RIGHT TO SELL?

If we have identified a promising market, exhibiting a consistent trend, been lucky enough to have entered at a favourable level and ridden it higher for a number of years, selling can be a difficult prospect. However, when we see prices becoming wildly overextended relative to a trend mean such as the 200-day MA, it is time to think about taking at least some money off the table.

We may still believe the market has further to go over the long haul or that the background story still has the potential to inspire more investors to participate. But even if this is the case, accelerations are unsustainable beyond the short term. A better entry point is likely to present itself in due course. The least advantageous time to think about selling is when prices have already declined to a trend mean. It is around such levels that we might expect support to be found if the medium-term uptrend is to remain consistent.

So how much do we sell? It will always be a judgement call. We can base the decision on the overall consistency of the move, how long it has already been trending for, where our average purchase price is relative to the current price and the potential size of a reaction which would retest the mean. Capital gains tax will also be a consideration for many investors.

The vast majority of people seek to latch on to a big trend, ride it higher and don't want to dabble too much with it: a classic buy-and-hold strategy. However, if we refuse to harvest profits when excellent opportunities such as upward accelerations present themselves, then when could be a better time to lighten? All investing and trading can be boiled down to some form of buy low and sell high.

When an acceleration occurs, prices are moving progressively higher as long as momentum persists. Using such opportunities to harvest profits takes advantage of this situation. The abundant liquidity that is associated with such aggressive buying also ensures a favourable fill on a sell order ,which might not be achieved when prices begin to pullback. This strategy leaves open the potential to reinvest the proceeds at more favourable levels when prices eventually pullback if the consistency of the trend supports that decision.

The alternative of using an acceleration to harvest some profits is to hold both during the advance and subsequent reversion in the hope that prices will surge even more in future. This exacerbates the conditioning process of being long and makes it that much harder to sell when the eventual climax is reached.

In my opinion, the best tactic would be to hold a core investment position and harvest profits at the margin. This would allow one to derive income from trading, which could be reinvested at opportune times following reversions to the mean. At a minimum, such a policy would ensure that we are resisting the temptation to increase the position irresponsibly as prices accelerate higher. The total position would have a lower average cost of purchase and a technical stop could be employed without being pressured by short-term considerations. The fact that an acceleration is used to let go of part of the position introduces greater analytical rigour and helps ensure we do not form an emotional attachment to the instrument.

KEY REVERSALS

- *Definition of an upside key day reversal* – a two-candle pattern where prices make a new low for the move but reverse and close above the high of the previous day.

- *Definition of a downside key day reversal* – a two-candle pattern where prices make a new high for the move but reverse and close below the low of the previous day.

Like so much in life, the interpretation of charts is overly complicated by those who refuse to accept a simple explanation. Many investors who come to candlestick analysis despair of ever getting a handle on the myriad patterns purporting to offer important information. I am a great fan of Ockham's razor, which can loosely be described as 'the simplest explanation is most likely the correct one'.

Rather than spending hours attempting to interpret the meaning of every individual day's trading, look for the days where something big happened. The importance of the move is in how much it affects crowd sentiment. The crowd only responds to force, so a dynamic move has to be big if it is to change investor sentiment. Taken in isolation, dynamic moves help to either reinforce the dominant sentiment or indicate that an important change has occurred. This is where key reversals come in.

In the case of an uptrend, assume prices have moved relatively uninterrupted for a period of time and even hit new highs or tested an area of previous resistance. If on the day or week of the key reversal, prices hit a new high and subsequently fall to close below the low of the previous day then something has happened to check momentum and bullish sentiment. In such circumstances, the power of the signal is all in its psychological impact on market participants. Therefore, as David Fuller says, "*the key to the key is size*". Simply put, the dynamic of the failure has got to be big enough to alert participants that something important has happened.

If one has to take out a magnifying glass and measure whether prices actually hit a new high and closed below the low of the previous day or week, then the psychological impact will obviously be less than a clearly defined formation.

Commonality is another important aspect to key reversals. If the change to the dominant crowd sentiment is real, then it is unlikely to hit just one instrument in a sector. If we witness key reversals across a range of related instruments within a short time frame then the efficacy of the reversal signal increases considerably.

Additionally, key reversals are often large moves, but the reversal needs to be held and improved upon to confirm the change of direction. Follow-through on subsequent sessions is essential to confirm the signal.

In summary we are looking for:

1. The conditions of the formation to be met.
2. Additional follow-through on subsequent trading sessions.
3. Ideally, commonality across related instruments.

Why are key reversals important? They happen often enough at major tops and bottoms to be a useful addition to one's analytical arsenal. Nike offers examples of both upside and downside weekly key reversals

Nike 2009

UPSIDE WEEKLY KEY REVERSAL

At the 2009 low, Nike had just broke downwards again and everyone was heralding the end of the financial system as we know it. However, something happened in mid-March. The price moved to a new low intraweek and closed above the high of the previous week. The rally followed through the week after. This constituted a failed downside break and the price shot right back up to test the upper side of the range before breaking upwards.

Nike 2011

DOWNSIDE WEEKLY KEY REVERSAL

1. At the December 2010 peak, prices had been rallying persistently for nearly four months and had become increasingly overextended relative to the trend mean. Having rallied to the psychological $90 area, the share moved to a new high intraweek only to pull back sharply intraweek and close below the low of the previous week.

2. The share found support above the 200-day MA and rallied right back to test peak where it formed another smaller weekly key reversal. On this occasion, downside follow was particularly abrupt and prices spent another six months ranging, albeit mostly above the MA.

Nike 2012

3. By late March 2012 Nike has become overextended relative to the 200-day MA again and posted a downside key reversal but failed to follow through to the downside. On this occasion the inconsistency of the downward dynamic formed part of the softening-up process that resulted in the reasonably deep reaction. Following the weekly key reversal, prices were held up for at least six weeks. The failed upside break in May and breakdown from the range two weeks later confirmed a swifter process of mean-reversion was taking place.

From the above examples we see that while key reversals are not a necessary condition when a market tops or bottoms, they do tend to foretell at least a pause in what might otherwise be a relatively consistent trend. They happen with sufficient regularity to be a useful tool.

I am often asked which is more important, a daily or a weekly key reversal. The answer lies in the size of the dynamics. Within a medium-term move, what happens on a weekly basis is of more importance than what happens on a daily basis. However, if the size of an individual daily dynamic is large enough it will show up on a weekly chart. Of more importance than whether the formation occurred on just one day or over a number of days is that the change of direction was sustained and that it was large enough to stand out on a weekly chart.

CONCLUSION

Accelerations represent wonderful money-making opportunities, where we have the potential to make a great deal of money quickly. However, they also represent episodes of emotional intensity that are unsustainable. Disciplined money-control tactics are required in order to profit from such occasions and to ensure we hold onto those profits.

CHAPTER 15:

TREND ENDING #2 –
THE MASSIVE REACTION
AGAINST THE PREVAILING TREND

What we will cover in this chapter:

"Broadening is seldom a reliable continuation pattern."

– David Fuller

- Failed breaks and loss of momentum are clues that the imbalance of supply and demand is changing. However, a massive reaction against the prevailing trend is categorical evidence that something big has happened. The size of the counter-trend move is such that it forces investors to reassess. In this case reassessment means reversal.

- The proverbial bolt from the blue can happen so fast that it takes time for the crowd to catch on, so type-2 endings are often followed by a period of ranging or 'right-hand extension' as the impact of the price action is digested.

HAVING THE CAPACITY TO IDENTIFY ACCELERATION as a trend ending is an invaluable tool in the arsenal of any analyst. However, while it would make investing and trading considerably easier if every market accelerated up and accelerated down, it just doesn't happen all that often and there is no way to know with any degree of confidence which markets are going to accelerate. Therefore we also need tactics to cater for those times when trends end without accelerating.

Let's review consistency characteristics: The below market has been trending steadily higher. Every time it consolidates it is within a similar band to previous occasions. Each one of the ranges is one above the other and it has just broken upwards once more.

No one long of this market will feel like they have anything to worry about. The trend is consistent and as we covered earlier "*if a market has further to go NOW, it will sustain the upward break*". Within this trend, upward breaks are being sustained – so the benefit of the doubt can continue to be given to the upside. Most investors would have a stop under the most recent low which would get triggered if something serious went wrong. There is nothing on the chart right now to indicate that a top might be developing because the price action is still consistent.

The market has now moved into a lengthier range. Most of the consistency characteristics remain intact but there are now some differences. The market has spent much more time ranging so there has been a loss of momentum. Failed upside breaks are beginning to occur which only means one thing – right now there is excess supply above the market. These are initial cues that something might be changing in how supply and demand are interacting.

However, nothing has yet happened to trigger any major stops. Most of those who have been long will still have their positions and because they have not experienced any kind of trauma they are unlikely to simply liquidate the position and move onto the next opportunity. In fact, they are more likely to suffer from boredom than anything else. If we have no reason to change our minds we are unlikely to do so. Why would we mess with something that has been making us money?

The only people in any danger of losing money in this market are those who were buying breakouts. Their strategy worked fine in the other ranges – wait for the breakout and rely on momentum. That's not working anymore because breakouts are failing. The other side of that equation is that those who were shorting rallies are now making money and will have a greater sense of conviction as a result.

Ranging phases are boring relative to trending phases primarily because traders are making less money and investors are sitting with a position that is not doing very much. In a range supply and demand are in balance and expectations go down. This is primarily because we tend to predict what we see, so if the market is ranging most people will predict more ranging. They'll be a little more bullish at the upper side of the range and a bit more bearish at the bottom. The longer a range goes on, the more people get bored with waiting. Arguments both for and against the prevailing market hypothesis will be evident and investors might not be ready to sell but more will be introducing stops to make sure that they hold on to the majority of their profit.

Here is lengthier range enlarged:

Lengthier range

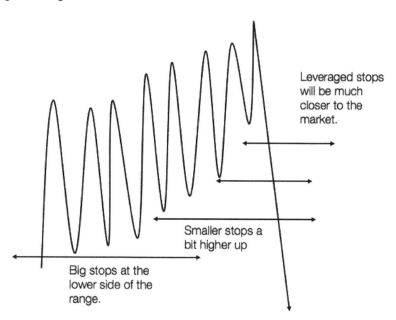

Large unleveraged investors, in for the long haul, are likely to have the loosest stops because they will only want to be taken out of the market if something really important happens. They will probably have a stop under the most recent major reaction low. Other investors might be reluctant to sell but their patience will be wearing thin as the market ranges for much longer than they have previously experienced. More leveraged traders who are not prepared to ride out even a small reaction will have stops even higher up and will be trailing their stops up behind each successive higher reaction low.

At this point the market could still sustain an upward break and reassert the overall uptrend. Even after the lengthier range and failed upside breaks demand could overcome supply at the upper side of the range and push higher. However, as we saw with failed upside breaks, *"if the dynamic of the failure is greater than the dynamic of the breakout the odds increase considerably that the lower side of the range will be tested".*

In this scenario the lows have continued to rise despite a significant loss of momentum. We know that most people tend to have their stops below the most recent low and as the market encounters supply above the market once more, it falls enough to trigger stops set by leveraged traders and those who had sought to buy the breakout. This source of additional supply causes the market to fall enough to hit stops set below the previous minor reaction low and a chain reaction is set in motion that hits the institutional stops at the bottom of the range. The market has just fallen farther and faster than anyone has seen for a long time.

This is the proverbial bolt from the blue and is the defining characteristic of type-2 endings. It is always this massive reaction against the prevailing trend that characterises the type-2 ending, so while lengthier ranges and failed breaks are indications that something may be beginning to change, the downward dynamic is confirmation that a pivotal event has occurred to change how supply and demand are interacting.

No one holding a long position was anticipating anything like this. The speed of the reaction is terrifying, and like deer in the headlights market participants are stunned into paralysis. Those with stops will have been kicked out of the market. Those still long will have to decide whether to sell or wait to see if the market recovers somewhat, offering a better exit opportunity.

This action is unlikely to have been as a result of a major fundamental change. As we have just seen with this example, the simple process of stops being hit has triggered this reaction and is forcing investors to make decisions. The violent price fall can probably be rationalised and a bigger story will coalesce if this turns out to have been a major trend ending.

Because of the shock value of the decline and the apparent lack of any serious change to the status quo that could be seen as a major inhibiting factor there will be a cohort of investors who view this as a buying opportunity. In the aftermath of such a traumatic event, those who had been looking for an opportunity to buy will ask whether they are being presented with just such a chance to participate. The market has pulled back violently but it is probably still possible to make a relatively convincing, though ultimately probably incorrect, argument for why an investment at this point could be profitable. This instinct in tandem with the absence of a well-defined reason for the pullback can often, though not necessarily, result in a range forming below or in the region of the type-2 top. This would be referred to as a type-2 with right-hand extension. This range might also be referred to as a 'first step below the top'.

We looked at first steps above the base as continuation patterns earlier, but here we have a first step below the top and it is an equally reliable continuation pattern. As with a first step above the base, this is because a sea change has occurred in the demand component of the market, but it takes time for sentiment to catch up.

The German DAX Index offers good examples of type-2 top and bottoming activity.

DAX Index 2006–2009

The index trended consistently higher from 2003 all the way through to 2007. Reactions were relatively similar-sized and the market found support in the region of the 200-day moving average on a number of occasions.

From early 2007 through to early 2008, the index encountered resistance in the region of the psychologically significant 8,000 level and posted failed upside breaks on a number of occasions. The first of these in July 2007 resulted in a reversion towards the 200-day MA. But the broad consistency of the almost four-year uptrend was sustained and the index rallied once more towards 8,000. It pulled back again to the 200-day MA and rallied briefly back above 8,000 but failed to sustain the upward break and pulled back once more. By early January 2008, the index had been in a clearly lengthier range and had posted at least two failed breaks above 8,000. Medium to longer-term investors had not experienced profit erosion and might have rationalised the price action as justifiable given the proximity of the round 8,000 level, which also represented the peak in 2000.

The fall from 8,000 to 6,500 in January 2008 was a wake-up call for investors. The progression of rising reaction lows had been broken. The 200-day MA had been emphatically pierced, and perhaps most importantly the complacency of major institutional buyers had been disrupted. This is the kind of environment when emergency investment meetings are convened. Some will say not that much has happened fundamentally, so they should buy more; others will say that they should become more cautious; and others will say it's a top so they should liquidate the position. In such cases all that has to happen is for a major source of demand such as a pension fund to stop buying and the market has just been robbed of one of its greatest supporters. Bull markets rely on new sources of demand continuing to invest. When that slows down, the previous dominance of demand over supply contracts.

However, following the sudden decline, there was no widely perceived understanding of why the market should decline. The US subprime debt problems were still a little-understood issue in early 2008. The market ranged mostly below 7,000 for another eight months in a first step below the top as sentiment caught up with the change that had occurred to the demand component. Then it overtook the problem and the market accelerated lower.

The October 2008 crash was a deeply traumatic event for most investors, as many people panicked out of their long positions. Fear was pervasive following the Lehman Brothers bankruptcy and cash was seen as the only safe haven. Subscribers of mine were writing in at the time asking if there was a bank secure enough to deposit one's cash in and I know of a few people who buried their cash and gold in safes in their gardens. However, as we saw in the last chapter, "*acceleration is always an ending but of undetermined duration*".

A globally significant index will not go to zero, so we know that such a violent downward acceleration has a limit in how far it can decline. The range that formed between October 2008 and July 2009 was not enough to convince many of the bears that the market was bottoming and some were waiting for the 'second shoe to drop'. However, there were a number of clues evident for the macro behavioural technical analyst to see that the market was bottoming.

The first of these was the downward acceleration which we have demonstrated is always an ending signal. The lengthier range mostly above 4,000 following a halving in value was a further indication that the demand component was beginning to return to dominance. The break below 4,000 in February 2009 was heralded by the bears as the beginning of the next down-leg but was in fact the last gasp of the bear market. The failed downside break indicated the return of demand and was signalled by a clear upside weekly key reversal. The failed break indicated that a retest of the upper side of the range was more likely and this had occurred by June amid short covering. The market subsequently paused below 5,000 before rallying persistently, and retested the 8,000 level at the time of writing.

CONCLUSION

Type-2 endings can happen with such suddenness that there is often a temptation to rationalise the price action because nothing will have apparently changed fundamentally. However, this would be to ignore the impact of the massive reaction against the prevailing trend on investor psychology and therefore their actions.

CHAPTER 16:

TYPE-3 ENDINGS – RANGING, TIME AND SIZE

What we will cover in this chapter:

- Type-3 tops are identified by lengthy periods of volatile ranging and can be characterised as wars between the competing forces of supply and demand.

- Type-3s never start out as type-3s but morph into these extremely difficult environments where the question really should be asked whether one should have a position at all.

- Type-3 bottoms represent the classic base formation. These are the foundations of bull markets once new sources of demand become apparent. As such they can be characterised as 'sleepers'.

TYPE-1 ENDINGS ARE SYMPTOMATIC of at least a temporary dramatic blowout in the dominance of supply over demand or vice versa. Type-2 endings are all about the shock value of a sudden powerful move against the prevailing trend and impact that has on crowd sentiment. Type-3 endings are formed by a war taking place between supply and demand. Just like in the real world, these can be lengthy, volatile, difficult exchanges where one would be wise to step aside and where collateral damage is almost unavoidable. In terms of price action, this war is evidenced by three primary characteristics: ranging, time and size.

Type-3s don't start out as type-3s but evolve into these patterns following an acceleration or marked loss of momentum. However, they all share the same characteristics. Type-3 patterns are difficult to make money in, particularly as they begin to unfold, because whatever the winning strategy had been in the prior trend, it will no longer work once a more volatile ranging environment takes over. This requires traders to adapt their tactics quickly. For investors the vital question will be whether one should really still be in the market at all.

Typical type-3 top

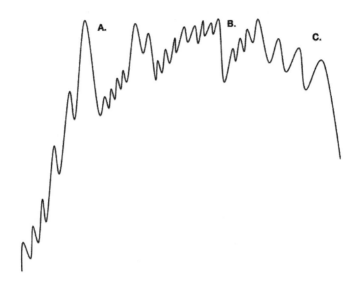

A type-3 is a *compound top*, containing elements of acceleration, loss of momentum and massive reactions against the prevailing trend – but it has unique aspects all of its own.

A. In this example a market which has been trending consistently begins to accelerate – the type-1 trend-ending characteristic. It then experiences a sudden deep pullback, which we would associate with a type-2 massive reaction against the prevailing trend. The market then finds support and rallies back up to retest the highs. At this point, those who have been stopped out will be rueing the decision to exit and will be tempted to re-enter the market. Those who did not have a stop and still hold their positions will be even less likely to implement such a strategy because they will not want to be kicked out of such a powerful uptrend, especially following the impressive rebound. However, from an objective standpoint, the risk premium attached to this market has now increased because the prior uptrend's consistency has, at a minimum, been questioned.

B. It fails to hold the advance to test the highs and falls back once more, only to find support above the previous lows and rallies back to test the high again, spending a lengthy period ranging below the peak. By this time the market has been largely rangebound for a considerable period. If it were a building, it could be described as top-heavy. Those seeking to buy into the market are being given ample opportunity to purchase but have to develop patience because the market is simply not breaking upwards to new highs. Participants with stops in this market are seeing them triggered. Relatively recent entrants will be seeing their positions move in and out of the money. Those seeking to short rallies have found a successful strategy and are making money.

C. The market falls back to test the lower side of what is turning into a very lengthy range, posts a failed downside break and rallies back towards the upper boundary. This time it does not succeed in retesting the high and falls away with a progression of lower rally highs before accelerating lower, completing the top formation.

One could spend a great deal of time attempting to describe the unique attributes of each and every big compound-top formation and hope that by learning what each looks like that history will repeat itself. However, history tends to rhyme more than repeat. Therefore it is probably more constructive to identify the characteristics common to all such tops. Once we observe the requisite signs we can make a diagnosis and employ the correct strategy to preserve capital and perhaps increase it.

Big tops such as that above spend a great deal of time ranging. In terms of supply and demand, ranging is evidence of indecision. Those making bullish arguments are counterbalanced by those making bearish arguments. However, when this occurs following a period where a market has trended consistently, it is often indicative of a change in how investors are interacting with the market.

The longer a market spends ranging following what had been a consistent uptrend, the more of its primary consistency characteristics will be lost. "*A consistent trend is a trend in motion*" means that a consistent trend is just about the best continuation pattern there is for as long as upward breaks are sustained. Once upward breaks are no longer being sustained and a market spends a lot more time ranging, it has lost what is perhaps the most important consistency characteristic for any uptrend.

When a war takes place between supply and demand, things tend to get messy and big patterns tend to unfold. Large percentage moves are common in type-3 patterns because of the increased volatility. This is particularly the case at tops more than bottoms because participation is much greater at the top than the bottom.

Head-and-shoulders tops, double tops, triple tops and any other compound top, while individual in their own right, all share the common characteristics of ranging, time and size. It is these characteristics that are important for planning how to deal with such patterns because they deal directly with how the interaction between supply and demand has changed rather than any other esoteric quality these formations might be presumed to have.

Copper (CMX) 1998–2009

Copper CMX 1st Month Continuation (HG1) 210.10 +5.35   www.fullermoney.com   1 May 2009

Between late 2006 and late 2008 copper offers an excellent example of a type-3 top. It had accelerated remarkably from just above $2 to $4 between March and May 2006. Therefore this type-3 started out as a type-1 accelerating trend ending. Having pulled back to $3, it ranged for five-months above $3: exhibiting a type-2 right-hand extension characteristic. It then broke downwards only to find support in February 2007 and rally back to test the $4 area. It formed a volatile range for the next ten months before pushing back up to post new highs above $4. However, it was unable to sustain these upward breaks, fell through the lower side of the short-term range, broke below $3, and subsequently accelerated lower to $1.25.

At the time, an argument raged as to whether the commodity secular bull market had ever really existed, whether copper's upward acceleration in 2006 was as a result of manipulation or whether this massive pattern was simply a lengthy pause in what was destined to be a massive bull market that would see prices rally even more impressively later.

When we consider the medium to long-term outlook for a commodity such as copper, one can't but also take note of the extremely lengthy type-3 base formation from which the original rally emerged. The bull market in commodities was always best defined in terms of the rising cost of production. This probably means that the low near $1.25 can now be considered a floor whereas once it would have been viewed as a ceiling.

TYPE-3 BOTTOMS – LENGTHY BASE FORMATION DEVELOPMENT – SLEEPERS

If a type-3 top is characterised by a violent war between supply and demand, then type-3 bottoms are characterised by uninterest and disbelief. As we covered in the psychological perception stages of bull and bear markets, the base formation phase of a trend evolves out of the disappointment associated with every market decline. It takes time to work through the excess of the prior bull market. It takes fundamentals strong enough to support another major advance to evolve. Not least it takes time for psychological wounds to heal.

Typical type-3 base formation

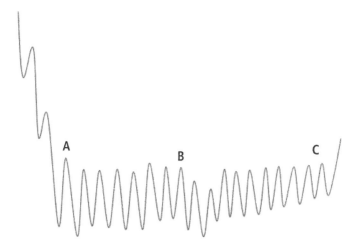

The formation of type-3 bottoms differs from tops because time and ranging are often more dominant characteristics than size, at least on an arithmetic scale. Type-3 bottoms tend to spend a great deal of time ranging and in some cases this can persist for years and even decades.

In a bear market, as prices decline leverage is squeezed out of the system. There is still a buyer for every seller but those with leveraged positions are forced to exit. Therefore by the time the market bottoms, participation has decreased.

A. In this illustration prices accelerate lower so this bottom begins as a type-1. A short covering rally takes place as value hunters predominate, at least for a while, which forms a type-2 massive reaction against the prevailing trend characteristic. However, as prices improve there are ranks of stale bull holders waiting for the first sign of a rally to liquidate inventory and the market deteriorates once more. The failed downside break, following this decline, signals that the demand side of the market perceives value and is willing to participate on dips. Another rally takes place. As the previous high is retested those who failed to take the opportunity to sell the last time this area was tested now lower offers into the market. This pattern persists and demonstrates that supply and demand have formed an uneasy equilibrium. As the range proceeds everyone gets the message that they need to adjust their expectations to the new reality. Sentiment deteriorates. Depression and resignation tend to be the dominant emotions in this environment.

B. As this range persists, those who no longer have a financial interest in this market – not least because they have taken losses on the decline – will have an emotional wish to see prices decline further. At a minimum they will be slow to participate again since they know what happened last time. Those still holding long positions opened significantly above where the market is now trading turn on their screens every morning and have a negative number to remind them of their mistake. As the market continues to range, other instruments will be outperforming and will be more attractive from an absolute and relative perspective, so the desire to write off the loss grows increasingly tempting. Prices may even break down from the range temporarily. However, if this is a base and value investors are still willing to increase positions on dips, the breakdown will not be sustained.

C. Stages A and B above can take anything from weeks to months, even years and decades, to unfold. However, the latter stages of a type-3 bottom are perhaps the most interesting from the perspective of investors looking for evidence that the base will be completed. Within a lengthy base formation, most participants have been conditioned by the ranging environment expectations of upside potential deteriorate. However, if a succession of higher reaction lows develops it tells us that the demand is willing to pay progressively higher prices for the instrument whenever it pulls back. The range will persist for as long as it takes a vacuum of supply to develop above the market but when that condition is met, the stage is set for a power breakout to occur, completing the base and indicating a new bull market.

Dollar Tree Stores offers an excellent example of a lengthy type-3 bottom. The share debuted near $2 in 1995 and hit a peak near $32 in 2000. The story that propelled Dollar Tree Stores was well and truly exhausted by the 2000 peak and it took nearly a decade to rejuvenate the company in the eyes of investors. Over the intervening years investors used rallies to liquidate positions and move on to fresher, more stimulating opportunities. Those with long positions were either completely passive or had to have a position because they needed to track an index. However, as with all ranges, bases are explosions waiting to happen.

Dollar Tree Stores (Nasdaq) 1995–2013

The price action in this chart has all the characteristics of a type-3 bottom: lots of ranging, time and size. While volatile, the size factor has been compressed in this chart by the subsequent impressive bull market. Type-3 bottoms are more often referred to as bases and are pregnant with potential for long-term investors.

With type-3 bottoms we look for signs that demand is slowly beginning to regain dominance. A sequence of incrementally higher major reaction lows represents evidence. When this occurs it tells us that investors are willing to pay successively higher prices for the share on pullbacks and are therefore demonstrating an increased desire to build positions. This type of activity is evident with Dollar Tree Stores, where progressively higher major reaction lows are evident in 2001, 2003, 2005 and 2008.

Prices then rallied steadily from the 2008 low to test the upper side of the base and broke upwards in August 2009.

Type-3 bottoms that spend a long time ranging can also be regarded as 'sleepers'. They often lie dormant, sometimes for decades, waiting for a new story capable of inspiring investors to participate. Secular bear markets depicted in the early to mid stages of type-3 bottoms are often the seedbeds for the next major bull markets. They are worth monitoring: when one major bull market ends, another is starting somewhere else. These seedbeds offer the best potential sources for new major bull markets to emerge. It is therefore particularly noteworthy that at the time of writing a number of stock markets such as the S&P500, Germany's DAX Index and the UK's FTSE-100 have been rangebound for 13 years, have experienced valuation contraction over that time as P/E ratios declined and could be at the dawn of new multi-year periods of demand dominance.

DAX Index 1992–2013

CONCLUSION

The volatile nature of type-3 tops ensures that participating in such market conditions is likely to be stressful and difficult to make money from. Since type-3s evolve from an earlier type-1 or type-2, they also represent the loss of consistency that those formations entail. We really need to ask whether we should have a position at all when a market we are interested in begins to behave in such a manner. At a minimum, position sizes need to be reduced to tailor to the new reality provided by the market.

Type-3 bottoms represent the seedbeds for new bull markets. Whether we decide to participate while the base is still developing will be a matter of choice and our tolerance of volatility. However, when a progression of higher reaction lows is evident within the base – and more importantly when prices breakout successfully – we are presented with evidence of demand dominance that could represent the genesis of a new bull market.

CHAPTER 17:

MONETARY POLICY

What we will cover in this chapter:

- David Fuller has stated for years that *"monetary policy trumps most other factors most of the time"*.

- The speed with which money moves around the economy (velocity of M2) has been declining across the G7 for more than a decade.

- Central banking 101 dictates that enough money be made available to allow growth to become self-sustaining.

- Therefore central banks can increase the supply of money without the threat of inflation provided the velocity of money continues to trend lower.

- When that situation changes, inflation becomes an increasingly important challenge.

- The yield curve spread for US Treasuries has been a lead indicator of US recessions for more than 30 years.

DURING THE EMOTIONAL ROLLERCOASTER that characterises the day-to-day activity of the financial markets, it is all too easy to ignore the big picture – the macro environment. As media plays an ever more pivotal role in the financial sector, the constant demand for soundbites and breaking news has contributed to ever-shorter time horizons for financial commentary. Leveraged traders spend the majority of their time assessing the short-term outlook and the advent of high frequency trading has reduced holding periods to nanoseconds. However, this short-termism does not obscure the fact that markets often form multi-year rhythmic trends and that monetary policy is a significant influence on how these moves progress and eventually end. Monetary policy doesn't change all that often, but it offers a priceless window on whether prices experience a headwind or a tailwind.

By way of comparison, if we were active in the orange juice market, we would be interested in how many oranges there are likely to be in any given season. It is for this reason that the US Department of Agriculture reports are so keenly anticipated by that market. In just the same way, in our constant effort to profit and to outperform, doesn't it make sense to attempt to gain some insight into what kind of monetary environment we are active in? If the supply of money is abundant it should be easier to make more of it than if supply is shrinking. How much it costs to borrow money is also worth knowing because it acts as a useful barometer of the perception of risk attached to leveraged positions. It is also helpful to know how easy it is to access credit. Short-term interest rates can be close to zero but if it is impossible to gain access to capital then the increase in liquidity required to fuel the next bull market is unlikely to develop.

MONEY SUPPLY AND THE VELOCITY OF MONEY

Depending on the country, a central bank has a mandate to promote growth and/or control inflation. In their efforts to achieve these goals, central banks accept, and in fact pursue, a moderate level of inflation in order to promote investment and foster growth. Short-term interest rates are kept at a comparatively amenable level and supply of money is increased to accommodate a growth trajectory for the respective economy. When inflationary pressures become more of an issue, interest rates can be raised and money supply (M2) choked off, to restrict the capacity for growth and dampen inflationary pressures.

Central bankers attempt to delicately balance the need to promote economic growth, high employment and moderate inflation. The lessons they learned from the Great Depression and Japan's experience since its property and stock market bubbles burst in 1989 is that *deflation* is to be avoided at all costs. The lessons carried over from Paul Volcker's time as Fed chairman in the early 1980s is that inflation, no matter how acute, can be squeezed out of the system. Therefore central banks tend to have an inflation bias – it is seen as a necessary ill which can be managed.

As of 2013, the USA has been the largest proponent of quantitative easing and the Fed's balance sheet has expanded to previously unimaginable extremes. Japan embarked on its own aggressive quantitative easing from early 2013 and relative to the size of its economy its easing programme has been even larger than the Fed's. The European Central Bank, the Bank of England, the Swiss National Bank and the Royal Bank of Australia have been making abundant liquidity available. Unsurprisingly, this has sparked a certain amount of disquiet among investors about the integrity of their respective currencies, particularly when the expansion of broad money supply occurs against a background of high fiscal deficits.

A debate has raged over whether inflation or deflation would prevail in a number of countries – especially in the USA. Those who cite inflation as the greatest risk look at their daily outgoings and can't help but see that the price of just about all staples has increased. Despite the fact commodity prices are volatile, the price of consumer goods only seems to trend upwards. Just about everyone is remarking on the higher costs of food and energy. Insurance, medical and education costs are not only at record highs but trending higher. Food price inflation was an important catalyst that spurred political upheaval in the Middle East. Those who predict a deflationary outcome point towards high unemployment, spare industrial capacity, wage compression and deleveraging to support their thesis.

Inflation is an enormously important subject for the prospective investor, whose aim is not only to profit in nominal terms but to make money faster than it is depreciating in real terms. Inflation is important to governments because social security payments and Treasury Inflation-Protected Securities (TIPS) or inflation linked bond returns are tied to inflationary measures. Inflation is seen as desirable to promote economic growth but not to the extent that it sparks higher wage demands. Therefore how inflation is measured and reported plays a significant role in how some assets perform.

The volatility of food and energy prices are an inconvenience for those attempting to model how an economy responds to stimulus. The prices for essential commodities both as raw materials in manufacturing and at the retail level tend to move considerably faster than economic measures which are updated at most monthly. In order to smooth inflation figures, how it is measured has been finessed considerably.

Hedonic methods originally ascribed to the real estate market have more recently been employed across just about every sector including energy and food. The theory runs that if one input cost is too expensive, the individual can substitute for something cheaper. This works comparatively well with housing because people often move to where they can afford or rent instead of buying. However, many essential items everyone spends money on do not stand up to this comparison. If I have a petrol car, I cannot simply begin to fuel it with diesel. How can I substitute milk in my breakfast cereal? It is impossible to make a sandwich without bread. I cannot heat or cool my house without electricity. I cannot survive without water. If I am sick, I will have to seek medical attention at some point. The list could go on.

By removing volatile elements from how inflation is calculated it becomes much easier to model inflationary expectations, but the result is that inflation is under reported. The Fed's preferred measure of inflation is the PCE Deflator. (The clue is in the name.) This index is particularly susceptible to missing large moves in commodity prices because they make up such a small weighting in it. This is justified by the assumption that commodity prices are highly cyclical, which was largely true during the triple waterfall bear market from 1980 to 2003. A more subtle interpretation is that commodities are prone to major bull and bear markets which play out over anything from years to decades.

Commodity prices have now held historically high nominal prices for the better part of a decade. Despite bouts of extreme volatility, there is no evidence that the low prices that prevailed before 2002 are about to be revisited for the commodity complex as a whole. The rise in the marginal cost of production for many commodities and the concurrent rise in per capita consumption of just about everything, support this view. A major fundamental shift in supply and demand would be required to question this hypothesis.

Inflation-adjusted charts for commodity prices offer perhaps the best example of how the pricing structure has changed. The below chart of the Reuters/Jeffries CRB commodity index, adjusted for inflation using the CPI, highlights the fact that commodity prices are substantially above where they were a decade ago despite the fact that central banks tell us that no inflation has occurred.

CRB commodity index adjusted for inflation using US CPIUS

Part of the reason commodities were excluded from inflation measures is because they were seen as too volatile and that their effect was smoothed out over time. However, what the above chart demonstrates is that commodities trended lower in real terms between 1973 and 2000. Ignoring the influence of commodities on inflationary expectations worked because prices fell more than they rose. However, since 2000 this has no longer been the case. Commodities have at least held their value in real terms. This raises the possibility that official measures of inflation are underestimating its influence.

In their efforts to provide an environment where growth can flourish, central bankers have increased the supply of money considerably over the last few decades and particularly since 2008. The pace of M2's expansion picked up during the financial crisis, and taken in tandem with the massive increase in the Fed's balance sheet this has been seen as an indication that medium-term inflationary forces are being stoked. Continued injections of money supply reflect the Fed's concerns about the slow pick up in employment and potential for a deflationary outcome. The commitment to do whatever it takes to avoid deflation had been picked up by an increasing number of central banks at the time of writing.

US M2 Index

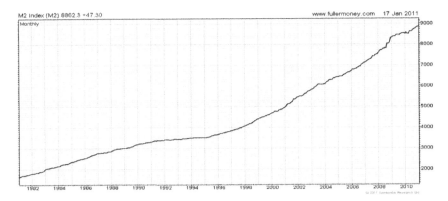

However, while it is tempting to conclude that the apparently unbridled expansion of M2 must necessarily result in massive future inflation, the situation is more subtle than it might first appear. Money supply cannot be looked at in isolation. The *velocity* of M2 plays an integral part in ascertaining whether the rapid expansion of M2 is likely to lead to significant medium-term inflationary pressures.

US velocity of M2

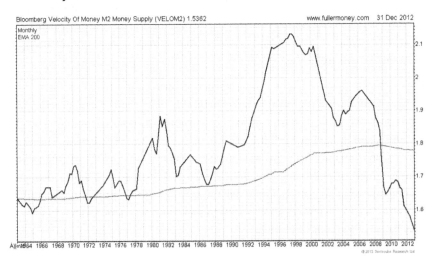

The velocity of M2 topped out in 1997, accelerated lower from July 2008 and hit new 55-year lows in 2013. It remains subdued, so the expansion in supply of money is helping to compensate for the slowdown in economic activity. Intuitively, if money is flowing through the financial system at an increasingly sluggish rate, then the supply of money needs to be increased in order to maintain a growth bias. When we multiply the velocity of M2 by M2 we get some interesting results.

The multiple of US M2 and the velocity of M2

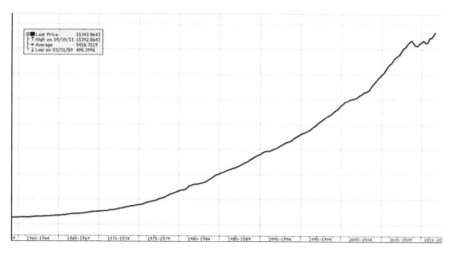

The almost unbroken line running from 1971 through to 2008 is a testament to the success of the Fed in matching the supply of money with the velocity of money to provide a favourable environment to promote growth. The credit crisis is clearly the most serious monetary event to have occurred in the last 50 years. The velocity of money shrunk at such a remarkable rate that it necessitated a massive infusion of new money to compensate. Even so, after more than five years, the long-term uptrend has not yet been reaffirmed. The above chart is heading in the right direction but central bankers will not have confidence that an environment amenable to sustained growth has been re-established until a new high has been sustained for a reasonable period. The reasonable period portion of this argument is where the potential for significant future inflation truly lies.

The ECB, Bank of England, Bank of Japan and Swiss National Bank are also dealing with declining velocity of money and are responding by increasing the supply of money. It is a reasonable bet that at least one of these organisations is not going to be able to sanitise their money supply quick enough when velocity of money eventually does return to a growth footing. A failure in that regard would be a clear indication that an inflationary outcome is inevitable.

THE COST OF MONEY

The previous example is concerned with the quantity of money in existence and the speed with which it moves through the financial system. However, the cost of borrowing is an equally important consideration. Modern central banking is based on the premise that a moderate amount of inflation is a good thing because it helps to promote economic growth by increasing the motivation to invest. Deflation is a hard cycle to break out of because individuals have to be convinced that they need to spend and invest to stimulate the economy when their experience tells them to defer spending because prices will fall. Managing inflationary expectations is therefore a major part of what a central bank does.

This means that following a major crash, where the velocity of money collapses, central banks are inclined to leave monetary policy loose for as long as it takes to ensure that inflationary pressures can take hold once more. Even as inflationary pressures begin to pick up, monetary policy is likely to be left loose until economic growth is deemed to be self-sustaining. Central bankers tend to believe that they have the tools necessary to squeeze inflation out of the system when it becomes a problem but are less confident about the corresponding ability to do the same with deflation.

The typical response to a major recession is to cut interest rates and increase the supply of money. More recently central banks have stepped in to purchase government bonds directly in an effort to force yields lower, cushion the financial and housing markets and to boost the prospects for recovery. The so called 'Greenspan Put', where investors came to rely on the Fed to bailout the worst offenders in a bust, remains a significant factor in the financial markets and can be graphically illustrated.

The spread between the 10-year and the 2-year Treasury bond is often referred to as the *yield curve spread*. When the spread is wide, investors and especially banks with access to funds via the Fed's discount window can borrow at a low interest rate on the short end of the curve and lend at the higher rate on the longer-dated side of the curve. For banks this is a risk-free trade and, for as long as the spread continues to widen, it allows them to recapitalise without directly receiving a politically sensitive bailout. This process is often referred to as bailing out the banking system via the yield curve.

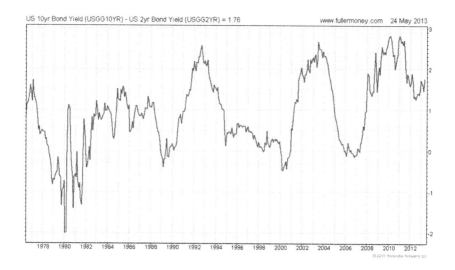

As late as 2011 it was still possible for banks to borrow for two years at close to 2% and lend for ten years at close to 5%, pocketing close to 300 basis points. When one considers the amounts of money employed in such trades it is little wonder how quickly TARP-assisted banks were able to pay back their loans.

The spread's previous peaks in 1992 and 2003 also corresponded with episodes of extreme monetary accommodation. Such periods when the price of borrowing is cheap and when the system is awash with liquidity are classic conditions to promote the evolution of a new bull market in a promising asset class. In 1992 technology, telecoms and media were just getting started. In 2003 banks, commodities and emerging markets were just getting started. In 2009, commodities and emerging markets were early leaders again. However, it is the outperformance of companies offering exposure to the growth of the global consumer class that have proven to be the most attractive vehicles from the perspective of global investors on this occasion.

The yield curve spread is useful from the perspective of pointing out just how accommodative monetary policy is relative to past occasions. However, it is even more important as a lead indicator for recessions. David Fuller has often said that "*bull markets don't die of old age; they are assassinated by central banks*". Every bull market thrives on a steady flow of new liquidity which propels prices to ever more impressive heights. However, when central banks deem that the benefits of the bull market are outweighed by the risks to the economy from imbalances and rising inflationary pressures they begin to restrict money supply and raise short-term interest rates. A powerful bull market can continue to hit new highs after monetary conditions turn into a headwind because the crowd remains enamoured with their investment story. However, central banks will continue in their efforts to curtail speculation until they are successful, so the environment is certainly riskier once central banks begin to intervene.

An important Rubicon for monetary policy is when 2-year yields rise above 10-year yields. This is often referred to as an *inverted yield curve* and is a reliable lead indicator for US recessions. When the yield on 2-year bonds is higher than that available on 10-year maturities then the carry from one to the other is reversed. It suddenly becomes more economic to borrow at longer maturities than shorter ones, with the implication that longer-term risk is less acute than the short-term risk. In the USA, every inversion of the yield curve since at least 1978 has been a reliable lead indicator of a recession.

- In 1978, the inverted yield curve anticipated the crisis that peaked in 1980.

- In 1988, the inverted yield curve anticipated the Savings & Loan crisis.

- The yield curve became inverted briefly in 1998 and again in very early 2000, anticipating the Nasdaq bust.

- In late 2005, the spread entered negative territory once more and remained there until early 2007 in anticipation of the credit crisis.

This is a great deal of empirical evidence to digest but there are some obvious conclusions. As of 2013, monetary conditions are still loose but not as loose as they have been. Based on the above evidence, a recession is an unlikely prospect in the short to medium term. Leveraged trades continue to pay off and are likely to continue to do so for as long as the yield curve spread remains above the zero bound. When this spread again becomes inverted – probably sometime in the next four or five years – then we will be presented with a reliable indicator that the next recession is anything from a few months to a couple of years away. It is at this juncture that a more disciplined approach to position-sizing and leverage will become not only desirable but essential. Breaks in the consistency of medium-term uptrends, against a background where monetary conditions are tightening, is a double warning that the cohesion of the investment crowd is dissolving.

CONCLUSION

While it is convenient to think of economies as self-contained entities in which money created stays put, the reality is altogether different. Abundant money supply in the USA, UK, Europe and Japan is required to support those respective economies, not least because of the slowdown in the velocity of money evident in all those markets. However, in a system of global capital, money flows with relative ease to the most productive assets. These are increasingly to be found in assets leveraged to the growth of the global consumer. Easy monetary conditions in one region help fuel major bull markets elsewhere.

Against this background, one can justifiably question whether the Fed, ECB or Bank of England are nimble enough to curtail the massive expansion of M2 quickly enough to cater for a pick-up in domestic growth. It is on this question that the supposition of massive future inflation rests. If they succeed in tailoring their monetary response to the pick-up in growth, then a truly significant inflationary problem can be avoided. However, while possible this is not likely. Central banks have demonstrated a blind spot for inflation. Higher inflation, particularly if it can be masked through hedonics, is in the interest of debt-ridden governments. Throughout history, the policy response to too much debt has been either to default, inflate or some combination of the two. We can count on one hand the number of times a government has paid back a massive debt burden without recourse to either of these options.

Choosing investments is in many respects a relative value decision. Assuming that a deflationary outcome is likely, bonds may yet post new yield lows and abundant money supply will continue to fuel interest in equities and other risk assets. Assuming an inflationary outcome occurs, fixed income is likely to underperform just about all other assets and companies that can increase their dividends should prosper. A benign environment where interest rates rise moderately in response to improving economic perceptions could set the stage for a secular bull market in equities. Of the three scenarios, the third is in my opinion the most likely by 2020.

CHAPTER 18:

GOVERNANCE IS EVERYTHING

What we will cover in this chapter:

- Emerging and developed market designations are outmoded. It is more appropriate to speak of *progressing* and *regressing* markets.

- Governance is not an absolute designation. Whether it is improving or deteriorating is a more important judgement call.

- Governance tends to be cyclical. Hubris is the enemy of all great success stories. It is also largely unavoidable and ensures the cyclical nature of governance.

- If deteriorating governance coincides with loosening of regulations or aggressive monetary easing it can have a short-term bullish effect on markets but will be a long-term headwind.

DAVID FULLER HAS LONG PROFESSED that "*in emerging markets, governance is everything*". Over the last decade we have amended that to "*governance is everything, for all stock markets*".

Where once it was assumed that the risk in emerging markets was clearly more acute than so-called developed markets, the delineation is no longer so cut and dry. Since the year 2000 alone, China has emerged as the second-largest economy in the world. Brazil has evolved from hopeless debtor to a creditor and host of both the soccer World Cup in 2014 and Olympics in 2016. The Philippines has become a creditor to the IMF rather than a perpetual supplicant. At the same time European countries, long lauded for the integrity of their institutions and stability of their democracies, have had to go cap-in-hand to the IMF for enormous bailouts. The USA, which has long been vaunted as a bastion of free enterprise, capitalism and the rule of law has gone through two massive busts in a decade and is the largest debtor nation on earth. When characterised thus, we need to ask ourselves if there is a disconnection between our perception of risk and where the risk actually lies.

I have never been happy with the emerging/developed paradigm. It leaves no room for markets such as Singapore, South Korea or Taiwan, which left the emerging designation behind a long time ago. It also clearly misrepresented the risk premium that should have been attached to Greece, Portugal or Ireland. The emerging/developing designation is additionally unfavourable because it is too rigid. There is no room for a country to move from one to the other, when in fact economies are changing and evolving all the time.

Rather than get hung up on how to define what is developed and what is emerging, David Fuller argues that it makes more sense to speak of *progressing* versus *regressing*.

Progressing jurisdictions offer the most fertile environment for risk-adjusted profits. Just as with caring for a plant, an investment needs a favourable environment in which to grow. A progressing country is one where the rule of law and property rights are upheld, where fiscal discipline is valued and government deficits are shrinking, where corruption is steadily being reduced, with favourable demographics, where economic growth is outpacing population growth and swelling the middle class, where the standard of education is consistent with a growth trajectory, where the government provides a business-friendly environment and where the regulatory framework is loose enough to enable innovation but tight enough to choke off excesses.

The opposite – a regressing jurisdiction – is a country where the rule of law is arbitrary, where poor fiscal discipline leads to high inflation and an interminable cycle of boom to bust, where deficits swell to unimaginable levels necessitating severe cutbacks and/or default, where corruption is rife, where the demographic dividend is being squandered because labour policies are too rigid, where education is expensive and limited to a small minority and where regulation is often wrong-footed to the extent that it is enforced at all.

Progressing Economies Have	Regressing Economies Have
Improving economic governance	Deteriorating economic governance
Relatively strong GDP growth	Relatively weak GDP growth
Current account surpluses	Current account deficits
Low levels of government debt	Increasing government debt
High personal savings rates	Low personal savings and high debt
Sound banking sectors	Weak, dysfunctional banking sectors
Young, motivated and educated workers	A shortage of skilled workers

No country fits exactly into either of the above categories. From an investment perspective the trajectory of how standards of governance are evolving is what is important. We are likely to find some of the best opportunities in countries that were once governance basket cases but which are turning over a new leaf and adopting fiscally sound policies. An additional risk premium needs to be attached to markets where the standards of economic, fiscal, corporate, civil, and regulatory governance are deteriorating.

IS GOVERNANCE AN ABSOLUTE OR RELATIVE TERM?

When one comes from a country with well-established institutions and the stability of decades of domestic peace and relative prosperity there is often a strong temptation to demand the most exacting standards of governance from countries we are potentially interested in investing in. This would be a mistake. Compare two different countries: in one the majority of people live on $1 a day, in the other the majority live on $50 a day. Now ask yourself how radical an improvement in governance is required for each country to double its GDP?

There are a large number of countries which have moved from $1 per person per day to $2 per person per day. There is a well-trodden path to development for such countries. The growth potential of a large number of economies has been unshackled by simply dispensing with failed economic programmes. Encouraging inward investment through lowering trade barriers, creating an attractive tax structure and making it easier to do business are all examples of relatively simple institutional changes that can have outsized results.

Compare this to a country which needs to raise the average wealth of its citizens from $50 to $100 per person per day. Their ambition is to move from a relatively well-off country to being among the richest in the world. They will have already made the easy changes. In order to progress further they not only need to leverage their national advantages but excel at what comes naturally and become good at everything else. This evolution will require original thinking, long-term planning, political and social stability, fiscal responsibility, low inflation, sustained growth, mature capital markets, sound banking and world-class education.

Let us now consider the country on $100 per person per day that seeks to move to $200 per person per day. It will already have done much of what the former countries aim to achieve. As a leader in every sense of the word, the hubris that comes with success will be a significant threat. They not only need to do everything well but also need to improve productivity in new innovative ways if they are to achieve their goals.

If we set aside feelings of patriotism and loyalty, assume the role of a global unbiased investor and ask ourselves to which of these countries should the most exacting standards of governance be applied? Logically our answer has to be the last one. The most successful country can least afford to slide in its standards of fiscal, corporate, civil or regulatory governance. Therefore when we consider the situation of a country, rather than obsess with the current situation, we need to address it with a basic question: are the standards of governance getting better or worse?

When we think of countries it is sometimes appropriate to take a relativistic approach to governance. However, when we deal with corporations the highest standards of governance should always be applied regardless of jurisdiction. If the managers are running the company for their self-aggrandisement, enriching themselves at the cost of shareholders, structuring bonuses for their own short-term gain, falsifying income statements, hiding bad news in arcane accounting or if the CEO is spending more time on one of his three yachts than at the office, or is swaggering about the global stage rather than running the company – then we need to be concerned. Where the company is based is irrelevant.

The most consistent trends in currency markets often appear when we match the strongest with the weakest countries. In this respect, currency trading is always relativistic because we make a value judgement rather than an absolute statement of strength. A currency is only strong when compared to a weaker one. In terms of governance the perception reflected in the price action is that a country's situation is improving or regressing versus another. In order to make an absolute judgement we would then examine the performance of our base currency against a large number of other currencies. If a high degree of commonality exists, we are in a much better position to make an absolute statement about whether the governance of one currency region is better than all others. Commonality can also be employed with government bonds spread over a benchmark such as US Treasuries, German Bunds or British gilts.

In the commodity markets, governance takes on an important aspect. This is primarily in how supply is affected by both the actions of nations and corporations. High prices encourage governments to plug deficits or raise capital by nationalising mining and energy assets. This almost invariably results in supply falling because the newly nationalised companies have no profit incentive and key personnel leave along with the exiled foreign companies.

At the other end of the scale, commodity company executives are in the business of making the most money possible for their shareholders. The perception of how best to do this changes as a bull market progresses. When prices are low, the company will be more interested in survival than maximising value. Running costs, exploration budgets, labour and inventory management are likely to be tightly controlled. However, as prices appreciate focuses tend to change. The perception is that promising assets need to be acquired at any cost because they may cost more later. New supply is brought online to maximise the benefit of higher prices. This can lead to reckless behaviour where record prices are paid for half-understood assets based on phenomenally bullish forecasts. When companies compete for market share in the commodity markets it is usually a signal that the bull market is coming to an end because when new mines open the market is flooded with new supply.

GOVERNANCE IS CYCLICAL

Human beings will generally only implement reform when forced to. There is always a good excuse to delay a tough decision. This is as true of individuals as it is of governments and corporations. Almost no one questions a winning strategy until it is proven faulty.

At the other extreme, discipline is difficult to sustain over the long term. Once the immediate need to abide by a dictum has passed, memory tends to fade and rationalisations for why an exception can be allowed become easier to make. The long history of the rise and fall of empires provides ample proof of the cyclical nature of governance.

As individuals we are free to govern our own actions. We have no one else to blame for our mistakes but ourselves, and yet facing up to our errors is difficult at the best of times. When we participate with a crowd we abrogate our sense of responsibility and become less questioning of the accepted norm. Therefore we are even less likely to question the status quo as long as it is seen to benefit us.

Recessions reflect pivotal times in the cyclical nature of governance because they force change upon an often unwilling administration. Growth declines, tax receipts dry up and tough decisions line up. The first recourse of almost every government is to devalue the currency and court inflation. This quickly resets international competitiveness, the financial sector benefits from government largesse at the expense of savers. In this regard devaluation and inflation are stealth taxes on savers. The manipulation of long-dated government bond yields is a new and unwelcome additional tool used by governments since 2007. These policies also allow political hot potatoes such as government waste, excessive perks, public sector wages and pensions, loss-making state-supported industries, health costs, defence spending etc. to be ignored or at least kicked down the road. Depending on the depth of the recession, even these subjects may become unavoidable and a newfound respect for fiscal responsibility is demanded.

A reform agenda requires imagination and very often a change of government, but is characterised by politicians being electorally rewarded for taking hard decisions. Some see it as a once-in-a-generation chance for change and grasp it with both hands. Balancing the books is resurrected as a glorious ambition and policies are put in place in the hope of cutting imports, boosting exports, generating growth, replacing lost government revenue and setting the country back on the road to prosperity.

However, as soon as the immediate crisis has passed and some of the above policies have been seen to work, those who feel they were unjustifiably deprived by the severity of the cuts, revenue-raising measure or loss of privilege begin to agitate for an exception to be made. Perhaps teacher pension contributions were raised more than those of policemen. Perhaps the military has been on active service overseas for a lengthy period and justifiably demands better conditions for returning heroes. Perhaps one favoured energy sector continued to receive credits and funding throughout the crisis and another didn't. The first exception could occur in any one of a host of vested interests but sooner or later the slide begins and is very often irreversible until the next crisis unfolds.

Corporations go through exactly the same process. When times are good, revenues are rising and sales are ballooning, workers demand what they consider a fair share of the wealth they are helping to create. The CEO is lauded as a person of foresight, skill and tenacity. Shareholders think nothing of granting increasingly lavish bonuses, perks and options to the management team. More and more of the sales people start travelling business class and stay in progressively plusher hotels. New business lines are launched, expansion at any price becomes a mantra. As the good news keeps coming, valuations become increasing optimistic. Fundamental analysts begin to give a present value to cash flows for increasingly distant future dates.

When earnings begin to miss already extravagant expectations, share prices can take a significant hit, analysts re-examine their forecasts and shareholders demand action. The pay of executives is questioned, corporate travel and perks are cut aggressively and the corporate jets are sold. A newfound respect for margins is discovered, workers are fired, labour-saving devices and methods are implemented, unproductive assets are sold off and a more disciplined tone permeates every structure of the company.

MARKET IMPLICATIONS OF DETERIORATING GOVERNANCE

When we consider the implications of deteriorating governance it is important to remember that the market doesn't care what is in the best long-term interests of a company or country. It is much more focused on the short to medium-term. A fascination with quarterly earnings reports, the fact that CNBC can now be viewed on your phone or iPad, that we get updates on price action instantaneously all conspire to compress the perception of time and expectations. Therefore when we think of a company or country which is implementing policies that are likely to have short-term benefit but a disastrous long-term outcome the market generally responds positively.

Think of using nitrous oxide aggressively in your car. It will undoubtedly make the vehicle go faster and it'll be a lot of fun for as long as the acceleration lasts. However, long-term damage is being done to the engine and the effect of nitrous oxide is cumulative. Economies and markets are not that different.

CONCLUSION

Governance is always an important consideration because it helps to frame market perceptions of a country, bond market currency or company. While, in an ideal world, every asset class we seek to invest in would represent the best possible standards of governance, the reality is very different. Rather than subject each to our own high personal standards, we need to address the market from an unemotional perspective and ask the simple question: are the standards of governance improving or regressing?

As of 2013, a significant number of countries are at important junctures. The USA faces a crisis of regulation which has reached a point where some real substantive measures are now essential. In tandem with the looming tidal wave of retirements and the unfunded liabilities in terms of medical care and pensions, significant reform is essential. How this is framed is likely to have far-reaching consequences, either bullish or bearish, for the financial markets.

The inherent contradiction of the eurozone has long been an accident waiting.to happen. A failure to insist on the highest standards of governance has been central to the problem. It is simply impossible for a currency union to persist where one monetary policy is balanced with 17 fiscal policies. Some form of federal taxation system and transfer mechanism is essential. Reform is in the pipeline and a United States of Europe, probably with most of the existing members intact, remains the most likely long-term scenario.

China has benefitted enormously since opening up its economy and has moved from a deeply impoverished to a middle income country. If it is to sustain its development trajectory, significant reforms will need to be implemented. The overarching reliance on infrastructure development must be superseded by development of human capital. The evolution of the healthcare, service and high-technology sectors are all steps in this direction.

Following important economic reforms in the early 1990s, India's economy emerged as one of the fastest-growing in the world. The stock market flourished. Indian companies became successful aggressive participants in the global economy and the country acquired a newfound confidence. However, a failure to tackle corruption, protectionism and bureaucracy damaged international perceptions of the country's governance. Bold actions by Manmohan Singh's government in 2012 kickstarted the reform agenda again, but the trajectory of reform will need to be sustained if the country's significant long-term potential is to be realised.

ASEAN member countries benefitted enormously from the improving standards of governance forced upon them in the aftermath of the Asian financial crisis in the late 1990s. The region plays host to some of the fastest-growing consumer classes in the world as a result.

Sub-Saharan Africa, which was once written off as a violent, disease-ridden and corrupt backwater, is emerging as one of the fastest-growing regions in the world because of steps to improve governance. The perception of the region as somewhere a middle class can become established is opening up the continent for unprecedented growth.

While sovereign governance has been under attack internationally, the corporate sector has embraced reform and is in a much healthier position as a result. The credit crisis of 2008 forced many corporations to reform their business practices and strengthen their balance sheets. The result, in many cases, is that they have considerably better fundamentals than the countries in which they reside.

If we address the international markets purely from a governance perspective, would you rather own the debt of dubiously governed countries or the bonds and equities of well-governed companies?

CHAPTER 19:

THE REGULATORY ENVIRONMENT

What we will cover in this chapter:

- While we spend a great deal of time looking at the potential of various markets, the regulatory environment in which we are forced to perform has a significant effect on the decisions of investors and therefore is worthy of consideration.

- More regulation does not mean better regulation. All rules should pass the basic test of whether they support the capital formation raison d'etre of markets.

- In the coming decades potential changes in how the regulation of high frequency trading, the size of the banking sector, client monies and lobbying could have outsized effects on financial markets.

TO THE EXTENT that monetary policy controls the amount and cost of money, the regulatory framework in which we invest has an equally important function because it dictates what is and is not permitted. It is thus in the interests of the vast number of traders and investors that the market is regulated in a fair and transparent manner.

In addressing the regulatory environment in which we find ourselves, investors tend to have very strong views as to what constitutes good governance. Many commentators stridently defend their personal positions and will on occasion tailor their portfolios to reflect the world as they think it should be rather than how it is. We may or may not be agitating for reform in the standards of governance but we should never mistake our wishful thinking or ambitions for the regulatory framework with reality.

From an investment perspective, we need to adopt a dispassionate attitude. Some take comfort from complaining about the state of the world and how everything was better in the good old days. I have even seen a number of commentators make comparisons about the way the world is today and the fall of the Roman Empire. This tells us more about how they have positioned their portfolios than how the market will react to the regulatory framework we find ourselves in today.

As globally aware investors, with some sensitivity to improving and deteriorating standards of governance, we will obviously have strong views about what constitutes a supportive regulatory framework. In the following pages I will highlight some of the more important aspects to the regulatory framework as it exists in 2013. However, when we come to make investment decisions, we must judge not how we would like to see the world *develop* but on how likely a favourable *outcome* is.

Let us approach regulation from first principles. Capital markets exist so that those seeking to grow their businesses have access to the capital they require and agree to compensate the lender with an agreed rate of return. Speculators and traders are vital for the smooth running of a market because they provide liquidity and allow a secondary market to function in financial instruments. However, the important distinction is that the market does not exist to provide speculators with an income. It exists as part of the normal capital-raising exercise active in almost every economy. When a piece of regulatory legislation is proposed we should ask ourselves whether it protects the capital-raising mechanism of the market or whether it benefits the ability of speculators to profit. The existence of speculators is a requirement for a smooth functioning market, but not to the point where the system is gamed in their favour.

In an industry as competitive as finance, it can be taken for granted that each and every opportunity to profit will be exploited by someone. Regulators are charged with making sure such efforts stay within the confines of the law. Strong regulation need not mean more regulation, but it does require a sensible approach. The strength of a framework cannot simply be measured by the number of pages it is written on. The aim of any regulatory environment should be to ensure that no practice is permitted which poses a systemic risk. Additionally, if this administrative role is to be taken seriously, agencies need to be equipped with the staff, tools and funding necessary to do their jobs. The challenge in many countries is that they are not equipped with the technology or expertise to track the increasingly swift evolution of automated trading systems. This is a concern for everyone participating in the market.

HIGH FREQUENCY TRADING

In this regard, high frequency trading (HFT) operations pose a number of potential threats. Perhaps most importantly, their impact is poorly understood by regulators, allowing them to act in a regulatory vacuum. Considering that such operations trade in terms of nanoseconds, regulators who still rely on faxes have a hard time keeping pace. However, there are some clear indulgences afforded high frequency traders that are not available to most traders and could quite easily be reformed, assuming the desire to do so.

Quantitative traders have the option to co-locate their servers inside the exchange building to ensure they have swifter access to data than anyone else. This is a major revenue stream for exchanges but fails the basic test of being better for traders than for capital formation.

Some HFT operations frequently flood the market with orders so that they can ascertain where sell stops and buy orders are placed and thus manipulate the price. As of 2013, HFT operations account for the vast majority of volume on a number of exchanges and other pools of liquidity. One has to question whether this is a testament to their success or their favourable treatment by a regulatory framework which appears to ignore their activities.

The most common defence proposed by HFTs is that on aggregate they contribute to market liquidity. They also claim that their actions have reduced the cost of trading for retail investors by compressing the spread between the bid and offer. However, these arguments obfuscate the facts. Stuffing the market with thousands of orders that expire in less than a second is not creating liquidity. In a rising market liquidity is never an issue. However, when prices fall, market makers are relied on to quote prices. Too many supposed liquidity providers absent themselves from this responsibility during declines and therefore cannot claim they are providing liquidity.

High frequency traders claim that the advent of technology has contributed to the tightening of spreads, a positive for retail investors. However, the fact that such strategies are constantly scalping cents from every trade means that the possibility they are contributing to market slippage has greatly increased. For those unfamiliar with such terminology, think of changing money at the foreign exchange counter in a bank or travel agent. There has been a massive compression in the spread between the bid and offer but when you ask for a quote the teller has to keep increasing the offer because the market slips away as he attempts to execute the transaction. I have talked to more than a few large investors who testify to spending an inordinate amount of time attempting to outwit automated trading systems. They witness the slippage of prices on a daily basis as they attempt to execute comparatively large orders.

Perhaps the greatest indictment of HFTs is that while they do not greatly affect the direction of the market they greatly contribute to increased peak-to-trough swings and a heightened state of volatility. This is frustrating the ability of normal investors to interact favourably with the market. The actions of HFTs do not promote the capital formation raison d'être of the market. In fact, how they conduct their business contributes to a loss of faith in the ability of the market to function and so is a direct threat to confidence. In this regard, while it would not be appropriate to vilify every individual HFT firm, there is no denying that the sector represents a risk to the financial system and not a great deal is being done at the time of writing to handle it.

THE GLASS–STEAGALL ACT OF 1933

The Glass–Steagall Act of 1933 passed the simple test of being better for capital formation than it was for speculators because it divided the operations of wholesale banks from those of securities firms.

The rationale was pretty simple. Wholesale banks were mostly concerned with asset-based lending, mostly via mortgages on residential and commercial property, car loans etc. as well as cash management and trust services. This limited the risk wholesale banks were exposed to, affording them the stability required by their customers. Investment banks were concerned with raising capital via the equity and bond markets, underwriting and taking positions on their own behalves. Many investment banks were organised as partnerships until the 1990s, which meant that position sizes were limited to the ability of the partners to cover liabilities.

Classically a securities business was only able to take positions with regard to the size of its balance sheet and its ability to cover margins. Following exceptions and the eventual repeal of the Glass–Steagall Act in 1999, securities firms were free to merge with wholesale banks. Examples such as Salomon Smith Barney with Citibank, JP Morgan with Chase Manhattan Bank occurred before the financial crisis of 2008. Following that event, the process reversed and wholesale banks such as Wells Fargo and Bank of America acquired securities businesses such as Wachovia and Merrill Lynch respectively. These types of mergers are desirable from the perspective of the various business units because the securities business gains access to a deposit-holding institution against which it can massively increase the size, sophistication and scale of its trading operations. The wholesale bank gains the ability to make the 'lumpy' profits often associated with investment banking. The problem for the wider market is that the position sizes of such behemoths can pose seriously destabilising systemic threats to the wider market.

Former Fed Chairman, Paul Volcker, attempted to reinstate the inability of deposit-taking institutions to hold proprietary positions. Some of his suggestions were implemented in the Dodd–Frank Wall Street Reform and Consumer Protection Act which came into effect in July 2012. However, despite his preference for a simple all-encompassing rule, lobbyists successfully implemented numerous exceptions and addenda to the extent that the resulting bill is practically incomprehensible. Mr Volcker voiced his frustration in a *New York Times* article in 2011. "I'd write a much simpler bill. I'd love to see a four-page bill that bans proprietary trading and makes the board and chief executive responsible for compliance. And I'd have strong regulators. If the banks didn't comply with the spirit of the bill, they'd go after them." I agree with every word, and the investing community as a whole would benefit from a curbing of position sizes. But at the time of writing, the Dodd–Frank bill represents reality and we must adjust our actions accordingly.

RE-HYPOTHENTICATION

Lest anyone suspect that broad based regulatory reform is essential, simply consider the implications of *re-hypothentication*. Many assume that by posting collateral for trading with a securities business, the money simply sits in a segregated account in order to cover hypothetical margin requirements. However, the securities business is free to increase the size of its proprietary positions using this 'hypothetical' money as collateral. This practice is referred to as re-hypothentication and was one of the main considerations in the failure of MF Global in 2011. The firm had been betting with its clients' money and lost it. As with other areas of the shadow banking system this practice allows firms to increase the size of their positions without actually using their own money and avoids the scrutiny of regulators. This is another area where a simple reform would greatly increase the faith of investors in the financial system.

LOBBYING

When a government or regulatory decision affects one's business it would be insane not to lobby for a favourable outcome. However, while the incentive for vested interests to engage in lobbying is self-evident, whether this is in the interests of citizens is a much more murky area. From an investment perspective this phenomenon can be viewed in two distinct lights depending on one's perspective.

If a company I have an investment in has a vested interest in legislation being tilted in its favour then lobbying can very much serve as a benefit in the narrow sense of the word. However, when competing lobbying interests gum up the legislative process with addenda, riders, exceptions and complication, where the ability of the country to enact effective laws is compromised, then the process can be identified as a threat to confidence and a symptom of deteriorating governance. As such it could represent a threat to my investment.

The activities of lobbyists in presidential elections, general elections or referenda are often seen in an unfavourable light because they seek to influence a decision to favour their particular interest group rather than the net benefit of the majority. Super Political Action Committees (Super PACs) in the USA, as well as lobbyists in just about every other country, damage the perception that legislators are free from undue corporate influence. In many respects it is irrelevant whether legislators were ever independent. The net effect of the boom in lobbying is that it damages the perception of impartiality. A loss of faith in the political establishment is therefore amplified by the very public success of lobbyists in achieving their goals.

While lobbyists can have positive effects on the outlook for the companies they represent, on aggregate their activities pose a risk for financial markets because when the cycle of governance turns against such activity it is likely to have a material effect on how investors and traders interact with the market.

CONCLUSION

Just as governance tends to move in cycles which vacillate from one extreme to another, regulation tends to do the same. The aftermath of the Great Depression was characterised by a desire to never let a situation where speculators could pose a systemic risk to ever occur again. By the 1980s institutional memory had corroded to such an extent that the rationale for such a restrictive regulatory environment was seriously questioned. The UK's Big Bang, which liberalised London's financial markets, the USA dispensing with the Glass–Steagall Act and the creation of the euro on a flimsy regulatory framework all represented extremes of regulatory laxity. As countries deal with the aftermath of the financial crisis in 2008, their answer has so far been to adapt half measures which serve more to complicate regulation than reform it. Loopholes through which banks, hedge funds, HFT firms and other financial intermediaries can easily squeeze are rife. This suggests that it is a matter of *when* rather than *if* another financially inspired crisis envelopes the global economy.

CHAPTER 20:

CRASHES, CONTAGION AND OPPORTUNITY

What we will cover in this chapter:

- Every crash creates the kind of wonderful investment opportunities value investors dream of. Where are they most likely to be found?

- Whatever represented the epicentre of risk is most likely to experience type-3 base formation characteristics and could spend years ranging.

- The collapse of an internationally traded vehicle results in contagion spreading to comparatively unrelated instruments that will recovery much quicker.

- Even within the market that has just crashed there will be instruments that dodged the excessive risk-taking characteristic of a mature bull market and they will find themselves in very favourable positions.

- Look for signs of early temporal leadership and relative strength.

- There is always a bull market in something. The decline of one market will create a bull market in something else.

IF WE HAVE BEEN DILIGENT WITH OUR CHART READING and position sizing we will have sold and/or initiated short positions either before a crash takes place or quickly after it begins. However, if we are still holding inventory once such an event has occurred there are a number of possibilities that need to be examined. The best way to think about the decisions that need to be made are in degrees of separation from the problem.

Major crashes deeply affect investors, particularly if they have lost money. No one wants to make the same mistake twice, so they are doubly cautious about investing following such an event. Analysts who failed to anticipate the crash seem to jump at shadows in the aftermath of a major decline, seeing signs of another massive fall at every turn. They don't want to miss the next one, so they predict loudly and often that the market has further to go on the downside. Sentiment deteriorates even further and people become even less likely to commit what cash they have left.

Despite the trauma, fear, disappointment, disillusionment, self-doubt, anger and betrayal investors feel following every crash, such events also offer wonderful buying opportunities. These potential entry points occur both within the sector which has just crashed as well as in other sectors because of the collateral damage inflicted by the crash.

THE CRASH

When a market crashes, the instrument which represented the hopes, dreams and unfulfilled wishes of the crowd during the bull phase will be the one that falls fastest and hardest. It now represents the epicentre of risk perception and will drag down anything else in the associated asset class. If it is an internationally traded vehicle the shockwave can extend into other asset classes, geographic regions or currencies. Ask yourself, is the asset that just crashed and which represents the epicentre of global risk more or less likely to provide the inspiration for the next bull market?

Every major bull market evolves through accommodative monetary conditions and a story that inspires investor interest. In the latter stages of a bull market, a large proportion of participants will be hoping prices have at least a few more years to run before a significant pullback occurs. They become like junkies – "Just give me one more new high". However, as the bull matures, central banks tighten monetary conditions and prices eventually begin to fall. By the time prices have deteriorated, losses have been taken, the contradictions of the bull market become evident and investors are often well and truly disillusioned with the story they had previously put so much faith in. The price action of the shares that were most closely identified with the bull market story will have crashed spectacularly and some will simply no longer exist. Sentiment towards the sector will be apocalyptic and a significant demographic will have been burned to an extent that they will be shy about investing for quite some time.

Financial market bubbles occur when a reasonable bullish story with sound fundamentals is inflated by a large dollop of liquidity and manic investor interest which takes it to incredible heights that can only be justified by the most ludicrous of rationalisations. Examples of market bubbles include:

- The railroad bubble of the Industrial Revolution, which promised to change the way people lived their lives and succeeded in its aims but not before massive bankruptcies and investor losses enveloped the sector.

- The Japanese bubble in property and stock markets, which occurred through the belief that Japanese management and business practices were going to allow Japan to become the largest economy in the world. Today, many of the business practices, inventory management and innovations that helped to fuel the Japanese bubble are ubiquitous in the global economy.

- The telecoms, media and technology bubble of the 1990s, which again promised to change the way we live our lives and succeeded in doing so. However, as with all good ideas taken too far, the bull market resulted in massive over-investment, terrible investment decisions and a belief that all the promised changes needed to happen immediately. When the bubble burst, it heralded a massive consolidation of the three sectors concerned, where there have been clear winners and losers.

- The 1987 crash, which was fuelled by the belief that new products such as stock market index futures offered portfolio insurance and allowed fund managers to hedge their market risk. When everyone shorted the S&P500 future at the same time, in an effort to hedge long exposure in their portfolios, they caused a crash. Two years later the S&P500 was at a new high.

- The credit bubble that burst in 2007 and 2008, which was fuelled by a number of assumptions but chief among these was that banks had developed tools allowing everyone to hedge default risk. They concluded they could take on as much risk as they wanted because defaults were no longer a threat.

Following massive bankruptcies, foreclosures, write-offs, nationalisations and bailouts we saw how spurious this claim was. However, credit default swaps (CDSs) do offer the ability to take a view on default probability which is a legitimate speculation in the market. Some of the abuses associated with CDSs, such as shorting a share then bidding up the price of the CDS to suggest a greater default probability, will need to be met with regulation. But CDSs are here to stay.

In all cases the crash represented a hugely traumatic event that created wonderful investment opportunities when it had run its course.

Those who have taken losses as a result of failing to manage their positions correctly often comfort themselves with the claim that they were lied to and cannot be blamed for their actions. However, almost every bubble eventually comes good on its promises, just not in the time frame investors might like. The stories driving major bull markets really do change the world. Major bull markets represent wonderful money-making opportunities. We just have to learn to view these developments dispassionately if we are to profit from them – and hold onto our profits.

When a market crashes, anyone holding a long position is either nursing a loss or at a minimum experiencing severe profit erosion. The disappointment of these people, coupled with the antipathy directed at the asset class from those who have sold or have short positions, will be such that the likelihood of the burst bubble mustering the wherewithal to represent the next major bull market is virtually nil. Crashes generally end in lengthy type-3 basing activity because those with stale long positions use any significant rally to liquidate some inventory. This means that if someone is sitting with a long position in an instrument that has just crashed – and which was the centre of the problem that caused the crash – they have very little chance of recouping the loss in a timely manner.

Consider the portfolio manager who has a long position in an investment that has just crashed. He resisted the temptation to sell on the way down and has to look at a big red negative figure on his profit and loss statement every time he turns on his screens. He has more than he wants of this instrument and it is entering a type-3 bottom defined by lengthy ranging. The chances of him being able to get out of the position flat at any time in the following few years are very slim. It may take time to accept the new reality provided by the market but he will eventually view any significant rally as an opportunity to liquidate the position so he can move onto another asset class and forget about this mistake. The technology shares that were most associated with the mania followed this pattern during the tech bust and the banks most associated with CDOs and property loans followed this pattern after the credit crisis. Other instruments have recovered much quicker.

CONTAGION

Instruments that experience contagion but which are not directly related to the problem market have a much better chance of bouncing and reasserting a demand-dominated environment.

Crashes are major market events, have a huge psychological impact on market participants but provide *just* the kind of environment value investors are looking for – i.e. low prices and attractive valuations. Major bull markets tend to attract investors from all over the world seeking to participate in whatever the inspiring story driving the uptrend is. When that market eventually begins to fall rapidly, investors are forced to sell and liquidity is prized above any other factor. As sentiment deteriorates, potential buyers lower their bids, liquidity dries up and prices fall further, increasing the likelihood that even more potential buyers will withdraw from the market. Margin calls need to be met. Inventory in the deteriorating market is often difficult to shift so investors are forced to sell not what they want but what they *can* in order to raise cash.

This contagion results in comparatively unrelated instruments experiencing aggressive selling pressure. The often dubious merits of a diversified portfolio have been preached religiously for decades. The result is that most investors now tend to hold a range of different assets and sectors in their portfolios. This means that instruments often touted as non-correlated can come under pressure *not* because they are particularly affected by the deteriorating fundamentals of the burst bubble but because investors are forced to sell them in order to meet obligations in *another* part of their portfolio. As losses mount in one part of the portfolio, investors look at where they have outstanding profits that could possibly be netted off against a loss or sold to fund a margin requirement. They sell what they can in order to narrow the developing loss or to ensure that they capture the profit now in case it evaporates later.

As prices for a wide array of investment vehicles deteriorate, investors are tempted to conclude, in the absence of evidence to the contrary, that these additional instruments must also be suffering from the same malaise as the crashing market. However, if we think rationally this is unlikely to be the case. Contagion-selling occurs during every major market crash. It needs to be recognised for what it is. It leads to the kind of mispricing of assets that value investors often wait years for. Opportunities for outsized gains abound following every crash if one has the tools to identify them and the strength of character to participate and hold on.

During the credit crisis of 2008, fear that the subprime mortgages problem was spreading to prime US mortgages led to a run on a number of banks and climaxed with the dramatic failure of Lehman Brothers. No one knew who had bought the packages of mortgages that were quickly going toxic so banks stopped lending to each other. This crippled the interbank market, leading to a deepening of the crisis.

Emerging markets, commodities and just about every stock market sector sold off aggressively as panic and uncertainty spread. In the cool realm of hindsight we can conclude that a large number of investment vehicles fell considerably farther than could have been justified and investors would have been better off simply holding on. However, during the riot of emotions caused by the incredible declines in October 2008, perspective was in short supply.

So let's assume that, following the next crash, opportunities are likely to exist. Let's look now at what they could be.

THE ASSET THAT HAS JUST CRASHED

Active traders may consider attempting to trade in the shares which have fallen hardest during the crash. These shares will likely never (or at least it will feel like forever) revisit their peaks, but that is irrelevant for someone investing after the crash once the base formation has begun. They will be more concerned about where the market goes next.

Bottom-picking among laggards does not come without significant risk, not least that a company could go bankrupt. Even if a sector is destined to range for a considerable period, such is the volatility evident in base formations (from the lower to the upper side) that active traders are often tempted to participate in such markets. This might be exciting but from a risk-adjusted perspective there are easier ways to make money. I would personally only recommend this approach for institutional participants who have to have a position in the asset concerned.

CLEAR LEADERS WITHIN THE SECTOR THAT JUST CRASHED

When a bubble bursts there will almost always be a few shares in the sector that avoid the slaughter. These few will have avoided the worst excesses of the bubble and so will survive the rationalisation that follows the bust. They will often have the opportunity to buy up premium assets during the bankruptcy of competitors and the mergers that ensue. Very few will pay attention to these companies because the massive failures grabbing headlines will be all anyone wants to talk about.

Companies which the crash avoids survive for a reason. Google didn't hold its IPO until well after the tech bubble bust. Amazon peaked early, bottomed early, showed early relative strength and was one of the first shares to surmount its bubble peaks. Apple was perhaps the greatest success story of the post tech bubble era and was also a clear relative outperformer from a very early stage. The share consistently outperformed the Nasdaq for almost ten years until its peak in 2012.

Apple / Nasdaq 100 1992–2013

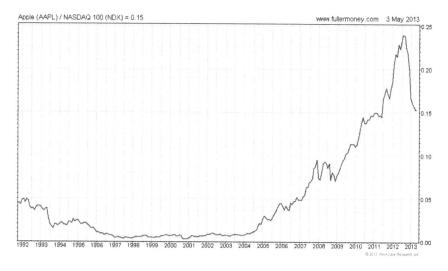

Following the credit crisis in 2008, Visa and Mastercard were two of the few financial companies to take out their pre-crisis peaks. They are exposed to the consumer but are internationally diversified and crucially do not take deposits and do not issue CDOs. Wells Fargo avoided most of the excesses that characterised the credit bubble. This put it in a favourable position in 2008 when it acquired Wachovia as well as a number of smaller banks. This allowed the company to become one of the four largest banks in the USA and a clear relative outperformer. Asset management companies also came through the credit crisis with flying colours.

Wells Fargo (NYSE) / S&P500 Banks Index 2003–2013

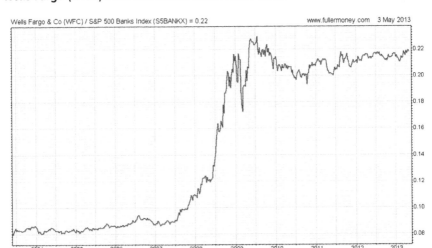

Both of the technology and banking examples demonstrate that the relative strength leaders following a crash offer comparatively low-risk opportunities to invest on a trend-running basis because they are comparatively unaffected by the malaise that caused the sector to decline in the first place.

THE NEXT BULL (OR BUBBLE)

Crashes create opportunity and perhaps the most important from the perspective of seeking to identify the next big investment theme is connected to the selling contagion that has occurred during the decline. As one market loses its allure, another is by definition gaining adherents.

Following any major decline, the majority of investors will understandably focus on the asset class that has just crashed. Media outlets will be running doom-and-gloom stories, others will be searching for someone to blame for their losses and a great number of people will be attempting to make sense of the experience. In the midst of this chaotic environment, a few assets will be outperforming. Investors who have just taken a huge loss will be chagrined at the thought of jumping back in and many will dismiss any whiff of a bullish story as Pollyannaish. However, any asset class that shows relative strength following a crash does so for a reason.

The Fed's response to the bust credit crisis was the same as it was for the 1987 crash, the Mexican debt default, the Russian debt crisis, the Asian financial crisis, Y2K and the tech bust. They cut interest rates aggressively, flooded the market with liquidity and left the stimulation in the system for far longer than was necessary, which helped to fuel another bubble. Nothing appears to have changed in the last decade, so this behaviour can be expected to continue. In fact the exact same policy has been adopted by just about every major central bank. Therefore as much as we might like to rail against the system, if we want to make money, the easiest way remains to accept the status quo and spend some time thinking about where the next bubble is going to be blown and how best to profit from it.

Bears and naysayers can rationalise it anyway they like but when everyone is worrying about another 'down-leg' or waiting for the 'the other shoe to drop' if the central bank is flooding the market with liquidity it is going to have a bullish effect on some market. We look for an asset class that is clearly outperforming. There has to be a reason it is favoured over others. Once we know what the reason is we can grasp the story that is inspiring investors to act.

The new outperformer may be a market that suffered a sharp decline due to contagion-selling during the crash, but rebounds not only more powerfully but sooner than other asset classes because it is well removed from the epicentre of the problem that caused that crash. It is perhaps best to examine some empirical evidence.

Following the Nasdaq crash of 2000, comparatively high-yielding shares briefly showed relative strength but paled when compared to the outperformance of US banks. They were able to leverage access to cheap credit and turned the securitisation and syndication of loans into a three-ring circus. This early relative strength helped to indicate that financials were going to be at the centre of the next bull market and ultimately at the centre of future big problem. Banks bottomed early, rose fastest in the early part of the bull market and importantly topped out early as some of the practices they were engaged in went sour.

Gold also began to show early relative strength following the tech bust for the first time in nearly 20 years. There were a number of reasons for this, not least because mine output had declined to such a stage that government sales were helping to keep the market in equilibrium. A new demand component was introduced as the continued debauchery of fiat currencies pursued by just about every government was beginning to take a toll on investor confidence and the purchasing power of their respective currencies was persistently eroded. In 2001, a trickle of investors began looking for a secure store of value. Many concluded that they wanted an asset that could not simply be lent into existence and resolved to increase the weighting of gold in their portfolios. That did not stop gold from experiencing contagion-selling in 2008, but it bottomed early and took out its previous peak, demonstrating that it was comparatively unaffected by the problems that caused the banking crisis. By 2013 it was affected by the liquidation of ETF holdings as government yields bottomed. This may have signalled the end of gold's bull market.

The ASEAN region was also susceptible to contagion selling but bottomed in 2008, nearly six months ahead of the S&P500. Indonesia completed its base early, retained a position of relative outperformance for a number of years and moved to new all-time highs in 2010. Indonesia is but one example in the ASEAN region, with a number of countries representing the emergence of a powerful consumer class.

These types of opportunities look glaringly obvious in hindsight when they are hundreds of per cent off their lows. They are much more difficult to appreciate when almost everyone around us is bearish. Let's look at some examples of crashes and the bull markets that rose phoenix-like from their ashes.

TYPE-3 BASE FORMATION COMPLETION

A market that has ranged for years in a type-3 bottom and suddenly not only begins to exhibit relative strength but also breaks upwards in nominal terms can be entering a new long-term bull market.

Following any major blow to our confidence we seek to learn from our mistakes. Someone who has taken a major loss will seek to reverse the kind of activity that got them into the mess in the first place. Close to a major market top they might have been paying any price for a position and failing to implement a stop strategy commensurate with the risk being taken on. Once prices started to deteriorate, they were left holding onto positions as they were unwilling to admit to a mistake and hoped prices would go back up. In the aftermath of a major decline, where positions have probably been sold at an unfavourable level, the temptation to reverse the strategy employed at the top is powerful. They will wait to initiate positions and sell at the first sign of trouble.

This strategy would have been appropriate closer to the peak but is not appropriate following a major decline. Bottoming activity is extremely volatile due to the war taking place between supply and demand. A stop placed anywhere within the base runs a major risk of being triggered by relatively insignificant swings.

Until a base has been completed, upward breaks are unlikely to be sustained, so waiting for a breakout will mean buying at the upper side of the range and running the risk of being immediately stopped out.

Even those that succeed in buying at the lower side of a base are often tempted to sell at the first sign of trouble because they fear making the mistake of enduring profit erosion again.

The most cautious investors will be aware of risks attached to attempting to bottom pick so they will wait for a successful breakout from a base before re-entering the market in the full knowledge they are balancing the potential of buying more than

100% off the lows with the peace of mind that comes with seeing a completed base and the demand-dominant environment that it reflects.

Taking this into account, once we see that a base has been completed and – more particularly – when it is accompanied by commonality in other related assets, we have clear evidence of medium-term demand dominance and the upside can be given the benefit of the doubt provided the breakout to new highs is sustained.

IBM is an excellent example of just such an occasion. The share rallied impressively during the 1990s and went through almost a decade of ranging in the 2000s. It bottomed ahead of the wider market in 2008, ranged in the region of the historic peak in 2010 and sustained a move to new all-time highs later that year. As well as the company's many other merits, such as a strong record of technological innovation, it is attracting interest because of its share buyback programme especially in an environment where investors feel starved of yield.

IBM (NYSE) 1992–2013

Biotechnology was among the darlings of investors as the promise of revolutionary treatments inspired investors in the 1990s, and Biogen also spent much of the decade from 2000 in a lengthy type-3 base where a considerable number of companies went bust or were taken over. By 2011, Biogen had completed a lengthy type-3 base, emblematic of increased investor interest in the sector generally.

Biogen (Nasdaq) 1992–2013

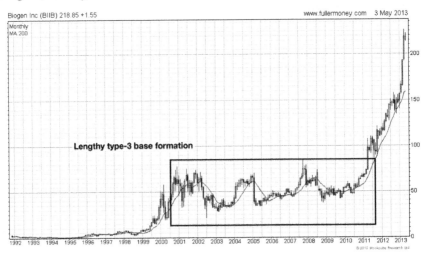

Participating while a market is still in a type-3 base formation can be emotionally wearing because of the volatility. However, once the base has been completed, we are presented with incontrovertible evidence that demand is resurgent. This is why lengthy bases can be considered the seedbeds for future bull markets.

If we return to first principles, ranges are explosions waiting to happen. Expectations go down the longer a market ranges and the volatile choppy activity becomes the accepted reality. But what we must not forget is that bear markets do eventually end – and when they do, major bull markets follow. When we see evidence of base-formation completion, the best tactic is to get long and use pullbacks towards the 200-day MA as opportunities to increase the position for at least the early stages of the advance.

CONCLUSION

Crashes are enormously traumatic events but they also help to re-instil analytical rigour. Following a crash, bargains emerge – and early leaders attract investor interest for a reason. Base-formation completion then gives us clues to where the next major bull market is likely to develop.

CHAPTER 21:

MAJOR MARKET CYCLES

What we will cover in this chapter:

- Markets tend to move in secular (long-term) bull and bear market cycles.

- Since it is easier to make money in a bull market it makes sense to have some understanding of where we are in the big market cycles.

- 2013–15 represents a turning point. Gold's decade long bull market could be ending. US Treasury yields have been compressing for more than 30 years and are becoming increasingly volatile. Equities ,and particularly those with solid records of dividend increases, have been an unloved asset class and represent the best potential to evolve into a new secular bull market.

ABOVE ALL ELSE MAJOR BULL MARKETS represent times when great wealth is accrued by those who participate. Many lose it all and more in the subsequent bust. Therefore, once we have equipped ourselves with the tools necessary to recognise consistent trends as well as major tops and bottoms, the next step is to identify the markets most likely to move into generation-long bull markets where a trend-running tactic will be most useful. As discussed in the last chapter, base-formation completion is one of the easiest ways to identify new bull markets in their early stages but appreciation of how asset classes interact with each other over the very long-term is equally important. In this regard long-term ratios give us some vivid insights into how various asset classes perform relative to one another.

As of 2013 there are a number of minor themes garnering investor interest but four major themes are evident:

1. US Treasuries had been in a major bull market for the last 33 years. At the time of writing we have the most compelling evidence in decades that the market has topped and a new secular bear is likely to ensue.

2. Gold posted a positive annual return for 11 consecutive years. 2013 will be its first negative year since 2001. This can be considered a major trend inconsistency.

3. Wall Street, represented by the S&P500, has been rangebound since 2000 in a secular process of valuation contraction and rising dividend yields and posted a new all-time high in May 2013. We are potentially at the dawn of a new secular bull market.

4. The Autonomies, which I define as large multinational companies with global brand recognition, strong balance sheets, good records of dividend increases – and which have outgrown their domestic markets – are increasingly breaking out of long-term bases and represent a major secular bull in its early stages.

Let us consider how these various markets are interacting.

**Dow Jones Industrial Average Total Return Index / Gold 1920–2013
(arithmetic scale)**

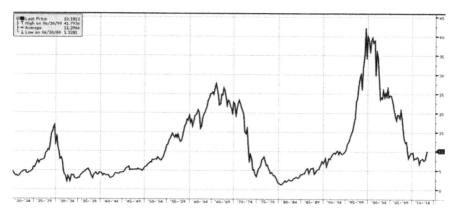

This chart highlights the large move that has occurred in the relationship between the Dow Jones Industrial Average since 2000 when the ratio peaked at a multiple of 40. In 2000, the acceleration in the outperformance of the Dow versus gold could have been considered a type-1 trend ending characteristic with some right-hand extension.

**Dow Jones Industrial Average Total Return Index / Gold 1920–2013
(logarithmic scale)**

This is the same chart except viewed in a log scale. This view highlights the large percentage changes in the constituents required to move the index one unit of scale the further it declines. From the 1999 peak near 40, the ratio compressed to below 6.5 by 2011. This reflected a largely rangebound Dow Jones Industrial Average and a decade-long advance for gold. Moving the scale from 40 to 39 did not require an especially large percentage change in either the price of gold or the Dow Jones Industrial Average. By contrast, for the ratio to move the Dow Jones Industrial Average from seven to six times the price of gold requires significant percentage changes in the underlying instruments.

These 90-year charts offer two competing scenarios for how the bull market in one asset class is reflected in the underperformance of another.

The mania that climaxed in 1929 is now more famous for the subsequent bust and Depression than the roaring bull market that created it. At the time, the price of gold was pegged. So when the Dow Jones Industrial Average crashed it outperformed by not falling as much as the index.

The stock market bottomed relative to gold in 1932. Following the Depression and Second World War, a secular bull market was evident from 1945 until 1965.

1965 represented the top of another major bull market in equities. On this occasion, the subsequent bear market was characterised by a generational long period of P/E ratio contraction and rising dividend yields. The Dow Jones Industrial Average was said to have had a 'glass ceiling' at 1,000 and failed to sustain a move above that level until 1981. While the Dow Jones Industrial Average mostly ranged, gold embarked on a historic bull market and soared from $37 to $835 between 1968 and 1980. In its history as a freely traded instrument, gold has been much more volatile than the stock market.

The Federal Funds rate hit 20% in 1980 and again in 1981, but this marked a peak in inflationary expectations. Gold and commodity prices collapsed as new supply hit the market. The Dow Jones Industrial Average embarked on a 20-year bull market driven by efficiency gains, technological innovation and moderating inflation.

1999 marked a manic peak in telecoms, media and technology (TMT) which resulted in a crash for those sectors. The Dow Jones Industrial Average entered another generational long period of P/E ratio contraction and rising dividend yields. This time it was the S&P500 with a glass ceiling at 1,600. The Dow Jones Industrial Average outperformed the S&P not least because of its concentration of multinational companies leveraged to the growth of the global consumer. Gold bottomed in nominal terms in 1999 and entered a bull market in 2001.

The ratio has posted three important peaks over the last almost 90 years. These were in 1929, 1965 and 1999. Each successive peak represents the zenith of bullishness in three major equity bull markets; two of which climaxed in manias. Following these peaks, gold outperformed the stock market for a generation. The last major bull market for gold climaxed in a mania and peaked in 1980.

Considering the percentage contraction from six to two, if the most bullish prognostications for gold are to be realised a mania will be required – but how likely is that to occur? The ratio trended consistently lower from 1999 until 2011. The failed downside break and rally in 2013 is the first higher high in the course of the 12-year downtrend. This represents two major trend inconsistencies for the secular decline.

The question at this juncture is whether this trend has ended or whether it is losing consistency at the penultimate low. In absolute terms, investors will be asking whether gold's bull market will have one last explosive hurrah. They will point to a similar counter trend rally in 1974 that presaged gold's mania phase. However, if those theories are to be supported by the price action then the ratio will need to sustain a move below eight. Without such a move, the case for long-term outperformance by the Dow Jones Industrial Average should be given the benefit of the doubt.

GOLD / MERRILL LYNCH 10-YEAR+ US TREASURY TOTAL RETURN INDEX

The 1980 peak in gold corresponded with a major peak in US Treasury yields. Treasury returns were being eroded by persistently high inflationary pressures during the 1970s and investors demanded a higher yield to compensate for the loss of purchasing power. As a non-interest bearing asset, gold outperformed on the supposition it was the only 'real money'. Higher interest rates eventually choked off investment demand for gold as Treasuries became more attractive.

Gold / Merrill Lynch 10-year+ US Treasury Total Return Index

This chart is in log scale and depicts the price of gold divided by the Merrill Lynch 10-year+ Treasury Total Return Index from 1982. It depicts just how fast, far and for how long gold prices fell relative to Treasuries on a total return basis when the 1970s commodity bull market ended.

US Treasuries outperformed gold on a total return basis throughout the 1980s and 1990s. The first downtrend inconsistency was the loss of momentum from 2001. The progression of higher reaction lows was another clue the imbalance between supply and demand had reversed. The ratio broke out of an 18-month base in 2003 and trended higher for the better part of a decade.

At the time of writing the trend's consistency is being challenged. The downward reaction, prompted by gold's decline, is larger than that posted in 2008 and the ratio has dropped back into the 2008 range. If gold's decade-long outperformance is to be reasserted it will need to hold above the April 2013 lows.

US TREASURY YIELDS

It is important to note that gold's decade-long outperformance occurred during what has been a powerfully bullish environment for bonds. In the decade from 2000, the tech bubble burst and the credit crisis crash shook investor confidence in equities. Increased volatility, boardroom scandals, political corruption, banker avarice, the housing market bust, slow economic growth and high unemployment have all conspired to sap investor appetite for stocks while government bonds have been perceived as more appealing by comparison. This is despite the US government's high deficits, increasing debt burden and massive off balance sheet unfunded commitments such as Medicare and Social Security. The advent of Fed tapering due in the last quarter of 2013, with a view to the eventual removal of extraordinary monetary accommodation, is likely to have an outsized effect on both bonds and gold. The potential for higher government bond yields and moderate inflation to be counter-balanced by a return to self-sustaining growth is unlikely to be positive for either asset class.

US 10-year Treasuries 1964–2013

Let us describe the above 30-year trend's consistency characteristics as if we were speaking to a blind person:

1. Yields peaked near 16% in 1981 and have posted a succession of lower major rally highs since.

2. While yields have been falling for a long time, the progression of lower lows is not unbroken. There have been periods when the outlook for yields turned positive but never to an extent where the progression of lower highs was seriously threatened.

3. Rallies of 2% or more occurred in 1984, 1987, 1994, 1999, 2003–2006 and 2009 and could be considered 'normal' reactions within the prevailing downtrend.

This is unlikely to remain a consistency characteristic. Due to the maturity of the decline, a rally of greater than 2% would probably break the progression of lower rally highs and would represent a 20% decline in government bond prices. At 2–2.5%, real yields are no longer negative but returns are uncompetitive without the promise of capital appreciation.

Is there any evidence of type-1, 2 or 3 trend ending?

a) Yields accelerated lower in 2009 and 2011 increasing the potential for a bounce back in the opposite direction.

b) Volatility has increased suggesting a war between supply and demand.

c) A sustained move above 4% would break the progression of lower rally highs.

d) A sustained move above 5% would represent a larger rally than seen in the course of the decline to date and confirm trend change.

We conclude that base formation might be underway but this cannot yet be confirmed.

Are there any other factors worth considering?

Supply explodes at the top of every bull market. If it were equities, companies would be rushing out to list on the stock market. If it were commodities, investors would be attempting to grab a piece of the action by opening a new mine. In bonds, issuers rush to lock in the lowest cost of capital they have seen in a generation and borrow as much as they can. Mexico, BNSF Railway and Coca-Cola among others issuing 100-year bonds are reflective on this trend. In absolute and relative terms, yields are low.

Spread of US Treasury yields over S&P500 yields 1971–2013

This chart depicts the spread between the yield on US 10-year Treasuries and the S&P500's yield. It illustrates the peak in 1981 when Treasuries yielded 10% more than equities, but the fact that it is now in negative territory is perhaps more important.

Market historians will testify that investors traditionally demanded an equity yield well in excess of that on Treasuries to compensate for the perception of additional risk in the stock market. Since 2008, the S&P500's yield has exceeded that of US Treasuries on a number of occasions. Investors are seeking a safe haven in US Treasury liabilities because of the perception of risk in the stock market and other assets. Two burst bubbles in a decade, increased volatility, malfeasance in the banking sector and deteriorating governance have all taken their toll on confidence. However, that is where the comparison with the post-war era ends.

The US government is heavily indebted and its programmes to close its deficits have been unambitious at best. The economy has been on a low growth trajectory despite the largest monetary intervention in history. By contrast, the USA is replete with globally oriented corporations which dominate their respective niches, are flush with cash and are not overly influenced by domestic considerations. While there are signals that the Treasury bull market is in its latter stages, it has not yet ended. In fact the success of the corporate sector and the country's competitiveness in energy might yet deliver the growth necessary to avoid a worst-case scenario for the bond market.

S&P500 Total Return Index / Merrill Lynch 10-Year + Treasury Index 1992–2013

The S&P500 index underperformed US Treasuries on a total return basis from 2000. However, it hit an accelerated low in 2009, spent the three years from 2010 ranging and broke out in 2013 to reassert the relative uptrend. Provided the ratio continues to hold its progression of higher lows, the benefit of the doubt can be given to outperformance by equities.

The previous two charts highlight not only that equities on aggregate yield more than Treasuries but that they have been outperforming on a total return basis since 2009. When we consider that the S&P500 is a highly diverse index it is worth considering the performance of an index made up of companies with strong records of dividend growth.

S&P500 Dividend Aristocrats Total Return Index / Merrill Lynch 10-Year + Treasury Index 1992–2013

The constituents of the S&P500 Dividend Aristocrats Total Return Index have increased their dividends for at least the last 25 consecutive years. The outperformance of this index has been considerably more uniform, not least because these companies have such solid balance sheets. The added appeal of companies that increase their dividends at a rate above that of inflation is powerfully attractive in an ultra-low interest rate environment, but perhaps even more so in the event that inflation becomes a problem in future. The previous chart may be in the process of completing a type-3 base formation.

CONCLUSION

There are some logical interpretations when we think about the above ratios:

- The S&P500 has been largely rangebound for more than a decade, so it is likely to be closer to the end of the secular period of valuation-contraction than the beginning.

- Once completed, a secular process of valuation expansion is likely to take place which could see the Dow/gold ratio hit new all-time highs over the next few decades.

- In a low-yield world, companies with solid records of increasing dividends and those leveraged to the growth of the global consumer are outperforming the wider stock market and US Treasuries by a considerable margin.

- Gold has outperformed both Treasuries and the Dow Jones over the last decade on a total return basis. Considering the maturity of the market, 'gold fever' would be required for that outperformance to continue.

- Treasuries and government bonds generally have bubbly characteristics and this could now be in the process of bursting. This event is likely to mark the onset of a generation-long period of yield expansion and underperformance of the asset class.

CHAPTER 22:

HOW SUPPLY AND DEMAND INFLUENCE PRICE AND VICE VERSA

What we will cover in this chapter:

- A short-term move in prices does not change the fundamentals of a market but when prices have been rallying for a number of years, a supply response is encouraged.

- When prices have been declining for a long time, demand retreats and supply eventually responds, which creates the conditions for a new bull market.

- The impact of sentiment on prices and vice versa ensures that markets move in long-term bull and bear market cycles.

EVERY INNOVATION IN GENERATING, TRANSFORMING or saving energy creates efficiencies. These are rapidly reinvested in labour-saving devices, which in turn lead to increased consumption. This 'rebound effect' is more commonly referred to as the *Jevons paradox*.

In 1865 William Stanley Jevons observed that the introduction of a more efficient steam engine resulted in a surge in coal consumption. He then used this fact to opine that the rate at which the UK's coal was being depleted would increase and that the UK would soon run out of the commodity. Over a century later, the UK's coal production was a multiple of where it had been when Jevons made his prediction. Where did he go wrong?

His incomplete conclusion assumed that the efficiency of production would remain constant. He failed to take into account that technological innovation is just as likely to affect supply chains as it is the demand component. Just as steam engines became more efficient, so did mining methods. Yes, demand for coal continued to trend higher, but the cost of producing more from deeper seams contracted.

In a capitalist system, the simple fact is that as prices for a commodity rise the incentive of suppliers is to produce more in order to maximise profits. And, on the demand side, consumers are forced to implement more efficient ways of using the commodity. Hence, as a bull market gets underway, prices move higher, fuelled by the inability of supply to keep pace with a previously unforeseen source of demand. The perceptions of what actions need to be taken to deal effectively with this new situation change as prices increase.

Prices will trend higher until the situation has changed to such an extent that supply overwhelms demand and the trend of pricing reverses. As prices trend lower, the incentive is for suppliers to reduce costs in order to maximise profits, and consumers are under less pressure to reduce use.

The long-term relationship of how price affects perceptions and influences supply and demand dynamics ensures that asset prices move in multi-year bull and bear market cycles. While the rebound effect is most often used to explain the cyclicality of the commodity markets, it also offers a useful template for how supply and demand dynamics evolve in relation to prices for all exchange-traded vehicles.

STOCK MARKETS

It is no coincidence that the pace of IPOs picks up as prices for a stock market sector appreciate. Every company needs capital with which to fuel expansion but the stock market is far from the only source of that capital. In addition the regulatory oversight, compliance costs and balance sheet disclosures that a stock market listing requires act as a disincentive to seeking an IPO. Therefore the most attractive time to seek a listing is when the valuation of the company is at a high enough premium to justify the effort of seeking it.

The evolution of technology as a major productivity driver in the early 1990s drove a major bull market where demand for investment opportunities surged. This wall of capital thrown at the market helped fuel a massive infrastructure build, particularly in the USA and Europe. As demand for equities trended higher, the premium at which companies could be listed on the stock market increased substantially. This gave an opportunity to those in the technology sector to float their companies on the stock market for significantly more than they might otherwise have been worth. The generous fees associated with such deals also created an added incentive for investment banks to encourage companies to seek a flotation. The result of this frenzy to list was that the supply of stock more than doubled on the NYSE between 1996 and 2001.

NYSE number of shares outstanding in absolute terms 1995–2013

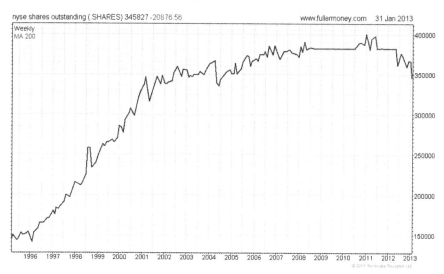

The bull market that was initially driven by a sound fundamental story and dearth of supply ended as supply flooded the market and as interest rates began to rise, which choked off the liquidity on which the bull depended. Not only was price the most expedient way of monitoring the market, it also directly contributed to the change in bullish perceptions that enticed supply into the market and eventually caused the market to falter.

The decade following the tech bubble saw the pace of new listings on the NYSE collapse as disappointment with the technology sector turned to ambivalence. Liquidity dried up as recession bit. Other sectors such as commodities and real estate attracted investor interest and served to diminish interest in the equity market. The response of exchanges faced with a collapse in listing activity was to seek ways to increase the volume traded. This contributed to their support for high frequency trading and co-location.

The policy response to the credit crisis of 2007/2008 led to negative real interest rates. This created a highly favourable environment to issue debt rather than equity. In fact, since the cost of debt dropped so much, a number of companies chose to issue debt in order to buy back their equity. Politicians wishing to be seen to do something to protect the interests of investors following two crashes in a decade greatly increased the compliance costs of listed companies. This contributed to companies taking the decision to delist. The net result was that the number of shares outstanding on the NYSE trended lower from 2011.

We can reduce this to how supply and demand respond to price action. The perception of investors is that the stock market has become prone to volatility and, in nominal terms, has ranged for 13 years; hence it must be more risky. Demand for equities has slumped relative to other asset classes and therefore the supply response has been to reduce inventory.

Declining inventory and an increasing number of privately held companies represents the pool from which new supply will emerge in the next bull market. Another way of thinking of this phenomenon is that the shares of quality companies are turning into collector's items as they buy back their own shares.

FIXED INCOME

US Treasury bonds have been in a bull market since 1980 and have greatly benefitted in the intervening years from the disinflationary environment that allowed the sector to generate reliable low-volatility investment returns. While Treasuries did not attract a great deal of attention in the latter stages of the technology bubble, their allure was burnished as equity markets entered a decade of volatile ranging.

To illustrate the declining allure of equities compared to bonds from 2001 to 2012 let us look at the average of suggested equity allocations by Wall Street analysts over that period. The index peaked at a suggested weighting of 72% in 2001 following one of the biggest bull markets for stocks in history. It then trended lower over the next 12 years, as disappointment with stock market performance sapped interest and the outperformance of bonds proved more alluring.

US stock market allocations 1997–2013

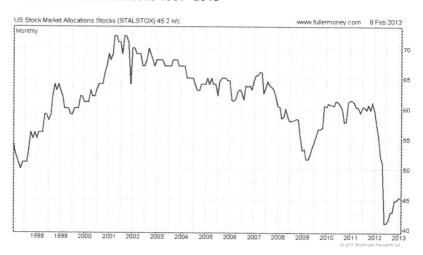

Governments have fostered the attraction of their bonds by engaging in quantitative easing. In so doing they have added a considerable additional source of demand to the market that would not otherwise have existed. The guarantee of government support gave new meaning to 'risk-free', and stoked a substantial momentum move. Additionally, the volatility in other asset classes bolstered the perception that Treasuries and other government bonds offer a safe haven. In an effort to ensure demand for bonds, governments increased capital-adequacy rules, compelling banks, insurance companies and pension funds to hold more government bonds.

As government bond yields fell to new lows, negative real interest rates became commonplace. In simple terms investors were willing to accept a negative yield in exchange for the possibility of an additional momentum move. Concurrently the balance sheets of corporations had improved substantially and they were presented with an historic opportunity to raise capital in the debt markets at highly attractive rates.

This all represents a massive swelling in the supply of bonds across the government and corporate sectors. Just as the response to high prices for equities was to increase supply, the same is true of the bond markets with ultra-low yields. When the liquidity on which the market depends is eventually removed, bond prices in particular will experience a steep decline.

CURRENCIES

The currency markets offer a slightly different example, since it is impossible to talk about the value of a currency without comparing it to something else. The persistent strength of one currency over another has a meaningful effect on *competitiveness* for the respective economies. No country is willing to tolerate a strong currency indefinitely. The stronger the currency becomes, the greater the incentive to increase supply in an effort to weaken it. Switzerland's adoption of a peg against the euro in 2011 and Japan's adoption of an inflation target in 2012 are both examples of this type of activity.

At the other end of the scale, a persistently weak currency raises questions about the ability of the country to meet its debt obligations, and results in more fiscally responsible policies being adopted or forced upon it. The US dollar is perhaps the most relevant example of where these points could have an outsized effect in the coming decade. The Federal Reserve is likely to be the first central bank to begin to raise interest rates, and the USA's competitive advantage in energy, technological prowess and the gradual imposition of fiscal responsibility enhance the attractiveness of the US dollar, particularly when other significant economies need a weaker currency.

COMMODITIES

The commodity markets represent a real-world example of how supply and demand dynamics are influenced by pricing and the perception of how prices will perform over time. The inability of global supply to respond to the advent of greater Asian demand resulted in prices for oil and other industrial commodities surging higher from 2003. This set in motion a significant reorganisation of the global energy sector, with significant changes occurring on both the supply and demand sides of the equation.

High prices greatly increased the incentive of oil companies to both produce as much as possible and invest in renewing their resources bases. The innovations that have led to record drilling depths and the combination of hydraulic fracturing and horizontal drilling have created new sources of additional supply that have not previously been thought economic. The potential implementation of these technologies outside of the USA's geography greatly enhances the possibility that supply will increase substantially over the coming decades.

On the demand side, consumers have been under pressure from higher energy prices. High gasoline prices have encouraged development of smaller vehicles, hybrid, natural gas and electric vehicles. High heating costs have been a tailwind for insulation and efficient heaters. High electricity prices have made CFL and LED bulbs even more attractive. Demand for less energy-intensive appliances and machines has also trended higher. The cost of producing energy has been an incentive to fund development of alternatives such as dual fuel power stations, wind, solar, biomass, geothermal, nuclear, coal and natural gas. More capital than ever has been invested in developing more efficient batteries.

Over time, as energy prices trend lower on an inflation-adjusted basis, countries such as the USA, who have pioneered lower energy costs, will benefit from increased investment. Energy intensive sectors such as chemical, advanced materials, fertiliser, aluminium, metal-refining, heavy industry and manufacturing sectors will all have a reason to relocate to the USA. The sustainability of this competitive advantage is based on the assumption that the spread between Brent crude oil, which represents global prices, and West Texas Intermediate pricing, which is the North American benchmark, will remain above the historical norm of at most $5.

The industrial metals complex represents another example of price declines reinforcing the perception that the sector was in terminal decline. The crash of the early 1980s forced the shuttering of capacity, rationalising of businesses and job losses. When demand began to improve in the early 2000s, companies were ill equipped and disinclined to respond. The scale of price advances eventually prompted massive investment, which sated demand and resulted in lower prices. Linear demand growth forecasts that were used to secure funding for expansion have often proved overly optimistic, as the net effect of increased supply is to ultimately satiate demand.

The precious metals markets represent an interesting interpretation from the perspective of supply and demand, because one of their principle appeals is their immutable quality. One of the bullish arguments used to support gold is 'most of the gold that has ever been mined still exists'. However, this represents both a virtue and the potential key to the eventual peak in the market.

Precious metal miners have been challenged to increase supply substantially because of declining ore grades and rising labour, energy, machinery and regulatory costs. Investment and industrial demand has exacerbated the supply deficit and prices responded with a decade-long advance. However, since investment demand is stored rather than consumed, it also represents a potential source of supply when inventory is eventually liquidated. Therefore, the integrity of the bull market rests not on the perceptions of the ultimate store of value but the trajectory of investment demand. This is why the consistency of the trend of all-known ETF holdings of gold is so instructive.

Total known ETF holdings of gold 2003–2013

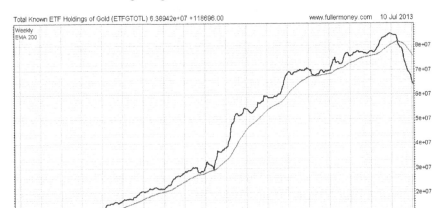

The index trended consistently higher from 2004, when ETFs represented a negligible gold holding, to a peak of more than 84,000,000 troy ounces in 2012. It dropped below the 200-day for the first time in 2013 and in the process posted its largest decline in a decade. In the absence of a sustained move back above 80,000,000 ounces, this can be considered a completed type-2 (massive reaction against the prevailing trend) top. What had once been a powerful tailwind for gold prices now represents a headwind.

Prices for agricultural products such as corn, soybeans and cotton peaked between 1973 and 1974 and trended lower in inflation-adjusted terms until the mid-2000s.

Earl Butz, US Secretary of Agriculture in the early 1970s, promoted corn production in particular. He alleviated supports for not planting on all a farmer's land and promoted the amalgamation of small holdings. In conjunction with advances made during the Green Revolution of agricultural innovation that took place between the 1950s and 1970s, this contributed to a surge in food production.

The introduction of the European Community's Common Agricultural Policy (CAP) in the aftermath of the Second World War introduced supports for the farming sector. Even though the Mansholt Plan of 1972 ultimately failed to implement the reform aims, it did succeed in introducing the modernisation of farm holdings, cessation of uneconomic activity and the training of farmers. In many respects these policies mimicked those that occurred in the USA around the same time and the result was similar. Food production soared over the next two decades.

In both systems farmers were incentivised through subsidy programs to produce as much food as possible. Blessed with some of the most fertile land in the world, both regions flooded global markets with cheap produce and were in turn protected by trade barriers. By the early 1990s this had created a situation, particularly in Europe, were food was being allowed to rot because of over-production.

Corn (CBT) / CPI Inflation 1964–2013

Overarching supply created by this situation locked agriculture prices into a decades-long inflation-adjusted bear market. As demonstrated previously, such a long period of cost-compression changes the perceptions of those involved in the enterprise.

By the late 1990s, the belief that food prices would remain permanently low had become pervasive. The embarrassment of a food-rich West, where a small sliver of the total population worked in agriculture, compared to a food-poor developing world, where 75% of the population worked the land, had become a political liability both at home and abroad. Additionally, the cost of farm subsidies had risen to such high levels, particularly in Europe, that reform became a priority.

One of the main aims of CAP reform was to remove the incentive to produce food. Subsidies were refocused on *custodianship* of the land instead. Unsurprisingly, food production began to trend lower.

One of the main successes of the Doha round of World Trade Organization negotiations was the agreement in 2005 in the Hong Kong round that all agricultural export subsidies would be removed by 2013 and that industrialised countries would open their markets to imports from poorer countries.

In the USA, the pollution of groundwater by MTBE was used as a justification for mandating the use of ethanol as an alternative oxygenate in transportation fuel from

2004. This acted as a fresh source of demand for excess corn production and is a non-trivial factor in the subsequent price appreciation of the commodity. The use of food commodities as fuel has since become a global phenomenon. The UN Food and Agriculture Organization expected 14% of total coarse grain, 16% of vegetable oil and 34% of sugar production to be used for biofuels by 2013; up from 11%, 11% and 21% in 2010.

In the absence of a subsidy-driven incentive to produce, the cost of key agricultural commodities is returning to a more realistic level.

On the demand side of the equation, the concurrent expansion both of the size of the global population and per capita spending power has created a situation where not only are there more people, but per capita consumption of calories has also increased. The change in spending power has driven a shift in demand towards more meat products, which requires roughly nine times more grains per calorie consumed. This means a nonlinear (with population change) growth in the demand for grains.

This has seen inflation-adjusted price downtrends broken, and food prices appreciate in real terms for the first time in 30 years. The result is that global inventories of key food commodities have been at record low levels since 2009. The risk of price spikes has increased because there is less slack in the global market to deal with failed crops or weather events. In 2003, David Fuller dubbed such conditions in the commodity markets as *"supply inelasticity meets rising demand"*.

CONCLUSION

How supply and demand interact affects prices. As prices trend they alter the perceptions of suppliers and consumers so that their subsequent actions cause prices to eventually reverse course and the cycle begins once more. This occurs in every liquid market and ensures that prices move in long-term cycles. It has always been this way and always will be.

CHAPTER 23:

THEMES FOR THE DECADES BETWEEN 2015 AND 2025

"It's hard to make predictions, especially about the future."

– attributed to Yogi Berra

What we will cover in this chapter:

- Productivity can be defined as the multiple of labour, technology, energy and debt.

- As of 2013, the greatest urbanisation in history is lifting billions of people out of poverty and into the middle classes. Therefore labour productivity on aggregate is improving.

- We are living through one of the greatest golden ages of technological development in the history of our species. Industrial automation/robotics, nanotechnologies, genetics, cloud computing and other developments have the capacity to fuel productivity growth well into the future.

- The high price environment in energy prices that has prevailed since the early 2000s has encouraged supply growth from unconventional sources, not least natural gas and solar. It has also contributed to efficiency gains in battery technology and consumption patterns.

- In the so-called developed world the use to which debt has been put since 1995 represents a headwind for the above factors to fuel a secular bull market. No such obstacle is evident in progressing economies, not least in Asia.

UNCERTAINTY IS A FACT WE HAVE TO ACCEPT if we are to engage with and profit from the markets. It has long been a tenet of David Fuller's that we need to *"foster the humility to accept the reality provided by the market"*. Giving in to the arrogance that we can in any way influence the direction prices are likely to take is a sure recipe for eventual losses. We might have strong personal opinions about a company, country, government, products, currency or management structure but these mean nothing if not confirmed by the market. In a war between our beliefs and the power of the market we will surely lose. However, even with these considerations in mind, if we can successfully identify a theme that has the power to shape perceptions of value over a number of years it greatly facilities the process of identifying promising investment opportunities.

At any time there are a considerable number of investment ideas vying for attention and that hold short-term profit potential. These play out continually as investor interest rotates from one sector into another. However, it is the big macro cycles that have the power to shape our lives over years. Major bull markets evolve from these cycles and disciplined investors can make fortunes. It is these events which are most interesting for macro behavioural technical analysts because it is simply easier to make money in a bull market.

Themes that have the power to create value generally share one common characteristic: they increase productivity. Rather than be bogged down by a discussion of how to exactly measure productivity, let us consider what might change the status quo enough to improve productivity. For these purposes I will assume that productivity equates to the sum of labour usage, energy costs, technology and debt/capital implementation. When a major improvement in any one of these considerations occurs, there will logically be an improvement in productivity.

You might ask why this is important? If we can figure out how to do more with less, we create value. Such leaps forward open up new avenues for intellectual creativity and as this growth trajectory is discounted by markets, prices rise to compensate. If we identify such events we are in a highly favourable position to profit from our analysis.

LABOUR

The UN expects the global population to increase from approximately 6.5 billion in 2010 to approximately 9 billion by 2050; a rise of almost 40%. That represents a massive jump in population and in the potential for hours worked, which will lead to greater productivity by virtue of size alone. This process would be greatly facilitated by improving standards of governance in high population countries that allow more people to achieve their productive capacity. As more countries move from a rural to an industrialising trajectory there is considerable scope for development of internal demand and export capacity which will facilitate global trade and promote growth. In the agriculture sector, the rollout of farm machinery, irrigation, seeds, fertiliser and knowhow are helping to increase productivity and yields. This frees up working-age populations for other activities in the manufacturing and services sectors.

Individual countries which succeed in lifting their populations out of poverty and create a middle class will improve productivity in the process. This fosters investor interest as valuations improve. Global companies that thrive in such an environment all stand to benefit from this trend.

The reasons for population growth give us an idea of where investment themes might evolve. On one side of the equation, life expectancy has increased substantially in the last 50 years. As the availability of improved diets and more advanced medical attention becomes a global phenomenon, demand for life-enhancing treatments, residential care, financial planning and ultimately funerals all increase.

On the other side of the equation, while global birth rates continue to trend lower, infant mortality is improving even faster so that the population continue to rise. At some point in the future, probably post 2030, as birth rates continues to decline and as mortality rates begin to plateau, global population growth is likely to stagnate and may even decline. However, between now and that event, population growth is likely to remain a significant contributor to labour pool growth. For the increasing number of countries that foster social mobility this is creating increased demand for just about everything. Infrastructure such as homes, offices, factories, roads, bridges, airports, railways, hospitals, schools etc. all need to be built. Utilities such as electricity, water, gas and telecoms all need to be upgraded.

On the consumer side, the evolution of Wal-Mart's business offers an interesting case study. The company dominates the supermarket sector in North America by competing on product range and price. However, its North American revenues have been static for a decade. Almost all of its growth has come from its international business, where it is expanding in Asia, Latin America and Europe. As supermarkets expand, demand for what they stock also trends higher. This helps to explain increased demand for processed and packaged foods, condiments, household cleaning products, detergents, cosmetics, soap, shampoo, deodorant and other consumer staples.

The confluence of these themes means we are living through the greatest age of humanism that is ever likely to occur. Not only are there more people, but their average standard of living is also improving and with it the productive capacity of the global economy. This has created a powerfully bullish force that is changing the lives of billions of people. In turn this is creating value and a reappraisal by global investors.

ENERGY

By some estimates, a $10 rise in the price of oil shaves 0.2% off real GDP in the USA. WTI Crude Oil prices have risen from an average of $20 in the last 1990s to an average of $90 between 2011 and 2012. This can be equated to loss of growth potential of 1.4%. However, this is an average figure. Energy producers' benefit in such a scenario and the impact falls most heavily on consumers. This has a negative impact on consumer demand and a material effect on the productive capacity of the economy.

Brent Crude oil, which is representative of global pricing, rose from similar levels in the late 1990s to an average of $110 by 2011/12. The energy efficiency of other countries varies widely, so it is impossible to estimate the tax high oil prices put on growth but it is almost certainly more than the USA's.

It is for this reason alone that anything which reduces the price of energy can be seen as a net positive for the productive capacity of the global economy and hence broad stock market valuations.

It has been my and David Fuller's view since 2009 that the advent of unconventional gas production is truly a game-changer for the global economy. The subsequent application of similar technology to unconventional oil production has amplified this trend considerably. The USA has pioneered the development of unconventional oil and gas and, as a result, benefits from a competitive advantage in energy pricing. There is a real possibility that the US economy will approach energy self-sufficiency at some point in the decade from 2015 to 2025 as a result of these innovations. Considering what is at stake, it is inevitable that other countries will eventually develop their own reserves of unconventional oil and gas.

The high price environment that prevailed from 2003 onwards also encouraged greater efficiency of consumption, which in turn has reduced the call on oil production. At the end of the last bull market in energy prices, new sources of supply and improved efficiency resulted in prices falling in inflation-adjusted terms between 1980 and 1999. In nominal terms, prices held at levels that were well above those that prevailed prior to the 1970s. We can anticipate that even in the most bearish scenario nominal prices for oil are unlikely to fall below $40 on a sustained basis over the coming decades, largely due to increased costs of discovery and production. Likewise the prospect of energy price spikes is being reduced in the absence of political upheavals in OPEC.

Assuming I am correct in the belief that the energy market will transition from a tight supply to an abundant supply environment, there will be clear winners and losers. The most significant losers will be those that depend on high prices to support their business or government models. This is particularly relevant for Canadian tar sands and exploration in the Arctic. The financial viability of renewables, which is already questionable in a high-price environment, would depend even more on political sponsorship for survival.

The winners in an environment where energy prices trend lower in real terms and on a sustained basis are both retail and corporate consumers. In the industrial sector the cost of energy is a major consideration in where to locate facilities. For ordinary consumers who have seen heating, cooling, transportation and food bills affected by high energy prices, the benefits are clear. This could then have an outsized effect on the cash available to drive increased consumer spending in non-energy areas, and exert a multiplier effect on employment.

TECHNOLOGY

"If I have seen further it is only by standing on the shoulders of giants."

– Isaac Newton

Every major leap forward in human development has been supported by innovation in the recording, storage, availability and transmission of information. Everything from cave paintings, papyrus, vellum, ink, paper, printing, the telegraph, telephone, computers, fax, email, the internet, cloud computing and social media have cumulatively increased our ability to communicate. Not only has technology advanced the rate at which we can transmit ideas and complete complex calculations, but it is easier than ever to accumulate the knowledge of others so that we can build upon it.

An additional benefit is that with the advent of the internet and cloud computing, humanity's collective knowledge is now more secure than ever. In antiquity, wars or natural disasters destroyed libraries, and it sometimes took a civilisation centuries to make up for the loss of knowledge, if they ever recovered. With the invention of the printing press, the risk of such events destroying centres of learning for good decreased. The internet not only fosters cooperation but also makes it much less likely that the collective knowledge built up by our species over centuries can be lost due to wars or natural disasters.

The rate at which new information is being created is rising exponentially. Patents are being lodged at an ever-increasing rate. New products, methods and innovations have become so commonplace as to be unremarkable. These form the basis of a golden age of information that we are privileged to be living through. Such is the pace with which discoveries are being made, products created, and the human experience of technology evolving, that we can reasonably expect ground-breaking productivity gains to continue to appear in the coming decades. Moore's Law states that the number of components that can fit onto a circuit will double every two years. It was assumed that the speed, efficiency and size of processors would improve by a similar margin – and in fact they have for more than 50 consecutive years. 2013 is likely a small turning point, moving the rate to every three years. However, as the size of 'gates' on a chip draws closer to the width of a silicon atom, the search for an alternative material has become more intense. By 2020 the width of a silicon node on a chip is expected to reach a physical limit of five nanometres. This means that a race is on for the discovery of an alternative.

In 2011 Intel released a tri-gate (3-D) chip which reduced leakage of power and increased efficiency beyond what might have been expected from conventional designs. Also in 2011 IBM created the first graphene-based circuit and used it to power a broadband frequency radio. In February 2013 at the International Solid-State Circuits Conference a team from Princeton University demonstrated the first working circuit manufactured from carbon nanotubes. While both these carbon based technologies represent potential breakthroughs, there is still a great deal of work to be done in developing products from them. However, the future for the sector looks bright and nothing has occurred to deter optimism.

As processors become smaller, faster and produce less heat, as software becomes more sophisticated, and as cameras become more sensitive, the stage is set for a revolution in the industrial automation sector. Robots have been the subject of science fiction novels for decades but are becoming an increasingly visible part of the industrial landscape. Leaps forward in optical technology in the last 20 years have greatly enhanced their capability to perform more complex operations.

At the time of writing, Philips Electronics employs hundreds of workers at a Chinese factory to manufacture electric shavers. At a new facility in the Netherlands it employs a few dozen workers per shift and 128 robots to produce its newer, more technologically advanced products for a similar cost.

Following what must have seemed like a terminal decline, General Electric has begun to expand its Appliance Park facility in Kentucky. It has moved production of water heaters and other appliances back to the USA, as energy costs, industrial automation, labour flexibility and transportation costs make the case for insourcing compelling.

Nike produces 96% of its running shoes in Asia. In a news item from March 2012, Charlie Denson, president of Nike's brand, hypothesised that as automated manufacturing progresses, he could envisage a time when a customer would walk into a shop, have their foot scanned, and a customised shoe would be manufactured in the USA or other major market to save time and transport costs.

ARM Holdings has been enormously successful with its chip designs that were most notably used for Apple's range of handheld devices. However, in the third quarter of 2012 the company generated more revenue from items other than mobile phones. Embedded processing is its fastest growing market and Intel is racing to increase its footprint in the sector. Embedded processing represents the practice of inserting circuits into products that have not previously had computational or communication applications. General Electric refers to the practice as "Industrialising the Internet" because it is introducing efficiencies to the industrial complex that were once unimaginable. The process represents a revolution for the industrial complex and has considerable potential for productivity gains.

From an investment perspective, the obvious beneficiaries of the march of technology are likely to be the leaders in their respective fields who can produce needed products that help their customers save money through efficiency gains. The less remarked on beneficiaries are the end users who can increase margins by doing more with less, and the retail customer who benefits from homogenisation of technologies, economies of scale and competition.

Technology is also changing the outlook for the healthcare sector, where genetics-focused therapies are approaching commercial viability. Genetics and biotechnology more generally represent an exciting area of medicine, with the capacity to enhance both our quality of life and life expectancy.

From the proposition in the 1860s that traits can be inherited, to the discovery of DNA's double Helix in 1953, to the first US approved gene therapy in 1990, to the cloning of a sheep in 1996, to the DNA sequencing of a fruit fly in 2000 to the completion of the Human Genome project in 2004 we can deduce that the pace of genetic discovery is accelerating. As additional products are brought to market, the potential for life-enhancing therapies and productivity growth among the wider global population is considerable. Additionally, the application of genetic engineering to agriculture has considerable potential to dramatically increase yields despite public opposition in some countries.

DEBT

Enhancements in energy, labour or technology can promote productivity growth, but debt is an additional avenue which allows us to borrow on the presumption that we can grow the capital faster than the rate at which we need to pay it back. The entire financial system is structured as a network of liabilities and creditors where one party accepts a risk and rate of return in exchange for their capital. While most people focus on the ability to repay debt, the use to which the capital borrowed is put has an effect on productivity growth and hence the outlook for investment themes.

Intuitively, governments, corporations and individuals would make the most efficient use of debt when they employ it to increase productivity. Investing in anything that enhances the return on capital invested can easily be justified and is a reasonable motive for committing to a debt burden. Borrowing to fund a takeover that will create synergies for both business, or to enhance energy or labour productivity, or to fund a potentially beneficial technology are common uses of debt that lead to capital formation, and are invaluable to investors.

However, when debt is used to compensate for deteriorating productivity in the energy, labour or technology fields, the risk of it eventually becoming a problem rises commensurately. A government or corporation that increases borrowing to raise benefits or salaries for employees without wringing out additional productivity is obviously putting itself at risk of budget shortfalls. A government, corporation or individual that borrows to fund pet projects with no financial basis or chance of return on capital invested is indulging in emotion rather than reason. Funding the development of energy ventures that may never be profitable in preference to more economically viable solutions is gambling rather than investing.

Following the credit crisis of 2008 a wide divergence emerged between the trajectory of debt to GDP ratios in Europe, the USA and Japan compared to those in much of Asia. On the one hand many Western economies raised debt levels to help compensate for the loss of economic activity following the tech bust. They doubled down on this policy following the credit crisis by taking on the debts of banks and engaging in quantitative easing. At the time of writing they are presented with the quandary of how to reduce their debt burdens in an orderly manner. Inflation, selective write-downs and growth appear to be the only solutions. Some mix of these alternatives will be necessary to fix the problem.

By contrast, many Asian countries experienced deep corrective phases following the Asian financial crisis in the late 1990s and have since tried to run surpluses and eschewed debt accumulation. The result is that not only are Asian and particularly ASEAN governments less leveraged, but their respective consumers are less leveraged. Therefore they have ample opportunity to increase their debt burden in order to fund productivity-positive strategies. This represents a powerful potential tailwind for growth and perceptions of value in their financial markets.

CONCLUSION

As we address the four broad areas from which investment themes might evolve we are presented with a confluence of powerfully bullish potential outcomes. The Greatest Urbanisation in History, The Golden Age of Technology and the game changing nature of unconventional oil and gas production mean that we are living through one of the most exciting periods in human history. The mountain of debt that has been accrued in the West and Japan represents a major challenge that will need to be tackled if their domestic markets are to respond effectively to these themes. The removal of extraordinary monetary measures and the potential for unrest in the Middle East's major oil producers represent potential threats to the bullish outlook.

From an investment perspective, once we have identified what the motivating theme is likely to be, we choose our investment vehicles based on where the greatest difference between supply and demand exists. Charts of price action represent the most expedient way of doing this.

CHAPTER 24:

THE GLOBAL MIDDLE CLASS

What we will cover in this chapter:

- In the last few years the global population has become more urban than rural.

- The adoption of capitalist economic systems is allowing more people to reach their productive capacity and to improve their standard of living.

- Progressing economies represent where the greatest opportunities for growth reside.

THE PATH TO ECONOMIC DEVELOPMENT is now well-trodden. Countries embarking on the road to industrialisation have the luxury of seeing how it is done from the experiences of those who have gone before. Additionally they can skip ahead in terms of development through installing the most up-to-date infrastructure without having to invent it themselves. This also allows the pace of development to increase.

As economies expand, they raise more people out of poverty and into the middle classes. As countries embark on development they tend to move from poor with high growth to wealthier with lower growth. An alternative perspective is that it becomes increasingly difficult for countries to sustain high growth rates as they become richer. This is logical since less is required to move from a GDP of $1 per person to $2 per person than from $1,000 per person to $2,000 per person.

Economic convergence

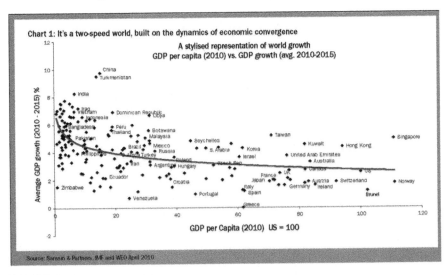

As a country embarks on development, it generally tends to lever a competitive advantage in labour costs in order to drive inward investment. Provided this policy is coupled with disinflationary policies, growth improves and wealth increases. As the pool of available labour is exhausted through economic expansion, increased productivity becomes more of a priority. Education, modernisation of plant, machinery and work practices, the development of an internal consumer market, expansion into alternative sectors etc. all become possible additional avenues to help fuel development and national wealth.

CHINESE CONSUMERISM

China's success since Deng Xiaoping's opening up of the economy offers both an excellent example of development from a low base and of the challenges faced in moving to a consumer-oriented growth model. The initial phase of China's development was characterised by liberalisation of labour laws and impressive support for foreign direct investment. Massive infrastructure development followed and came to dominate the economy by the early 2000s. As the country followed an export-oriented and capital investment growth model, the state built up savings of more than $1 trillion while the consumer was estimated to have more than $2 trillion in savings. Such was the success of the growth model that the economy went from a relative backwater to the world's second-largest in 30 years. Property became the investment vehicle of choice for many people and the risk of a bubble became increasingly pressing.

By 2010 China had reached a Rubicon in terms of its development. According to the World Bank it would garner more economic growth by investing in human capital than infrastructure over the following decades. This crystallised a major challenge for the Chinese: how to rebalance an infrastructure and export growth model with a vibrant consumer class without causing a property crash?

A vibrant consumer class has obvious attractions, not least because it would help buffer the economy from external shocks to the export-oriented manufacturing sector. A strong services sector also tends to contribute to greater productivity, which is always desirable. By 2013, boosts to the welfare state, investment in healthcare, increases in the minimum wage, the development of a newfound respect for the environment, and the easing of travel restrictions had all been implemented.

One of the main aims of these reforms was to reduce China's domestic savings rate, one of the highest in the world. Consumers have previously been forced to hold high percentages of their income in cash in order to provide for potential medical costs and possible job loss. Reforms to create support for citizens should help reduce the need for savings and open up the potential for increased consumer demand for goods and services. This should help to even out the economy's growth drivers and increase productivity. As China becomes richer, the evolution of its economy depends on successfully evolving into a consumer-oriented society.

INDIAN ASPIRATIONS

India offers another example of rapid economic growth but from a vastly different perspective. The failed 'Hindu' economic model of protectionism and self-reliance persisted for longer than many anticipated. Saddam Hussein's invasion of Kuwait in 1990 was the eventual catalyst for change, because the remittances from Indian workers in Kuwait were cut off, initiating a budget and balance of payments crisis. Sweeping economic reforms were instituted, which spurred economic growth for more than a decade.

The Indian economic miracle has relied on the ingenuity of its people in prospering despite widespread corruption and the government being mired in bureaucracy. Perhaps its greatest institutional strength is the independence of the courts and protection of property rights, which has allowed a vibrant and globally oriented corporate sector to evolve.

India's consumer sector is more developed than might otherwise be expected for a country with a comparatively low GDP per capita. On the one hand this has allowed the economy to weather turmoil on the global stage better than most. However, the corollary is that the failure to develop a significant manufacturing sector has inhibited the country's export potential and contributes to a persistent trade deficit.

The lack of infrastructure development and the slow pace with which new permits can be attained acts as a drag on GDP growth. This contributes to the perception that India is not a welcome host for manufacturing investment.

What China has attained in term of its infrastructure, India aspires to. The pace of public-private partnerships to promote infrastructure development in the decade from 2000 has been impressive but the pace of development will need to pick up if India's global ambitions are to be realised.

In 2012, the rupee briefly traded at an all-time low of almost 58 rupees to the US dollar. This weakness was the result of foreign investors taking flight at deteriorating governance, widespread graft and a loss of faith in the ability of Manmohan Singh's government to push through reform. When he unilaterally pushed through reform of the financial sector, fuel subsidies and the retail sector, it set in motion a catalyst for additional investor interest. The currency can be viewed as a barometer for global investor confidence in India's prospects. Improving standards of governance, a streamlined permitting process, a crackdown on graft and continued liberalisation of the domestic economy would all support the currency, improve perceptions, foster growth and inhibit inflationary pressures.

A MIDDLE CLASS OF BILLIONS

China and India represent a third of the global population. As their populations continue to move from a rural to an urban environment and as they become more urbane, demand for consumer goods increases. However, not only is this a trend evident in two countries – it is a global phenomenon.

Brazil is a middle-income country which has turned from being a serial defaulter to a creditor to the IMF since 2000. The confluence of improving economic governance and higher commodity prices multiplied the positive effects on the economy. Property prices have risen, the currency has become one of the world's firmest and standards of living are increasing rapidly.

South Africa is another commodity exporter with a large domestic population which, despite political upheaval, has held to an anti-inflationary economic policy and has the historic benefit of an independent judiciary.

Indonesia threw off its dictatorial past with the ousting of President Suharto in 1998 and adopted an economic policy strongly influenced by fiscal rectitude. Its large domestic population and considerable commodity exporting sector have combined to spur impressive economic growth and rising living standards.

Mexico has benefitted enormously from NAFTA (a free-trade agreement with the USA and Canada), its considerable natural resources, not least oil, and its proximity to the world's most affluent consumer market in the USA. As economic growth persists, its large domestic population is experiencing rising living standards on aggregate.

The Arab Spring that began in late 2010 highlighted the failure of many Middle Eastern governments to provide the chance of an improving standard of living for their populations. Favourable demographics represent an opportunity for any country but also an enormous challenge. Those who rise to the challenge succeed; those who fail will probably be mired in economic limbo until they reform.

On frequent trips to China, I've been surprised by the number of African business people I meet. I've spoken with business people from Nigeria, Uganda, Kenya, Tanzania, Guinea, Ghana, Malawi and Mozambique who were in China sourcing cheap consumer goods to supply nascent consumer sectors in their own markets. Improving standards of economic governance, albeit from a very low base, are promoting impressive growth rates for many of these countries. They also teach us that any country can prosper provided stability and improving governance are realistic policy objectives. It is never too late.

The examples illustrate that in a global economy it is not appropriate to allow one's perceptions of a single country to frame one's opinion of the whole world. There are billions of people who aspire to a better standard of living for themselves and, more importantly, their children. The trend of improving governance is evident across Asia, Africa and Latin America and it is no surprise that these regions represent some of the world's highest growth markets.

URBAN, WEALTHY, INTERDEPENDENT

In the 2011, for the first time ever, the global economy went from mostly rural to mostly urban. This represents a major shift in the course of human history and a major investment theme. When we consider the path to development of the world's population centres, improving standards of governance irrespective of the starting point are a prerequisite. Subsequently, the needs and priorities of different countries will take precedence. Some will need to build infrastructure, others improve education, others foster a manufacturing sector, others will need to invest in commodity export capacity etc. However, on aggregate, there are some clear conclusions.

Per capita demand for commodities has a strong correlation with per capita income. If we return to the chart at the beginning of the chapter, as countries become richer and standards of living increase, per capita consumption of energy, steel, industrial resources, grain, meat, cotton, chemicals etc. embark on a long-term upward trajectory. Those with the ability to increase supply were slow to respond from the early 2000s and prices for these commodities surged out of long-term type-3 bases. New sources of supply began to reach market from 2009 and China's change of focus from infrastructure development to promoting the consumer has had an impact of the demand growth profile of industrial resources. Additional price appreciation will depend on large new sources of demand evolving, potentially from India, ASEAN, the Middle East or Africa. There is every chance that this will occur, not least because infrastructure development is an increasingly urgent priority for a considerable number of countries. The question from a pricing perspective is whether it will occur before major new sources of supply are brought to market or after.

One of the first things poor people do when their income increases is buy more food. The treats that were once reserved for holidays such as Diwali in India or New Year and the Mid-Autumn festival in China become everyday delicacies. Let us assume that everyone has a preference for either sweet or savoury foods but not everyone has the financial resources to satiate those desires. While there are clear examples of people who have an innate ability to control their dietary intake, a great deal of evidence suggests that as disposable income increases so does calorie intake. Demand for processed foods experiences a jump as the pace of life increases, as more women go to work and as the demand for convenience increases. Demand for ready-meals, salty, sweet and spicy treats increase. People quickly develop a taste for sugary drinks and demand for these increases in line with incomes.

When I was a college student I used to run a tour boat on the Lakes of Killarney in Ireland. My partner who had been a boatman for 40 years had a saying: "I have a drink problem … the problem is getting money for it." As disposable incomes rise, the per capita consumption of alcohol tends to increase where it is not inhibited by cultural or religious factors.

Per capita demand for basic consumer goods such as soap, shampoo, toothbrushes, floss, toothpaste, toilet paper, tampons and sanitary napkins, condoms, moisturiser, shaving foam, razors, deodorant, aftershave, hairspray and make-up, washing detergent, softener, dish cleaner, utensils, household appliances, furniture, etc. all increase as populations become richer. The companies that can profit from this development are those with the reach, experience, brand recognition and healthy balance sheets to fund such expansion.

As disposable incomes rise, consumption of mobile phones, computers, hi-fis, internet, motor cycles, cars, trucks, vans, international travel, luxury goods such as jewellery, watches, bags and clothes increase as well.

Once people have access to potable water, a better class of shelter, as many calories as they want and all the gadgets they might desire, their attention turns to how to build their wealth and how to live long enough to enjoy it. At this point, demand for banking, asset management and healthcare kick in.

If we look back at the development of the USA's consumer class in the post-war era, the evolution of demand for consumer goods is readily observable as incomes rose. This process is being mirrored across emerging markets today as the more enlightened governments attempt to offer their populations a modern version of the American Dream.

As the global middle class becomes more urban and increasingly wealthy, trade between regions is multiplying at a prodigious rate. Whereas once the rest of the world depended on North America and Western Europe for demand growth, the evolution of literally billions of new consumers over the coming decades is likely to see a truly global trade network develop where intra emerging market trade becomes a much more potent force. Over time this should decrease the reliance of asset markets in Asia, Latin America, the Middle East and Africa on Wall Street. In tandem, following a decade of economic malaise, the potential for the USA, Europe and Japan to get back on a sustainable growth footing is dependent on improving governance and is more likely than not in the next 15 years. A period of synchronised global economic expansion is a real possibility.

CHAPTER 25:

THE AUTONOMIES

A COMPARATIVELY SMALL NUMBER of companies have outgrown their respective domestic markets to become truly multinational participants in the global economy. These companies will be less unduly influenced by the travails experienced by their respective domestic markets because their revenue is more diversified. Companies with a global reach, that dominate their respective niches, have brand recognition, strong cash flows, reliable dividends and leverage to the growth of the global consumer are capable of profiting even when their domestic market might be in difficulty.

David Fuller christened such large multinationals "*mobile principalities*" or "*Autonomies*" because they are independent, powerful, mobile "*mini countries*" that focus where the best potential for profit exists. What country they consolidate earnings in is less important than the source of their income. They should therefore prosper as long as the global economy is expanding. Following the credit crisis of 2008 many such companies demonstrated considerable resilience despite uncertainty in many areas of the global economy. The majority are leveraged to the growth of the global consumer, where they have established brands and possess the capital necessary to expand aggressively in the world's major population centres.

These companies embody the adage: you don't buy countries, you buy companies.

From an investment perspective, and in the context of our macro behavioural analysis, why are the Autonomies so special?

They possess a truly inspiring story – they are supplying the goods and services facilitating an improving standard of living for hundreds of millions, if not billions, of people. They are the financial representation of the greatest urbanisation in history, technology's golden age and the beneficiaries of the boom in unconventional oil and gas production.

- Autonomies are highly exposed to the growth of the global consumer.
- Autonomies share a high degree of commonality in their share performance.
- A number have long records of maintaining and increasing their dividends.
- They offer some of the most consistent trends.

As of 2013 Wall Street is in the latter stages of a more than decade-long process of valuation contraction, but many of the Autonomies have already broken upwards to new all-time highs, represent leadership and are establishing *secular bull markets*.

One could have a lengthy conversation about what does and does not qualify as an Autonomy so I have compiled a list of the most attractive candidates. I consider these a menu from which we might choose, provided they continue to exhibit consistent uptrends.

RESTAURANTS: MCDONALD'S AND YUM BRANDS

Fast food can be considered a consumer staple. Those who frequent such establishments tend to be loyal customers. Companies such as McDonald's and Yum Brands (KFC, Pizza Hut and Taco Bell) have strong cash flows. Both exhibit impressive records of increasing dividends. McDonald's is an S&P500 Dividend Aristocrat, which means it has increased its dividend every year for at least the last 25 years.

In Asia, going to McDonald's, KFC or Pizza Hut is not about the speed of service but about the experience and what it says about your financial position. These are not cheap restaurants compared to local fare. In fact, by local comparisons, these restaurants are at the upper end of the cost bracket. People eat there because they want to foster an image of wealth and sophistication. KFC, in particular, has tailored its menu to Chinese tastes and is somewhere families go for a treat or where a boy takes a girl to impress her.

Yum Brands' (YUM on NYSE) Chinese revenues overtook those of its US operations in 2012.

Yum Brands 1998–2013

277

McDonald's (MCD on NYSE) derived 68% of revenue from outside the USA in 2012 with Europe being its largest market followed by North America and Asia.

McDonalds 1992–2013

ALCOHOLIC BEVERAGES: DIAGEO, SABMILLER, RÉMY COINTREAU, ANHEUSER-BUSCH INBEV, HEINEKEN

Across Asia and Latin America people have more money for socialising, and alcohol plays an important part in many occasions, not least business meetings.

Diageo has a primary listing in the UK (DGE on LSE) and an active secondary listing in the USA (DEO on NYSE). It is also an S&P Europe 350 Dividend Aristocrat, which means it has increased its dividend every year for at least the last ten years. Diageo is globally diversified and is represented by brands such as Guinness, Baileys, Smirnoff, Captain Morgan, Johnnie Walker and Smirnoff among others.

Diageo 1992–2013

Anglo-South African brewer *SABMiller* (SAB on LSE and JSE) is another globally diversified brewer with a solid record of raising its dividend. Its brands include Amstel, Carling and Löwenbräu.

SABMiller 2002–2013

France-listed *Rémy Cointreau* (RCO on Euronext) is one of the only, if not the only, European or American alcoholic beverage company where Asia Pacific is both its largest and fastest-growing market. (38% in 2012 versus 33.75% in 2011.) The company's best-known brands include Rémy Martin, Cointreau and a number of cognacs.

Rémy Cointreau 1992–2013

ANHEUSER-BUSCH INBEV

Belgian and US-listed Anheuser-Busch InBev (ABI on Euronext and BUD on NYSE) is the world's largest brewer, dominating the US market with Budweiser. It is also represented internationally by brands such as Bass, Becks, Hoegaarden and Stella Artois.

Anheuser-Busch InBev 2001–2013

The company also dominates the Latin American market through its separately listed subsidiary *Companhia de Bebidas das Americas* (ABV on NYSE or AMBV4 on BM&F). The company's main brands are Antartica, Brahma and Skol. It is also the sole distributor of Pepsi in Brazil.

Ambev (NYSE) 1997–2013

Mexico-listed *Grupo Modelo* (BMV in Mexico) produces Corona beers and is the exclusive importer and distributor of Anheuser-Busch in Mexico. The company was the subject of an acquisition attempt by its parent in 2012/13.

By acquiring Singapore's Asia Pacific Breweries (Tiger beer), *Heineken* (HEIA on Euronext) clearly signalled its global aspirations, setting its sights on Asia.

Heineken (Euronext) 1992–1993

NON-ALCOHOLIC BEVERAGES: STARBUCKS, COCA-COLA, PEPSI

During China's Cultural Revolution coffee was considered a bourgeois beverage so people were disinclined to drink it. That attitude is changing rapidly and consumption is increasing. US-listed *Starbucks* (SBUX on Nasdaq) might be famous for good but expensive coffee in the West but it is so much more than that in the East. Free wi-fi access in Asia is also an important attraction. This is something McDonald's also offers. Where better to demonstrate how cosmopolitan one is than at Starbucks, where people vie to be seen with the latest technological gadget?

Starbucks 1992–2013

US listed *Coca-Cola* (KO on NYSE) is an S&P500 Dividend Aristocrat and epitomises the idea of a multinational company. There is practically nowhere on earth where the Coca-Cola brand is not recognised and this is the company's greatest strength. North America is still its largest division but its internally defined 'Pacific' region represents one of its fastest-growing.

Coca-Cola 1992–2013

US listed *PepsiCo* (PEP on NYSE) might be considered a beverages company but generated almost as much revenue from snack foods as drinks in the USA in 2012. Its All Other Countries category, which it defines as the world excluding the USA, Mexico, Canada and the UK, is its fastest-growing area.

Pepsi 1992–2013

PROCESSED FOODS AND SNACKS: NESTLÉ, MONDELEZ INTERNATIONAL, UNILEVER, ARCHER DANIELS MIDLAND, DANONE

Per capita calorie consumption remains on a secular upward trajectory. From an investment perspective, the most important factor is not that the global population is expanding but the ability to pay for more food is also improving. Asia's rapid economic growth, coupled with mass migration to urban areas, is helping boost incomes and is fuelling demand for food. This is a massively diverse sector but a comparatively small number of companies are ideally placed to benefit.

Nestlé (NESN on SIX, NESTS on Euronext and NSRGY on the USA's OTC Pink) is an S&P Europe 350 Dividend Aristocrat. Its business units include coffee, chocolate, milk, infant nutrition and water. The company has more than 200 brands in total. It is globally diversified and its Asian revenue overtook that of Europe in 2011. It is also one of a group of multinationals with majority owned subsidiaries listed in Asian and African countries.

Nestlé 1992–2013

Mondelez International (Kraft's international businesses, MDLZ on Nasdaq), through 143 brands, concentrates on candy, snacks, beverages, cheese and other processed foods. Its Europe and 'Other Business' units are its fastest-growing.

Mondelez International 2002–2013

285

UK and Netherlands-listed *Unilever* (ULVR on LSE, UNA on Euronext, UL on NYSE) derives more revenue from Asia and Africa than any other unit of its business. The company's revenue is split almost equally between foods and home and personal care, making it ideally placed to benefit from both the improving ability to afford higher calorie foods as well as the rising standard of living that goes with such progression. While headquartered in Europe, Unilever has individually listed, majority-owned subsidiaries in a large number of Asian and African countries.

Unilever (ULVR) 1992–2013

US-listed *Archer Daniels Midland's* (ADM on NYSE) revenues are split almost 50/50 between the USA and international. The company is a global leader in food production and commodity trading. Through its acquisition of Australia's GrainCorp in 2013 it has set its sights on further Asian expansion.

Archer Daniels Midland 1992–2013

Danone is listed in France (BN on Euronext and DANOY on the USA's OTCQX) and is a global leader in dairy products, baby food, bottled water and clinical nutrition. The company derives almost as much revenue from the rest of the world as it does from Europe.

Danone (BN) 1992–2013

INGREDIENTS: INTERNATIONAL FLAVORS & FRAGRANCES, INGREDION, KERRY GROUP, MCCORMICK

US listed *International Flavor & Fragrances* (IFF on NYSE) is globally diversified, earning more than 75% of its revenues outside the USA in 2012. The company creates, manufactures, and supplies flavours and fragrances for the food, beverage, personal care and household products industries.

International Flavors & Fragrances 1992–2013

US-listed Corn Products International was renamed *Ingredion* (INGR on NYSE) in 2012. The company processes corn, tapioca, wheat, potatoes and other raw materials into ingredients for the food, beverage, brewing and pharmaceutical industries as well as numerous industrial sectors. The company derived 44% of revenues from South America, Asia/Africa and EMEA in 2012.

Ingredion 1992–2013

Kerry Group's primary listings are in Ireland and the UK (KYG on ISE and LSE & KRYAY on the USA's OTCBB). It is an S&P Europe 350 Dividend Aristocrat. The company processes and distributes consumer foods and food ingredients internationally. It specialises in dairy products and food ingredients, deriving 49% of revenues from North America and Asia Pacific in 2012.

Kerry Group (ISE) 1992–2013

US-listed *McCormick* (MKC on NYSE) manufactures spices, herbs, and flavourings for the retail, commercial and industrial markets. The company derived 42% of revenue from outside the USA in 2012.

McCormick (NYSE) 1992–2013

NUTRITION AND SUPPLEMENTS: DSM NV, MEAD JOHNSON NUTRITION, HERBALIFE

The lack of a widespread network of general practitioners in many developing countries has created an environment where a large number of people self-medicate. Supplements, teas and nutrition are part of the culture in many countries. Companies with a reputation for quality and integrity are benefitting as disposable incomes increase. Additionally, as life expectancy improves in much of the developed world demand for supplements that can enhance quality of life also represents a growth avenue for the sector.

Dutch listed *DSM NV's* (DSM on Euronext) nutritional products division is one of the world's largest suppliers of nutritional ingredients, supplying vitamins and other chemicals to the feed, food, pharmaceutical and personal care industries. The company also has operations devoted to production of pharmaceuticals, resins, polymers and plastics.

DSM NV 1992–2013

US listed *Mead Johnson Nutrition* (MJN on NYSE) concentrates on infant nutrition and supplements for expectant mothers. The company's Chinese revenues overtook those from the USA in 2011, while its Rest of the World designation is its largest.

Mead Johnson Nutrition 1992–2013

US-listed *Herbalife* (HLF on NYSE) concentrates on weight-management and targeted nutritional supplements. Asia Pacific represents its largest and one of its fastest growing segments. China also represents a dynamic growth market for the company.

Herbalife 2005–2013

Herbalife Ltd (HLF) 37.45 -0.33   www.fullermoney.com   28 Mar 2013

COSMETICS AND TOILETRIES: PROCTER & GAMBLE, COLGATE PALMOLIVE, KIMBERLY-CLARK, RECKITT BENCKISER, UNI-CHARM, ESTÉE LAUDER, L'ORÉAL, NU SKIN ENTERPRISES

When people move from earning $1 a day to $2 they experience a massive increase in relative spending potential. Some of the first items people choose to spend their extra cash on are soap, shampoo, deodorant, toilet paper, sanitary napkins and other toiletries many in the West simply take for granted.

As incomes improve, people move steadily higher on the disposable income ladder. As per capita GDP rises, demand growth for bigger ticket items begins to kick in. Perfume, various forms of makeup and diapers for children become not only desirable but essential items for middle class consumers.

US-listed *Procter & Gamble* (PG on NYSE) is an S&P500 Dividend Aristocrat and reports via three different units. Household care represented 52% of revenue, beauty and grooming 34% and health and well-being 14% in 2012. North America is still the company's largest market but its other global business units are growing faster. The company manufactures laundry, cleaning, paper, beauty care, food, beverage and healthcare products. As such it is one of only a few truly diversified globally oriented businesses.

Procter & Gamble 1992–2013

US-listed *Colgate Palmolive* (CL on NYSE) is an S&P500 Dividend Aristocrat and its products include toothpaste, toothbrushes, shampoo, deodorants, soaps, dishwashing liquid, laundry products and pet nutrition. Latin America is its largest market and Greater Asia/Africa is its fastest-growing.

Colgate Palmolive 1992–2013

US-listed *Kimberly-Clark* (KMB on NYSE) is an S&P500 Dividend Aristocrat and describes itself as a global health and hygiene company. Its products include diapers, tissues, paper towels, incontinence products and sanitary napkins. North America is the company's largest market but Asia, Latin America and 'Other' represent its fastest-growing.

Kimberly-Clark 1992–2013

UK-listed *Reckitt Benckiser* (RB/ on LSE) is an S&P Europe 350 Dividend Aristocrat. The company manufactures and distributes a range of household goods, toiletries, pharmaceuticals, condoms and food products. Its European and US revenues accounted for 48.9% of the total in 2012.

Reckitt Benckiser 1992–2013

Japan listed, *Uni-Charm* (8113 on TSE) is an S&P Pan Asia Dividend Aristocrat. The company is well represented in Asia and is a leading manufacturer of diapers for both adults and children. It also has a range of female hygiene products.

Uni-Charm 1992–2013

Estée Lauder (EL on NYSE) manufactures skin care, makeup, fragrance and hair products. EMEA and Asia Pacific represented its fastest-growing markets in 2012, accounting for 37% and 20.7% of revenues respectively.

Estée Lauder 1996–2013

L'Oréal (OR on Euronext) is listed in France and is the world's largest cosmetics and beauty company. It is globally diversified and active in the hair care and colour, skin care, sun protection, makeup and perfumes sectors. The company is also involved in the dermatological, tissue-engineering and pharmaceutical fields and is a major nanotechnology patent-holder in the United States.

L'Oréal 1992–2013

US-listed *Nu Skin Enterprises (NUS on NYSE)* concentrates on anti-aging skin treatments and splits out its Asian revenue into North Asia, South Asia/Pacific and Greater China. North America and Europe accounted for 21.8% of revenue in 2012.

Nu Skin Enterprises 1997–2013

LUXURY BRANDS: LVMH, CHRISTIAN DIOR, COMPAGNIE FINANCIÈRE RICHEMONT, TIFFANY, SWATCH

The term *nouveau riche* or 'new money' was developed to describe the first wave of newly wealthy upper class people during the Industrial Revolution. These were primarily industrialists, who were not part of the established hierarchy, but progressed through their own effort and built fortunes within their own lifetimes. They often lacked the education and social sensitivity of the established elite and rather than admit a sense of insecurity they attempted to buy respect. Those who envied their wealth or felt threatened by a challenge to their own prestige described them as vulgar and uncouth. However, over generations, the new rich became unrecognisable from 'old wealth' as their offspring were educated at the best institutions and affected an air of having been born to money.

Every major bull market creates another cohort of newly wealthy individuals who define themselves by their ambition. They break down previously impregnable social barriers. They do not respect the status quo and set out to carve a place for themselves in the world. Among such people there is often a sense of insecurity because not only do they want to possess wealth but they often want to fit in with those who move in such circles. The prevailing sentiment is: what good is wealth if people do not know you are wealthy?

Outward signs of wealth are therefore prized. They represent the totems of success. Phones, bags, shoes, clothes, jewellery, gold, cars, houses, boats and planes are all viewed as progressively more important reflections of success.

LVMH (MC on Euronext) is listed in France and famous for its champagne, cognac, perfumes, cosmetics, luggage, watches and jewellery. It is the largest luxury goods group in the world with globally diversified revenues. 2009 was the first year its Asia ex-Japan revenue exceeded that of the USA.

LVMH 1992–2013

Christian Dior is also listed in France (CDI on Euronext) and its cross-shareholding with LVMH confers it with more than 50% of the voting rights in LVMH. Christian Dior's Asian revenues became its largest as early as 2009 led by fashion, leather goods and selective retailing. Wine and spirits also represent a thriving business unit.

Christian Dior 1992–2013

Compagnie Financière Richemont is listed in Switzerland (CFR on SIX and JSE) and produces jewellery, watches and pens. Some of its brands include Cartier, IWC International Watch, Baume & Mercier, LeBlanc and Piaget. The group's Asian revenues became its largest in 2010 and remained on a growth trajectory at the time of writing.

Compagnie Financière Richemont (SIX) 1992–2013

US listed *Tiffany's* (TIF on NYSE) largest business unit is its gold and silver jewellery segment followed by its engagement ring and wedding band businesses. North America remains its largest market but revenues were quite variable between 2008 and 2011. Its Asian operations on the other hand reflected a solid growth trajectory and accounted for 37.8% of revenue in 2012.

Tiffany 1992–2013

Perhaps more famous for its retail offering, *Swatch* (UHR and UHRN on VTX) is also the world's largest manufacturer of luxury watches. The company derived more revenue from Asia in 2010 than from any other unit in the past decade.

Swatch (UHR) 1994–2013

ENTERTAINMENT AND TOYS: 21ST CENTURY FOX, DISNEY, MATTEL, HASBRO, ACTIVISION BLIZZARD

USA and Australia-listed 21st Century Fox (FOX on Nasdaq and NWS on ASX) is involved in cable network programming, movies, television and satellite television. The company generated almost as much revenue from Europe and Australasia as from the USA and Canada in 2012.

21st Century Fox Inc (1995–2013)

US-listed *Disney* (DIS on NYSE) is perhaps the best-known entertainment brand in the world and occupies a dominant position in the USA's parks and resorts sector. Media and networks represent its fastest-growing segments.

Disney 1992–2013

US-listed *Mattel* (MAT on NYSE) is the largest producer of toys and conventional games in the world and generated approximately half its revenue from outside the USA in 2012.

Mattel 1992–2013

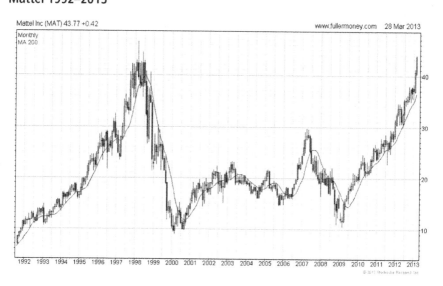

US-listed *Hasbro* (HAS on NYSE) is the second-largest producer of toys and conventional games in the world and its revenues have a similar geographical split to Mattel's.

Hasbro 1992–2013

US-listed *Activision Blizzard* (ATVI on Nasdaq) is majority owned by French-listed Vivendi and was the world's largest video game producer by market cap in 2013. Its revenues are evenly split between the USA and Europe and its Asia revenues almost doubled in the three years to 2012, albeit from a low base.

Activision Blizzard 1994–2013

RETAIL AND SUPERMARKETS: WAL-MART, TESCO, DAIRY FARM INTERNATIONAL HOLDINGS, CASINO GUICHARD-PERRACHON SA

One-stop-shopping is a novel concept to the majority of newly minted middle class people in Asia. Less free time and a desire to maximise what leisure time people have makes the allure of hypermarkets irresistible. Supermarkets offer choice, affordability and convenience and the sector has a prosperous future in high-growth economies.

US listed *Wal-Mart* (WMT on NYSE) is an S&P500 Dividend Aristocrat. The company has a dominant position in the USA's retail market and is increasingly dependent on its international division for growth. Its stores are widely evident in China's major cities and it has a toehold in India. The company has an additional listing in Mexico.

Wal-Mart 1992–2013

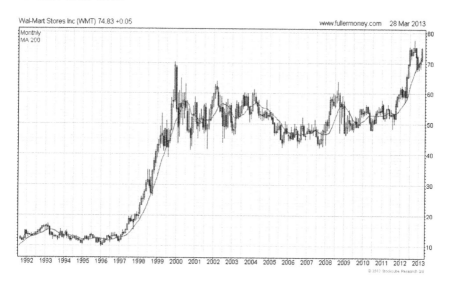

UK-listed *Tesco* is the dominant retailer in the UK (TSCO on LSE) and is an S&P Europe 350 Dividend aristocrat. The company's fastest-growing regions are in Asia, where it is expanding in South Korea, Thailand, mainland China, Malaysia and India.

Tesco 1992–2013

Amazon (AMZN on Nasdaq) is the world's largest online retailer and one of the most recognisable e-commerce companies. It is also active in the data warehousing sector. The company generated 43% of revenue from outside the US in 2012.

Amazon 1997–2013

Singapore-listed *Dairy Farm International Holdings* (DFI on SGX, DFIB on LSE) is a separately listed subsidiary of Jardine Matheson. It operates supermarkets, drugstores and convenience stories in Hong Kong, Taiwan, China, Singapore, Malaysia, Indonesia and India.

Dairy Farm International Holdings (SGX) 1992–2013

Casino Guichard-Perrachon SA is listed in France (CO on Euronext) and its international revenues almost equalled those of its domestic market in 2012. South America represents its largest overseas market but Asia is also on an impressive growth trajectory.

Casino Guichard-Perrachon SA 1992–2013

FOOTWEAR AND SPORTSWEAR: NIKE, ADIDAS

Sport becomes a priority for people when they have free time, a hallmark of people who have moved out of subsistence living and into the middle classes. The sedentary lifestyles so often associated with the middle classes also ensures that sport and physical activity become more important from a health and wellbeing perspective as incomes improve.

Nike (NKE on NYSE) is by far the largest sports goods company in the world. The USA, greater China and emerging markets represent its three fastest-growth markets.

Nike 1992–2013

Adidas (ADS on DB) is the second-largest sporting goods manufacturer in the world, but it is globally diversified and all its units expanded in 2012.

Adidas 1996–2013

CLOTHING: INDITEX, HENNES & MAURITZ, SHENZHOU INTERNATIONAL

As disposable income increases, shopping turns from a necessity into a pastime and the size of one's wardrobe increases commensurately. Clothing is one of the key sectors to benefit from an increase in demand for a 'modern look' to demonstrate how cosmopolitan someone is.

Inditex (ITX on BMAD) is listed in Spain and is perhaps best known for its Zara brand which accounts for two thirds of revenues. The company's rest of the world category – which excludes Spain, the EU and OECD – was its fastest growing in 2012, representing 22.5% of revenues.

Inditex 2002–2013

Hennes & Mauritz (H&M) is listed in Sweden (HMB on OMX). The company's rest of the world category – which excludes the eurozone and nordic countries – is its fastest growing. Its US, UK and Chinese revenues are its largest growth markets in that category.

Hennes & Mauritz 1992–2013

Shenzhou International is listed in Hong Kong (2313 on HKSE) and is one of China's largest manufacturers and processors of textiles. The company produces, dyes, finishes, prints, embroiders, cuts, and sews various kinds of fabric. 79% of revenues are sourced outside China, while Japan is its largest market accounting for a 35% share.

Shenzhou International 2008–2013

HEALTHCARE: JOHNSON & JOHNSON, BRISTOL-MYERS SQUIBB, NOVO NORDISK, BAYER, BIOGEN, PFIZER, ALLERGAN, NOVARTIS

The healthcare sector is remarkably wide-ranging, spanning everything from cutting-edge technology to end-of-life residential care. Healthcare, along with energy and technology, represents an arena where real value can be created from nothing. The ability of companies in this sector to develop life-enhancing and life-prolonging treatments, which were previously unimaginable and that improve aggregate productivity and quality of life, is highly attractive from an investor's perspective.

Growth in the healthcare sector can be broken down into those companies developing the next big thing and those accessing the next big consumer market. Occasionally both these traits are evident in the same company. The expansion of the global middle class represents a phenomenal growth opportunity for healthcare companies. Once consumers no longer have to worry about where the next meal is coming from, they begin to think about how to enjoy life. Healthcare becomes an increasingly important component of one's routine.

What follows can by no means be considered an exhaustive list considering the global prowess of pharmaceutical companies.

US-listed *Johnson & Johnson* (JNJ on NYSE) is an S&P500 Dividend Aristocrat specialising in medical devices and diagnostics, pharmaceuticals and consumer products. While its USA and European revenues slid between 2008 and 2010, its Asia-Pacific, Africa and Latin America segments allowed it to continue to grow on aggregate.

Johnson & Johnson 1992–2013

Bristol-Myers Squibb (BMY on NYSE) describes itself as a biopharmaceutical company and provides therapies that address cancer, heart disease, HIV/AIDS, diabetes, rheumatoid arthritis, hepatitis, organ transplant rejection as well as nutritional supplements.

Bristol-Myers Squibb 1992–2013

Novo Nordisk is listed in Denmark (NOVOB on OMX and NVO on NYSE). The company represents the most accessible pure-play on the global diabetes epidemic. Rising per capita calorie consumption has led to a massive jump in the number of people developing diabetes, estimated at approximately 200 million in both India and China respectively. Rising incomes mean that people are now also in a better position to pay for treatments with fewer unpleasant side effects. While almost all of the company's units grew in 2012, the USA represented the fastest expansion.

Novo Nordisk (OMX) 1992–2013

Germany-listed *Bayer* (BAYN on DB) is primarily a pharmaceuticals company with interests in fields ranging from diabetes to aspirin. It also has operations in crop science and animal care. The company is internationally diversified and all of its operations expanded in 2012.

Bayer 1992–2013

US-listed *Biogen* (BIIB on Nasdaq) commercialises therapies focusing on neurology, oncology and immunology. The USA remains its dominant market but all of its units expanded in 2012.

Biogen 1992–2013

US-listed *Pfizer* (PFE on NYSE) is one of the largest drug companies in the world. The company describes itself as a research-based, global pharmaceutical company that discovers, develops, manufactures, and markets medicines for humans and animals. While the USA is still its largest market, its emerging markets designation almost equalled its European revenues in 2012.

Pfizer 1992–2013

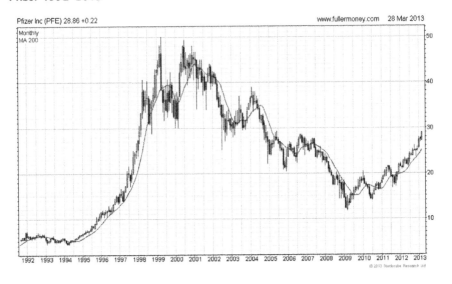

US-listed *Allergan* (AGN on NYSE), famous for its Botox anti-wrinkle product range, grew across all its geographic regions in 2012, with the USA accounting for 59%.

The USA is *Novartis'* (NOVN on SIX and NVS on NYSE) largest individual market, with 32.8% of revenue in 2012. Its rest of the world designation, which excludes much of Europe, accounted for 45%. The company focuses on pharmaceuticals but also has generics, consumer healthcare and vaccine businesses.

Novartis (SIX) 1992–2013

TOBACCO: PHILIP MORRIS, BRITISH AMERICAN TOBACCO

US-listed *Philip Morris International* (PM on NYSE) was spun off from Altria in 2008 and represents its parent's ex-USA revenues. The company holds more than a 15% share of global tobacco sales with Europe and Asia representing its largest markets on 35% and 23% of revenues respectively in 2012.

Philip Morris International 2009–2013

British American Tobacco (BATS on LSE, BTI on JSE and NYSE) is internationally diversified and Asia Pacific is its largest market with 27.7% and East Europe, Middle East and Africa represents 26.8%. It also holds a 30% share in India's largest company by market cap: ITC.

British American Tobacco 1999–2013

TECHNOLOGY: APPLE, GOOGLE, IBM, LENOVO, INTEL, ARM HOLDINGS, MICROCHIP TECHNOLOGIES, LAM RESEARCH, HEWLETT-PACKARD, SAMSUNG, SONY, TAIWAN SEMICONDUCTOR, MEDIATEK

In common with healthcare, technology-focused companies offer the promise of changing our lives for the better and delivering productivity efficiencies that revolutionise business practices. The sector went through a phenomenal bubble during the 1990s and most companies that survived the bust spent much of the next decade in deep hibernation, concentrating more on survival than growth. A small number took out their 1999/2000 peaks early and represent the cutting edge of commercial technological development. A second wave broke out of almost decade-long bases in 2009 and 2010.

US-listed *Apple* (AAPL on Nasdaq) has made music stores obsolete and is quickly doing the same to game stores. Design elegance and ease of use have always been its hallmarks. From its peak in 2012, the competing forces of dealing with Steve Jobs' demise and questions about the company's product development pipeline reined in animal spirits. At the same time, the announcement of a competitive dividend and its international revenue spread ensures that it remains a company of interest to a wide number of investors.

Apple 1992–2013

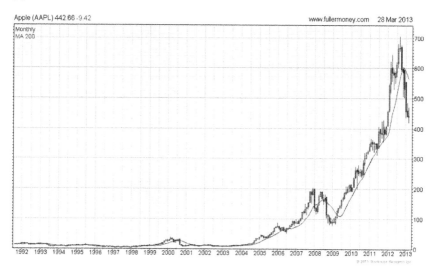

US-listed *Google* (GOOG on Nasdaq) bypassed the tech bubble, only listing in 2004. It is well known for its search engine and advertising, and has successfully branched out into operating systems for mobile phones and tablets. The company appears to be following a similar strategy to Microsoft in the 1990s by competing with Apple to develop an operating system – but then making it available to any company who wants it installed on their devices, rather than confining it to their own. It is now also committing a significant proportion of revenues to research and development of a range of unrelated products. The US accounted for 46% of the company's revenues in 2012.

Google 2005–2013

US-listed *IBM* (IBM on NYSE) sold its way out of the personal computer business in 2005 to concentrate on business solutions. As well as being the world's second-largest software company, IBM is also dominant in commercial hardware. The company is a leader in the cloud computing sector. Asia represented its fastest-growing market in 2012, while the US accounted for 34.7% of revenues.

IBM 1992–2013

Hong Kong-listed *Lenovo* (992 on HKSE) took over IBM's personal computer business in 2005 and is now one of the largest manufacturers in the sector.

Lenovo 1995–2013

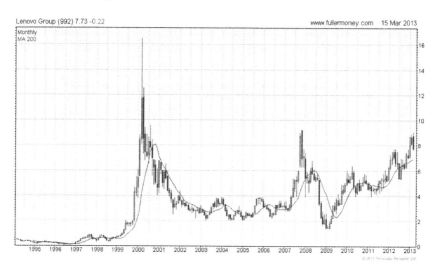

US-listed *Intel* (INTC on Nasdaq) is a global leader in microchip manufacturing. Asia Pacific is by far the largest contributor to the company's gross revenue and the company has been steadily growing its dividend since 2003.

Intel 1992–2013

UK-listed *ARM Holdings* (ARM on LSE) has been enormously successful with its chip designs, which have most notably been used for Apple's range of handheld devices. In the third quarter of 2012 the company generated more revenue from items other than mobile phones for the first time. Embedded processing is its fastest growing market. The company is internationally diversified and grew across all of its segments and geographies in 2012.

ARM Holdings 1998–2013

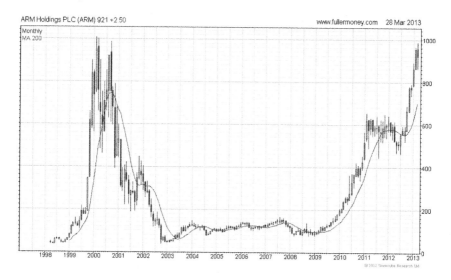

US-listed *Microchip Technology* (MCHP on Nasdaq) sold its ten-billionth microcontroller in September 2011. Asia represents both the company's largest and fastest-growing market.

Microchip Technology 1994–2013

US-listed *Lam Research* (LCRX on Nasdaq) develops, manufactures, sells and services the equipment required to manufacture chips and semiconductors. Asia represents the bulk of the company's revenue-generation.

Lam Research 1992–2013

US-listed *Hewlett-Packard* (HPQ on NYSE) has been the world's largest manufacturer of PCs since 2007 and is globally diversified in terms of its revenues.

Hewlett-Packard 1992–2013

South Korea and UK-listed *Samsung* (005939 on KRX and SMSD on LSE) manufactures a wide range of consumer and industrial electronic equipment and products such as semiconductors, personal computers, monitors, televisions and mobile phones. China represented the company's largest market from as early as 2007, but North America has been its fastest-growing market over the same period.

Samsung Electronics 1992–2013

Sony (6756 on TSE and SNE on NYSE) has a globally recognisable suite of brands but suffered more than most from the strength of the yen in the decade to 2012. It should benefit from an improving competitive edge as the yen weakens and from internal rationalisation. The company is involved in mobile products, communications technology, home entertainment and audio, motion pictures, games and music.

Sony 1992–2013

Taiwan Semiconductor (2330 on TWSE) is the world's largest semiconductor foundry and also one of the lowest-cost producers of chips. Some of its largest customers by value include Applied Materials, ASML Holdings, KLA-Tencor, Advanced Semiconductor and Hitachi.

Taiwan Semiconductor 1995–2013

MediaTek (2454 on TWSE) is a leading fabless manufacturer of semiconductors, particularly for the wireless communications sector. Its largest customers include TSMC, Google and Qualcomm.

MediaTek 2002–2013

SOFTWARE: MICROSOFT, ORACLE, SAP, TATA CONSULTANCY

Nothing encapsulates the digital age more than the role of software in industry, commerce and everyday life. From an investment perspective, software takes time to build, but is infinitely scalable – therefore once a product is accepted by customers, margins tend to be wider than in other sectors. For example, Microsoft's margins are typically in the 30% range compared with 20% for McDonald's or 2.5% for a company such as General Motors.

US-listed *Microsoft* (MSFT on Nasdaq) has long had the world's dominant operating system, as well as a number of additional products. It moved into the PC hardware space for the first time in 2012, with the launch of its tablet computer the Surface (before that it had produced videogame hardware and computer peripherals). The company's revenues are evenly split between the USA and the rest of the world.

Microsoft 1997–2013

US-listed *Oracle* (ORCL on Nasdaq) derived 42% of revenues from the USA in 2012, while 32% was sourced from its 'Other Foreign Countries' category, which excludes the UK, Japan, Germany, Canada, Australia and France.

Oracle 1992–2013

SAP became Germany's (SAP on DB) largest company by market cap in 2013, illustrating the dominance of its enterprise software and database management products. The company derives at least 40% of its revenue from outside Europe.

SAP 1992–2013

Tata Consultancy (TCS on BSE) is India's largest IT company and derived more than 90% of revenue from outside its domestic market in 2012. The company is primarily involved in IT solutions and services, business process outsourcing and infrastructure services.

Tata Consultancy 2005–2013

Tata Consultancy Services (TCS) 1473.8 +19.75   www.fullermoney.com   17 May 2013

ADVERTISING: WPP, PUBLICIS, OMNICOM

In July 2013 the second and third largest advertising companies announced a friendly merger which allow the combined company to become the largest global advertiser. Prior to the merger, France-listed *Publicis* (PUB on Euronext) was the second-largest advertising company in the world, with a similar international spread of revenue to *WPP* as well as strong commonality in the chart pattern. *Omnicom* (OMC on NYSE) was the largest advertising and public relations company with a primary US listing. Its revenues were split almost evenly between the Americas and the rest of the world. Its Asian unit overtook its EMEA unit in terms of revenue generation in 2011.

WPP 1992–2013

Publicis 1992–2013

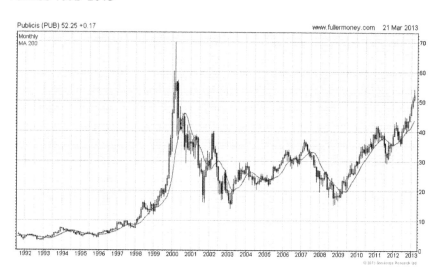

Omnicom 1992–2013

BANKS: HSBC, STANDARD CHARTERED, BARCLAYS, CITIGROUP, GOLDMAN SACHS, BBVA

As liquidity providers, banks are an essential component of any economy and often represent significant weightings in national indices, which adds to their importance from the perspective of a global investor. In the decade from 2000, many financial sector companies in the USA and Europe were subject to deteriorating standards of corporate governance, which saw a number declare bankruptcy during the credit crisis. A significant number of additional institutions would have disappeared were it not for the concerted efforts of global central bankers to save them. The sector has been ravaged by scandal, avarice, irresponsibility and criminal intent for much of the 2000s and investors remained ambivalent towards the sector at the time of writing. However, despite their poor record on the governance front, banks are a vital component of the global economy and some have truly global businesses. From an investment perspective, evidence of improving standards of governance, not least in the regulatory arena, would be desirable before initiating long positions.

UK-listed *HSBC* (HSBA on LSE) is one of the world's largest banks and almost certainly its most globally diversified. The company's revenues are split almost equally between Europe, North America, Asia Pacific, Hong Kong and Latin America.

HSBC (LSE) 1992–2013

Whereas *Standard Chartered* (STAN on LSE) has traditionally been considered a UK-listed Hong Kong centric bank, the rest of the world accounted for 40% of its revenues in 2012.

Standard Chartered 1992–2013

Barclays is another UK-listed bank with significant global operations. In 2012 more than 60% of its revenue was derived outside the UK. Much of its African and Middle East income is derived from its ABSA Group South African franchise.

Barclays 1992–2013

North America is still *Citigroup*'s (C on NYSE) largest market, but as of 2012 only accounted for 41% of revenues. The bank was one of the hardest hit following the credit crisis, but as it recovers represents significant potential for dividend growth.

Citigroup 1992–2013

US-listed *Goldman Sachs* (GS on NYSE) is one of the world's largest investment banks and over 40% of its revenue was generated outside the Americas in 2012.

Goldman Sachs 2000–2013

While Spain and Portugal probably represented the majority of *BBVA*'s (BBVA on BMAD and NYSE) losses in 2012, they only represent 27% of revenue, making it the most international of the eurozone banks.

BBVA (BMAD) 1992–2013

INSURANCE: AMERICAN INTERNATIONAL GROUP, CHUBB, AXA, PRUDENTIAL

One of the hallmarks of the middle class is an ability to hedge risks against life, health, fire, theft, property, unemployment, travel and credit. As well as being a highly profitable endeavour, insurance is a growth sector, since the millions of people who are moving into the disposable income bracket have a vested interest in ensuring that they stay there. Insurance lends certainty to one's financial position and therefore frees up savings for consumption.

American International Group (AIG on NYSE) would have disappeared in 2008 due to its reckless underwriting practices in the collateralised debt obligation markets, were it not for the intervention of the USA's Federal Reserve. It has since paid back its loans and remains one of the world's largest general, corporate, industrial and aircraft insurers. It is also involved in life insurance, financial planning and asset management. The company's international operations are spread over more than 130 countries and account for approximately a third of revenues. The below charts are in both arithmetic and log scale in order to depict the more relevant data subsequent to the 2008 crash.

AIG 1992–2013 (arithmetic scale)

AIG 1992–2013 (logarithmic scale)

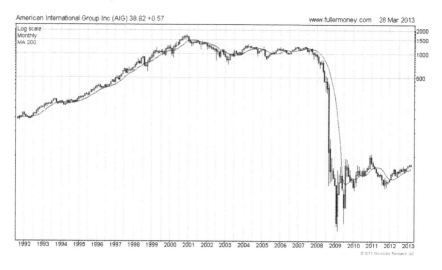

US-listed *Chubb* (CB on NYSE) is an S&P500 Dividend Aristocrat and is engaged in property and casualty as well as reinsurance. While the USA is its largest market, the company has operations in Europe, Canada, Australia, Hong Kong, Indonesia, Thailand, Argentina, Brazil, Chile, Colombia and Mexico. When combined, these account for approximately 25% of revenues.

Chubb 1992–2013

AXA (CS on Euronext) is listed in France and is one of the most globally oriented insurance companies in the world, with operations in North America, Europe and Asia. It is engaged in life, health and other forms of insurance, as well as asset management.

AXA 1992–2013

Asia represents 20% of *Prudential*'s (PRU on LSE) revenue, while the USA and UK are its largest markets. The company is engaged in pensions, annuities, savings and investment management and life assurance.

Prudential 1992–2013

CREDIT CARDS AND CREDIT SCORES: MASTERCARD, VISA, EXPERIAN

Consumerism moves hand in hand with urbanisation, as time is freed up for leisure and the pursuit of a higher standard of living. Convenience depends not only on access to a wide array of goods and services but quick access to credit in order to pay for them. Credit cards fill that role by facilitating instant gratification. Their fee structures, while usurious, are highly attractive from an investment perspective.

US listed *Mastercard* (MA on NYSE) derives almost twice as much revenue from its international business as it does from the USA.

Mastercard 2008–2013

US-listed *Visa*'s (V on NYSE) revenues are split almost equally between its US operations and the rest of the world, but the latter is growing faster.

Visa 2008–2013

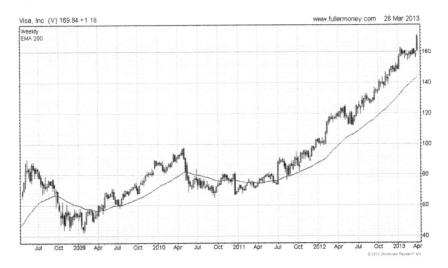

Debt represents an important constituent of the financial lives of an increasing proportion of the global population. Companies that help lenders ascertain just how creditworthy an individual is fill a valuable niche. Since there are a small number of such companies, they represent something of an oligarchy.

Experian is listed in the UK. Its revenues are split almost evenly between North America and the rest of the world.

Experian 2007–2013

AUTOMOBILES: BMW, VOLKSWAGEN, NISSAN, TOYOTA, KIA, GREAT WALL MOTORS

With the advent of a disposable income class in much of Asia and Latin America, the dream of car ownership has quickly become a reality for hundreds of millions of people. China overtook the USA as the world's largest car market in 2009. This has seen auto manufacturers tailor their product offering to a more global audience as they refocus on growth in the world's major population centres.

It is debatable whether Audi or BMW was the fastest-growing luxury car brand in Asia in 2012. *BMW* (BMW on DB) as an independent company is a more liquid share than Audi, which is a brand of Volkswagen, and its share price better reflects the company's growth potential. China represents BMW's third largest and fastest growing market behind the USA and Germany.

BMW 1992–2013

Volkswagen (VOW3 on DB) is one of the world's largest car brands. North America and Asia represent its fastest growth markets and accounted for 40% of revenue in 2012.

Volkswagen 1993–2013

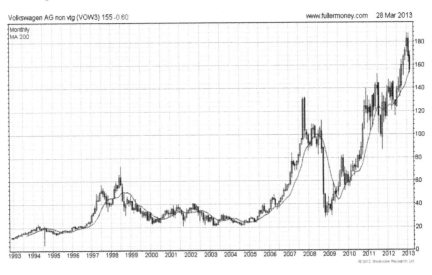

Nissan (7201 on TSE) is not the largest of Japan's automobile manufacturers but it is the most internationally diverse. Japan is its third largest market behind both North America and Asia, which accounted for 31% and 20% of revenues respectively in 2012.

Nissan 1992–2013

Japan-listed *Toyota* (7203 on TSE) is one of the world's largest auto manufacturers, as well as one of the most internationally diversified. Almost 70% of revenue was sourced outside Japan in 2012.

Toyota 1992–2013

More than 60% of *Kia*'s revenue is generated outside of its domestic South Korean market. Middle East/Africa, Europe and Latin America represented some of its fastest-growing markets in 2012. One of the company's greatest challenges in future will be how to maintain a competitive edge as the Korean won / Japanese yen exchange rate moves against it.

Kia Motors 1992–2013

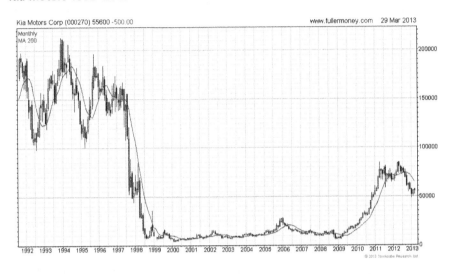

Great Wall Motors (2333 on HKSE) was in an exponential growth phase at the time of writing and was among the first of the Chinese automotive manufacturers to begin exports. Geely Automotive has a less impressive growth trajectory but also began to export in 2009.

Great Wall Motors 2004–2013

AIRPLANES: BOEING, EADS

Expanding trade links between emerging markets, as well as the prospect of synchronised global economic expansion in the decade between 2015 and 2025, are supportive of demand growth for planes. Additionally, the growth of the disposable income bracket suggests increased demand for foreign holidays and therefore more airline seats. The significant position such companies also occupy in the defence sector is also noteworthy, considering that arms exports represent major industries for the USA and Europe.

Commercial airplanes accounted for 60% of US-listed Boeing's (BA on NYSE) revenue in 2012, and more than 55% of its revenue was generated outside the USA in the same year.

Boeing 1992–2013

Commercial aircraft represented 65% of France-listed European Aeronautic Defence and Space's (EADS on Euronext) revenue in 2012, and 62% of that revenue was generated outside of Europe.

EADS 2001–2013

MACHINERY AND INDUSTRIALS: GENERAL ELECTRIC, ROLLS-ROYCE, UNITED TECHNOLOGIES, HONEYWELL, 3M, BERKSHIRE HATHAWAY, SIEMENS, EMERSON ELECTRIC, INTERTEK, ECOLAB, TYCO INTERNATIONAL, FANUC, ABB

The advent of embedded programming, coupled with the greatest urbanisation in history, has created both additional efficiencies and demand for industrial machinery.

US-listed *General Electric* (GE on NYSE) is one of the most diverse engineering and manufacturing companies globally and derived 53% of revenue from outside the USA in 2012. The company's two largest segments, Energy Infrastructure (33.8%) and GE Capital (31%) dominate the group's activities but it also has interests in aviation, healthcare, home and business solutions and transportation.

General Electric 1992–2013

UK-listed *Rolls-Royce* (RR/ on LSE) is a major power systems company. It is the second-largest producer of aircraft engines behind General Electric, as well as producing propulsion systems for the marine sector and turbines for power stations. The company's revenues are internationally diversified.

Rolls-Royce 1992–2013

US-listed *United Technologies* (UTX on NYSE) produces climate control systems, flight aircraft engines, elevators, escalators and fire and safety equipment. Its largest market is North America, accounting for 55% of revenues in 2012. Europe (20%) and Asia (15%) accounted for the majority of the remainder.

United Technologies 1992–2013

Honeywell (HON on NYSE) is listed in the US and provides aerospace products and services, control, sensing and security technologies, turbochargers, automotive products, specialty chemicals, electronic and advanced materials. In 2012, Europe and its other international businesses accounted for 41% of revenues.

Honeywell 1992–2013

US-listed *3M* (MMM on NYSE) is a highly diversified multinational conglomerate with interests in adhesives, abrasives, laminates, fire protection, dental products, electronic materials and circuits, medical products, car care products and optical films. The company's Asia Pacific revenues almost rival those of its US operations and they both expanded in 2012.

3M 1992–2013

Berkshire Hathaway (BRK on NYSE) is a difficult company to pigeonhole, not least because its operations are so diverse, ranging from insurance to manufacturing, haulage to consumer goods, distribution and food wholesale. Its acquisition of Heinz in conjunction with other investors in 2013 gives it a leading position in the processed foods sector and expands its international reach beyond what is a predominately US-related business.

Berkshire Hathaway 1992–2013

Germany-listed *Siemens* (SIE on DB) gave up the mobile phone business following the tech bust to refocus on its core engineering competencies. The company is synonymous with global engineering projects and Siemens India, a separately listed affiliate, is an S&P Pan Asia Dividend Aristocrat.

Siemens 1992–2013

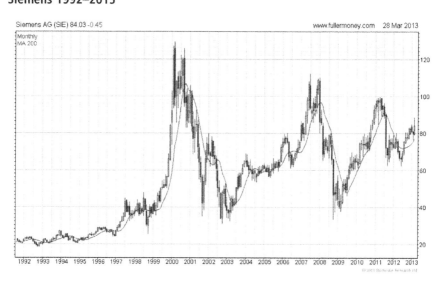

US-listed *Emerson Electric* (EMR on NYSE) is an S&P500 Dividend Aristocrat. The company's Asian revenues overtook Europe's to become its second largest in 2010 behind the USA. The company produces heavy industrial solutions for power plants and environmental concerns.

Emerson Electric 1992–2013

UK-listed *Intertek* (ITRK on LSE) is a global leader in quality control. All of its business units grew in 2012 and its largest markets are Asia, the Americas and EMEA respectively.

Intertek Group 2003–2013

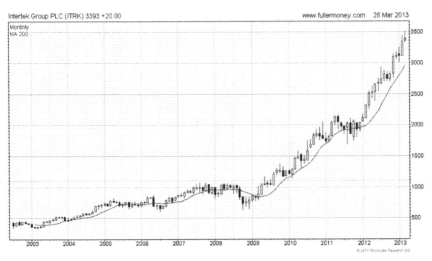

US-listed *Ecolab* (ECL on NYSE) is a world leader in water, hygiene and energy solutions for the food, energy, healthcare, industrial and hospitality markets. Its revenues are internationally diverse.

Ecolab 1992–2013

Tyco International is an internationally diverse manufacturing corporation with interests in fire safety systems, alarms, sprinklers, security systems and safety products.

Tyco International 1992–2013

Fanuc (6954 on TSE) is the world leader in robotics and generated more than 75% of revenue from outside Japan in 2012. Factory automation represents nearly half of the company's business interests.

Fanuc 1992–2013

ABB (ABB on OMX and NYSE, ABBN on SIX) generated more than 65% of revenue from outside Europe in 2012. Its largest business units in 2012 were Power Products (22%), Discrete Automation and Motion (21%), Process Automation (20%), Power Systems (19%), and Low Voltage Products (16%).

ABB (SIX) 2000–2013

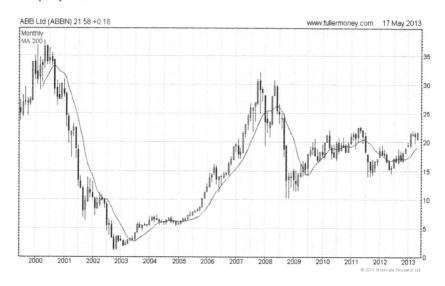

PACKAGING: ILLINOIS TOOL WORKS, REXAM, BRAMBLES

US-listed *Illinois Tool Works* (ITW on NYSE) is an S&P500 Dividend Aristocrat and is one of the largest producers of fasteners and components, arc welders and other engineered products. The company holds more than 20,000 patents and derived almost 60% of its revenue from outside the USA in 2012.

Illinois Tool Works 1992–2013

UK-listed *Rexam* (REX on LSE) is the largest manufacturer of beverage cans in the world and is a leading producer of rigid plastic packaging. The company is internationally diversified.

Rexam 1992–2013

Brambles (BXB on ASX) is listed in Australia and is the world's largest pallet and container-pooling services business. The company generated almost 90% of its revenue outside Australia in 2012. Amcor (AMC on ASX) is a similarly internationally diverse Australian packaging company producing a broad range of plastic, fibre, metal and glass products.

Brambles 2007–2013

Brambles Ltd (BXB) 8.44 +0.24   www.fullermoney.com   27 Mar 2013

CHEMICALS AND INDUSTRIAL GASES: LINDE, BASF, DOW CHEMICAL, DUPONT DE NEMOURS, AKZONOBEL, PPG INDUSTRIES, MONSANTO

The industrial gases sector represents an oligarchy where Praxair (PX on NYSE), Air Liquide (AI on Euronext) and Linde (LIN on DB) dominate the global market. Because it is uneconomic to transport gases over long distances, the business tends to be comparatively local and these three companies possess the global heft to express a presence just about everywhere. Of the three, *Linde* has the greatest exposure to Asia's growth markets.

Linde 1992–2013

Germany-listed *BASF* (BAS on DB) is the world's largest chemical company producing solvents, amines, resins, glues, electronic-grade chemicals, industrial gasses, basic petrochemicals and inorganic chemicals. It also produces raw materials for detergents, textiles, leather chemicals, pigments as well as catalysts, construction chemicals, adhesives and coatings.

BASF 1993–2013

US-listed *Dow Chemical*'s (DOW on NYSE) revenue was split almost equally between North America, EMEA and Asia Pacific in 2012. The company's products include plastics, synthetic rubber, pesticides, seeds, styrofoam, paper coatings, water purification products, petrochemical products to name but a few.

Dow Chemical 1992–2013

In 2012, the USA accounted for 38% of *DuPont's de Nemours* (DD on NYSE) revenue while Europe and Asia Pacific represented 23% each. The company is organised along a number of product segments including but not limited to electronic and communication technologies, performance materials, coatings, dyes, genetically modified seeds and is the world's largest producer of titanium dioxide. DuPont successfully acquired Danish listed Danisco in 2011, which also gave it exposure to the food ingredients sector.

DuPont 1992–2013

Approximately half of *AkzoNobel*'s (AKZA on Euronext) revenues are sourced in Europe, while Asia Pacific is its second largest market. The company produces paints, performance coatings and speciality chemicals.

AkzoNobel 1992–2013

US-listed *PPG Industries* (PPG on NYSE) derives more than half its revenue from outside the USA. It is involved in paint, speciality coatings, sealants for the aerospace sector as well as automotive, marine, industrial and packaging sectors. As with a number of US-based chemical companies, it has been among some of the greatest beneficiaries of the USA's low energy costs.

PPG Industries 1992–2013

US-listed *Monsanto* is one of the world's largest genetically engineered (GE) seed and glyphosate (Roundup) producers. The USA accounts for 55% of Monsanto's revenue, while Latin America represents its second largest market with 22.5%.

Monsanto 2001–2013

MINING AND ENERGY: BHP BILLITON, RIO TINTO, POTASH CORP OF SASKATCHEWAN, EXXONMOBIL, CHEVRON, ROYAL DUTCH SHELL, SCHLUMBERGER

Companies in the mobile and energy sectors are global by definition, exploiting resources in one region to sell in another. They are not mobile in the same sense as other companies because they have no choice but to focus production on where their resources are concentrated. Nevertheless, there are a number worthy of the Autonomy designation.

BHP Billiton is an S&P Europe 350 Dividend Aristocrat and is the world's largest diversified miner, with interests in iron-ore, base metals, petroleum, metallurgical and energy coal, aluminium, manganese, diamonds and potash. With Rio Tinto and VALE, BHP Billiton (BLT on LSE, BHP on ASX & NYSE and BIL on JSE) forms an oligarchy that dominates the global iron-ore market.

BHP Billiton 1998–2013

Rio Tinto (RIO on LSE, ASX and NYSE) has interests in iron-ore, aluminium, copper, borax, coal, gold, lead, silver, tin, uranium, zinc, titanium dioxide feedstock, diamonds, talc and zircon.

Rio Tinto 1992–2013

Canada-listed *Potash Corp of Saskatchewan* (POT on TSX) is the world's largest producer of crop nutrients. In 2012 its product categories were split between potash (41.4%), nitrogen (29.6%) and phosphate (28.9%). The USA was its largest market at 58.6% of revenues, but the remainder is spread throughout a range of countries.

Potash Corp of Saskatchewan 1992–2013

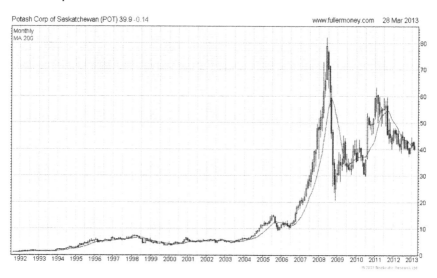

US-listed *ExxonMobil* (XOM on NYSE) is an S&P500 Dividend Aristocrat and has produced more natural gas than oil since at least 2009. The company is globally diversified and is a technological leader in its field. Resource nationalisation has been a challenge which it handles by leveraging its technological prowess and concentrating on non-oil assets.

ExxonMobil 1992–2013

UK and Dutch-listed Royal Dutch Shell (RDSB on LSE and Euronext) is also globally present, is intent on developing its relationship with China (now the world's largest energy consumer), produces more natural gas than oil and has a solid record of dividend growth.

Royal Dutch Shell 1992–2013

Chevron (CVX on NYSE) is perhaps not as large as the previous two energy companies, but it is equally present globally and has focused on developing technology to access difficult-to-reach resources.

Chevron 1992–2013

US-listed *Schlumberger*'s (SLB on NYSE) revenues are evenly spread globally. Together with Halliburton and Baker Hughes, the company dominates the oil service sector.

Schlumberger 1992–2013

CONCLUSION

These shares represent my best guess for a pool from which secular bull markets may emerge. While certainly not an exhaustive list, they represent some of the firms best-placed to drive and benefit from the greatest urbanisation in history, the golden age of technology, and unconventional oil and gas. These are the themes that are likely to have a meaningful impact on investment results over the decade from 2015 to 2025.

While a considerable number of base-formation completions and consistent trends are evident in these charts, there is also some evidence of inconsistency and trend-ending signals in some. In addressing them as macro behavioural technical analysts, we must foster the humility to accept the reality provided by the market. Even instruments in secular bull markets are capable of large pullbacks from time to time. The questions we need to ask ourselves when such events occur are whether medium-term trend ending signals are evident and what tactic is appropriate to our circumstances.

CONCLUSION

"It is better to know some of the questions than all of the answers."

– James Thurber

THE FOUR PILLARS OF macro behavioural technical analysis – price/crowd psychology, liquidity, governance and fundamental value/investment themes – give us a framework to assess the potential of investment ideas as they are proposed. Since we are living through an incredibly exciting period of human history there is no shortage of potential themes to examine using these criteria.

Billions of people are being lifted out of poverty, the pace of technological innovation is changing our lives in ways we can't even imagine and we are moving out of an era where energy is in short supply. Concurrently, the debt super-cycle that has been in evidence since 1980, and in a mania since 2008, is ending.

These themes have the capacity to create wonderfully rhythmic trends we can all participate in. Major themes have the power to instil powerful emotions among the investing crowd. We might even be tempted to fall in with our own pet theory. However, while we all have strong opinions, price is the only arbiter in markets. Our greatest challenge will be to remain dispassionate, particularly when others are letting their emotions run riot.

Differing perceptions of value create markets regardless of asset class. Charts of price action allow us to assess the rhythm of how supply and demand are interacting. Over the course of a market cycle price will influence sentiment and vice versa. A disciplined factual approach to chart reading, employing filter questions, allows us to assess the consistency of that relationship. By participating in consistent trends we avail of an environment where risk and reward are in our favour. When consistency deteriorates we are forced to ask if trend ending characteristics are evident. We will have an objective answer to that question.

In an uncertain world, identifying when one major market cycle ends and another begins is perhaps the most important thing we can do in our analysis. The group of companies I refer to as Autonomies represent a stable of shares I believe are likely to benefit from the new secular bull market that is developing on the world's stock exchanges. The only way to monitor whether that call is correct will be to monitor the consistency of their trends using price charts. At **FT-Money.com** we devote ourselves to monitoring these trends and identifying opportunities. *Crowd Money* provides you with the tools to do the same.

FT-MONEY.COM

EOIN TREACY joined David Fuller in 2003 to lend a hand in migrating the world-renowned Fullermoney investment letter from hard copy to a fully online interactive experience. In 2013 they founded FT-Money.com in order to further enhance the service's features and to provide a totally up-to-date user interface.

At FT-Money.com, they showcase the macro behavioural technical analysis pioneered by David Fuller at *The Chart Seminar* on Wall Street from 1969 and explained by Eoin Treacy in *Crowd Money*. Eoin took the seminar over from David in 2008 and has taken it back on sell-out tours to four continents since.

At FT-Money, the strategists take their cues from a study of market history and liquidity cycles, trends in standards of governance and behavioural psychology, then apply the methodology to stocks, bonds, currencies and commodities on a daily basis. Consequently, their views are original, practical, concise and frequently controversial. They write extensively on markets, focusing on topical and timely issues, addressing the crucial questions that everyone is asking.

In addition to writing and recording on FT-Money, David Fuller and Eoin Treacy provide a tailored consultancy service to some of the world's largest investors.

Empowerment Through Knowledge remains the service's theme. David and Eoin empower subscribers through their experience as career analysts and investor/traders. Similarly many subscribers help to empower David and Eoin through their own experience and insights, and the many commentaries they forward. This collective wisdom is pooled in Comment of the Day. This gives a voice to the community of users who are further empowered through the opportunity to learn, not only from research, but also from each other, thus creating an ever increasing pool of shared experience and knowledge.

David or Eoin record a daily podcast, which includes a review of market action on the day, in terms of trends, opportunities and risks. They tell you exactly what they think and why. Crucially, they also tell you exactly what they are doing with their own trades and investments, including tactics.

FT-Money's chart *library* has more than 12,000 instruments. Charts are customisable with a wide range of ratios, spreads, multiples and studies. One of the chief benefits is the breadth of options available: with every country index in the world, more than 200 currency pairs, bond yields for major and emerging markets, all liquid commodities and some which are not so liquid. This is not to mention the more than 10,000 equities from a host of countries which are also available. With an ever increasing range of filters the chart library is an indispensible tool to help identify the next big trend.

INDEX

21st Century Fox (mass media
multinational) 302

3M (engineering/manufacturing
company) 350

A

ABB (engineering/manufacturing
company) 354-5

Abe, Shinzō 61

abrupt decline 70-1

acceleration

and forecasts 165-6

identifying 166-7

and massive reactions against trend
182

and ranging phases 168-9

and trend endings 163-5, 169

and type-3 endings 187

and when to sell 170-1

acceptance (psychological perception
stages) 43, 44,

54-8, 66-71

accumulation phase 51

Activision Blizzard (video game
producer) 304

Adidas (sports manufacturer) 309

advertising 24, 25, 330-2

aesthetics 14-16, 100

African economic development 271

Aggreko (power company) 156-7

agriculture prices 254-6

AIG (American International Group)
101, 336-7

airplane autonomies 345-6

AkzoNobel (chemical production
company) 360

alcoholic beverage autonomies 278-82

Allergan (healthcare company) 316

Amazon (online retailer) 306

anchoring 142-3

anger 81-2

Anheuser-Busch InBev (brewer) 280-1

anonymity 22

anticipating price action

and banking sector leadership 113,
125-7

and commonality 113, 119-21

and consistent trends 113-19

and dynamics 113, 128-9

and leadership 113, 121-5

and relative strength 113, 121-5

Apple Inc. (technology corporation) 65-6, 228-9, 319

Arab Spring 271

Archer Daniels Midland (food producer) 286-7

Ariely, Dan 142-3

ARM Holdings (technology company) 263, 322-3

ASEAN countries 214, 232, 264, 272

Asian financial crisis (1997) 83, 264

AstraZeneca (pharmaceutical company) 69-70

automobile autonomies 341-5

Autonomies

    advertising 330-2

    airplanes 345-6

    alcoholic beverages 278-82

    automobiles 341-5

    banks 332-5

    chemicals/industrial gases 357-61

    clothing 309-11

    cosmetics/toiletries 292-7

    credit cards 339-41

    definition of xv, xvii, 276

    entertainment 302-4

    footwear/sportswear 308-9

    healthcare 312-17

    ingredients 288-90

    insurance 336-8

    luxury brands 298-301

    machinery/industrials 347-55

    mining/energy 362-6

    non-alcoholic beverages 282-4

    nutrition/supplements 290-2

    packaging 355-7

    processed foods 284-7

    restaurants 277-8

    retail/supermarkets 305-7

    software 328-30

    success of 276-7

    technology 319-27

    tobacco 317-18

AXA (insurance company) 338

B

banking autonomies 332-5

banking sector 113, 124-7, 332

Barclays (bank) 334

base formation

    and psychological perception stages 47-8, 51-4, 73

    and stops 150-1

    type-3 189-90, 223, 232-4

BASF (chemical production company) 358

Bayer (pharmaceuticals company) 314-15

BBVA (bank) 335

bear markets

    acceptance stages 43, 44, 54-8, 66-71

    and anticipating price action 115, 120

    and blind questioning 103, 107, 111-12

    depression stage 44, 71-5

    disbelief/dismissal stage 43, 46-54

    and dynamics 128

    and emotional intelligence 38-9, 41

    euphoria stage 43, 58-62

    and fundamentals 96

    and influences of crowds 28-9, 31, 33

and leadership 122

and massive reactions against trend
182-3

and overextension 136

relationship with bull markets 2-3

turning point stage 43-4, 62-6

and type-3 endings 190

Bear Stearns (investment bank) 120

Berkshire Hathaway
(engineering/manufacturing
company) 350-1

BHP Billiton (mining company) 362

Biogen (biotechnology company) 233-4,
315

blame 35, 41

blind questioning 102-12

BMW (auto manufacturer) 341-2

Boeing (aircraft manufacturer) 346

bottom-picking 228, 232

Brambles (packaging company) 356-7

Brazilian economic development 271

break-even stops 149, 153

breakouts
and acceleration 168-9

and blind questioning 103-5, 109-12

and commonality 120

and consistency characteristics 178

and consistent trends 116-19

failed 90-3, 118, 154, 180

and fundamentals 94-6

and key reversals 173

and psychological perception stages
51-3, 54-5

and ranging phases 87-90, 93-4, 178

and stops 154

and type-3 endings 187-8

Bretton Woods Accord 48

Bristol-Myers Squibb (healthcare
company) 313

British American Tobacco (tobacco
group) 318

brokers 79-80

Browne, Lord 50-1

bubbles 225-6, 230-2

Buffett, Warren 4, 67-8, 72

bull markets
and acceleration 165-7

acceptance stages 43, 44, 54-8, 66-71

and anticipating price action 115

and banking sector 125-7

and blind questioning 103, 107,
110-12

and central banks xiv, 4-5, 203

and contrary indicators 144

and crashes 223, 224-7, 230-2

depression stage 44, 71-5

disbelief/dismissal stage 43, 46-54

and dynamics 128

and emotional intelligence 37, 39

euphoria stage 43, 58-62

and fundamentals 96

and governance 211

identifying 1-9

and influences of crowds 28-30, 31,
32-3

and leadership 122

and market cycles 235-44

and massive reactions against trend
182

and 'nouveau riche' 298

and overextension 135-6

relationship with bear markets 2-3

and supply and demand 249-50

turning point stage 43-4, 62-6

Butz, Earl 254

C

candlestick analysis 171

CAP (Common Agricultural Policy) 254-5

Capital Gains Tax 170

capitulation 71

Casino Guichard-Perrachon SA (retail group) 307

'catching a falling knife' analogy 68-9

CDOs (collateralised debt obligations) 30, 226, 229

CDSs (credit default swaps) 226

central banks
and bull markets xiv, 4-5, 203
and crashes 225
and interest rates 61
and liquidity 4-5
and monetary policy 195, 196-205

chart reading
and aesthetics 14-16
blind questioning 102-12
common mistakes 97, 100-1
comparison with technical analysis 11, 12-13, 132
disciplined/responsive interpretation 16-18
and price action 11-14, 132-3
and psychological perception stages 45
and rhythms of the market 13-14
and supply and demand 11, 13-14

Chart Seminar xiii, xviii, 37, 45, 54, 65, 78, 82, 369

cheap credit 70-1, 73, 231

Check Point Software Technologies 53-4

chemicals/industrial gas autonomies 357-61

Chevron (energy company) 365

Chinese economic development 269, 271

Christian Dior (luxury goods group) 299

Chubb (insurance company) 337

Cisco Systems 167, 169

Citigroup (financial services group) 73-5, 168-9, 334

clothing autonomies 309-11

Coca-Cola (drinks group) 283

Colgate Palmolive (cosmetics/toiletries producer) 293

commodities
and anticipating price action 120-1
and base formation development 47-8
and fundamentals 94-6
and governance 211
and per capita income 272-3
and supply and demand 248, 252-6
and volatility 197-9

commonality 113, 119-21, 172

Compagnie Financière Richemont (luxury goods group) 300

compound tops 187-8

compromise 20

consistency characteristics
and anticipating price action 115-16, 118
and blind questioning 102-12
and breakouts 178
and chart reading mistakes 97, 100-1
identifying 98-100
and market cycles 241
and ranging phases 99-100, 178
and supply and demand 98-100

consistent trends 113-19, 145, 188

consolidation 54, 104-5, 109, 115

contagion 19, 23-4, 223-4, 227-8

contradictory ideas 27, 29-31

contrary indicators 143-4

cosmetics/toiletry autonomies 292-7

cost of money 202-4

cost-averaging 149, 159-61

crashes

and bubbles 225-6

and bull markets 223, 224-7, 230-2

and contagion 223-4, 227-8

and opportunity 223-4, 226, 228-32

and type-3 base formation 223, 232-4

credit card autonomies 339-41

criminality 67-8

currency markets 210-11, 252

cyclical nature of governance 211-13

D

Dairy Farm International Holdings (retail group) 307

Danone (food producer) 287

de Backer, Wouter 72

debt (as future theme) 263-4

deflation 197-9, 202, 205

demand dominance 14, 17, 93, 120, 151, 191-3, 233

Deng Xiaoping 269

denial 81

Denson, Charlie 263

depression 40, 44, 71-5

developed markets 207-8

Diageo (drinks group) 279

disappointment 35, 40, 46

disbelief/dismissal 43, 46-54

disciplined chart interpretation 16-18

Disney (entertainment brand) 302-3

disposable income 272-3, 290, 292, 309, 336, 341, 345

Dodd–Frank Act (2012) 219

Dollar Tree Stores (US chain store) 191-2

Dow 100,000 (book) 32

Dow Chemical (chemical production company) 359

downside key day reversals 171, 172-4

DSM NV (nutrition/supplements producer) 290-1

DuPont (chemical production company) 359-60

dynamics 113, 128-9

E

EADS (European Aeronautic Defence and Space) 346

Ecolab (engineering/manufacturing company) 353

economic convergence 268

economic development 268-73

Eliot, George 80

emergency meetings 66

emerging markets 144, 203, 207-8, 273, 308, 316, 345

Emerson Electric (engineering/manufacturing company) 352

emotional capital 67

emotional intelligence 35-41

emotional responses 27-9, 33

energy (as future theme) 260-1

energy prices 61, 197, 253, 257, 260-1

Enron (energy company) 67

entertainment autonomies 302-4

Estée Lauder (cosmetics/toiletries producer) 296

ETFs (exchange-traded funds) 231, 253-4

euphoria (psychological perception stage) 43, 58-62

Experian (credit provider) 340-1

exponential MAs (moving averages) 133-4, 135

ExxonMobil (energy company) 364

F

facts 27, 32-3

failed breakouts 90-3, 118, 154, 180

fallacy of control 144-5, 148

Fanuc (engineering/manufacturing company) 354

fear xvii-xviii, 23, 35-6, 40, 67-8, 72, 81

fellow feeling 19, 20-1

financial stops 157-8

food prices 197, 254-6

footwear/sportswear autonomies 308-9

force 27, 31-2

forecasts 31-2, 59, 165-6

Freud, Sigmund
and crowd influence 29, 30, 31, 32, 165
and emotional intelligence 37, 39, 40
and group formation 20, 23
and psychological perception stages 59

FT-Money.com xiii, xix, 368, 369-70

Fuller, David
and Autonomies xv, xvii, 276
and central banks xiv, 5, 203
and chart reading 12-13
and Chart Seminar xviii
and commonality 119, 120
and consistent trends 116, 145
and dynamics 128
and essence of investing 159
and failed breakouts 91, 154
and fallacy of control 148
and FT-Money.com xiii, xix, 369-70
and governance 208
and harvesting financial markets 2
and humility 258
and key reversals 171
and leadership 127
and MA 133
and mean reversion 132
and mid-point danger line stops 153
and monetary policy 195
and objectivity 8
and progressing/regressing markets 208
and psychological perception stages 45
and ranging phases 78, 88
and roundophobia 145
and supply inelasticity/rising demand 50, 256
and unconventional gas production 260

fundamentals 94-6

G

General Electric (engineering/manufacturing company) 262-3, 347

genetics 263

Glass–Steagall Act (1933) 218-19

global middle class 267-73, 292, 305, 308, 312, 336

gold 3, 61, 102-6, 158, 231, 235-40, 253-4

Goldman Sachs (bank) 335

Google (technology corporation) 320

governance
as absolute or relative 209-11
cyclical nature of 211-13

and emerging markets 207-8

and identifying bull markets 6-7

as pillar of macro behavioural analysis xiv, 1, 367

standards of 213-14, 216

gradual acceptance 56

Graham, Benjamin 4, 14

'great moderation' theory 41

Great Wall Motors (auto manufacturer) 344-5

greed 35-6, 72

'Greenspan Put' 202

Greenspan, Alan 51

group formation

characteristics of 19-25

and contagion 19, 23-4

and fellow feeling 19, 20-1

and heightened emotional states 19, 22-3

and psychological perception stages 58-9

and responsibility 19, 21-2

and segregation 19, 21

and suggestion 19, 24-5

Group Psychology and the Analysis of the Ego (book) 20

Grupo Modelo (drinks group) 282

H

Hasbro (toy manufacturer) 304

healthcare autonomies 312-17

Hegel, G. W. F. 62-3

heightened emotional states 19, 22-3

Heineken (brewer) 282

Hennes & Mauritz (clothing retailer) 310-11

Herbalife (nutrition/supplements producer) 292

Hewlett-Packard (technology manufacturer) 324

HFT (high frequency trading) 217-18

holistic market analysis xviii, 1, 8, 18

Honeywell (engineering/manufacturing company) 349

hope 82

HSBC (bank) 332-3

Hussein, Saddam 270

hypnosis 24

I

IBM (technology corporation) 233, 320-1

Illinois Tool Works (packaging company) 355

Indian economic development 270

Inditex (clothing retailer) 310

Indonesian economic development 271

inflation 195, 196-9, 202, 205

influences of crowds 27-33

infrastructure development 214, 249, 259, 268-70, 272

ingredients autonomies 288-90

Ingredion (ingredients producer) 288-9

insurance autonomies 336-8

Intel (technology manufacturer) 322

intentional transmission 24

interest rates 61, 196-7, 202

International Flavor & Fragrances (ingredients producer) 288

Intertek (engineering/manufacturing company) 352

inverted yield curves 204

investment banks 218

J

Jerry Maguire (film) 37
Jevons, William Stanley 248
'jilted lover' effect 35, 38-9
Jobs, Steve 65, 319
Johnson & Johnson (healthcare group) 312-13
Journal of Behavioral Finance 142

K

Kadlec, Charles W. 32
Kerry Group (ingredients producer) 289
key reversals 163, 171-4
Keynes, John Meynard 3, 29
KFC (restaurant chain) 277
Kia (auto manufacturer) 344
Kimberly-Clark (cosmetics/toiletries producer) 294

L

L'Oréal (cosmetics/toiletries producer) 296-7
labour (as future theme) 259-60
Lam Research (technology manufacturer) 324
Le Bon, Gustave 28
leadership 113, 121-5, 228-30
learning lessons 73
Lehman Brothers (bank) 22, 30-1, 101, 182, 227
Lenovo (technology manufacturer) 321
Linde (industrial gas company) 357-8
liquidity
    and banking sector 332
    and central banks 4-5
    and contagion 227

and high frequency trading 217-18
and identifying bull markets 4-6
as pillar of macro behavioural analysis xiv, 1, 367
lobbying 220
long-term data 101
love 35-9
luxury brand autonomies 298-301
LVMH (luxury goods group) 298-9

M

MAs (moving averages)
    and anticipating price action 117-19
    and blind questioning 105-6, 108-12
    definition of 131, 133
    and key reversals 173-4
    and massive reactions against trend 181-2
    and mean reversion 132, 135, 138-40
    and overextension 135-8
    and stops 157
    and technical analysis 132
    and trend direction 140
    and trend mean 13
    types of 133-4
    use of 133-5
machinery/industrials autonomies 347-55
Madoff, Bernie 67
Magnit (Russian supermarket chain) 92
market bottoms 32, 46, 72-3, 120, 159-60, 137, 140, 174
market cycles
    and gold 235-40
    and US Treasuries 235-6, 240-4
market declines 81-3
market tops 63, 120, 140, 174, 232
marketing 24, 25

massive reactions against trend 177-83, 187

Mastercard (credit provider) 339

master-slave dialectic 62-3

Mattel (toy manufacturer) 303

McCormick (ingredients producer) 290

McDonald's (restaurant chain) 57, 277-8

McDougall, William 21, 28

Mead Johnson Nutrition (nutrition/supplements producer) 291

mean reversion 132, 135, 138-40, 174

media 196

MediaTek (technology manufacturer) 327

melancholia 40

Merrill Lynch (wealth management arm of BoA) 107-10, 239-40, 243-4

Mexican economic development 271

MF Global (brokerage firm) 219

Microchip Technology (technology manufacturer) 323

Microsoft (software corporation) 122-3, 328

Middlemarch (novel) 80

mid-point danger line (MDL) stops 149, 153-4, 156, 157

mining/energy autonomies 362-6

'model myopia' 101

Mondelēz International (food group) 84, 285

monetary policy
    and cost of money 202-4
    importance of 195
    and inflation 195, 196-9, 202, 205
    and supply of money 196-201, 204
    and velocity of money 195, 200-1, 204

Monsanto (genetically engineered seed producer) 361

Montgomery, Henry 142

Moore's Law 262

myopia 101, 120

N

NAFTA (North American Free Trade Agreement) 271

Nestlé (food producer) 285

Nike (sports manufacturer) 172-4, 263, 308

Nissan (auto manufacturer) 343

non-alcoholic beverage autonomies 282-4

'nouveau riche' 298

Novartis (healthcare group) 317

Novo Nordisk (pharmaceuticals company) 314

Nu Skin Enterprises (cosmetics/toiletries producer) 297

nutrition/supplements autonomies 290-2

O

OAPEC (Organization of Arab Petroleum Exporting Countries) 48-9

objectivity 8, 20, 100, 187

Ockham's razor 171

oil prices 48-52, 155-6, 260-1

Omnicom (advertising company) 330, 332

opportunity 223-4, 226, 228-32

optimism xviii, 25, 46, 72, 144

Oracle (software corporation) 328-9

orderly decline 69-70

overconfidence 64, 142, 144

overextension 13, 105, 109, 135-8, 169-70, 173-4

P

packaging autonomies 355-7

panic 35, 39-40

PCE (Personal Consumption Expenditures) Deflator 198

PepsiCo (drinks group) 284

personification of markets 60

pessimism xviii, 4, 41

Pfizer (pharmaceuticals company) 316

Phenomenology of Spirit (book) 62

Philip Morris International (tobacco group) 317-18

Philips Electronics 262

population growth 259

position sizing 149, 157-9

Potash Corp of Saskatchewan (crop nutrients producer) 61-2, 363

PPG Industries (chemical production company) 361

Prince, Chuck 73

processed foods autonomies 284-7

Procter & Gamble (cosmetics/toiletries producer) 292-3

productivity 210, 249, 257-9, 262-4, 269, 312, 319

profit erosion 39, 67-8, 70, 150-1, 167, 226

progressing/regressing markets 207, 208-9

protectionism 270

Prudential (insurance company) 338

psychological levels 145-8

psychological perception stages

acceptance 43, 44, 54-8, 66-71

depression 44, 71-5

disbelief/dismissal 43, 46-54

euphoria 43, 58-62

turning point 43-4, 62-6

Publicis (advertising company) 330-1

Q

quantitative easing 197, 251, 264

R

ranging phases

and acceleration 168-9

and anticipating price action 114-19

and blind questioning 103-5, 107-9, 111

as 'boring' 77, 87, 88, 119, 179

and breakouts 87-90, 93-4, 178

and consistency characteristics 99-100, 178

and failed breakouts 90-3

forming the range 79-81

and market declines 81-3

and stops 179-80

and supply and demand 78, 88-93

and support/resistance levels 77-8, 79-81, 84-5

in trending markets 78

and type-3 base formation 232-4

and type-3 endings 187-92

rationality 29-32, 38, 58

'rebound effect' 248

recessions 202-4, 212

Reckitt Benckiser (cosmetics/toiletries producer) 294-5

regulatory environment 215-21

re-hypothentication 219

relative strength 113, 121-5

religion 21, 28, 60, 62

Rémy Cointreau (drinks group) 280

responsibility 19, 21-2

responsive chart interpretation 16-18

restaurant autonomies 277-8

retail/supermarket autonomies 305-7

revenge 41

Rexam (packaging company) 356

rhythms of the market 13-14

Rio Tinto (mining company) 362-3

risk

    and crashes 224

    and influences of crowds 28, 30

    and psychological perception stages
        49-50, 55-6, 60, 63, 68-9

    and stops 149, 150-1

Rolls-Royce
    (engineering/manufacturing
    company) 348

roundophobia 141, 145-6

Royal Dutch Shell (energy company)
    364-5

S

SABMiller (brewer) 279

Samsung (technology manufacturer) 325

SAP (software company) 329

Schlumberger (energy company) 365-6

securities firms 218-19

segregation 19, 21

self-recrimination 35, 40, 82

shape of recovery 73-5

Shenzhou International (clothing
    manufacturer) 311

shock 82

short-sellers 33, 80

short-term data 101

Siemens (engineering/manufacturing
    company) 351

Singh, Manmohan 214, 270

'sleepers' 192

software autonomies 328-30

Sony (technology manufacturer) 326

speculators 216-17, 218, 220

'stale bull' inventories 71-2

Standard Chartered (bank) 333

standards of governance 213-14, 216

Starbucks (coffee chain) 282-3

step sequence uptrends 92-3, 104-5,
    153-4

stop losses 149, 152-3

stops

    and cost-averaging 159

    implementation of 156-7

    and massive reactions against trend
        180

    placement of 150, 151-2

    and position sizing 157-9

    and ranging phases 179-80

    and risk 149, 150-1

    sequence of 152-6

stories 3-4, 47, 55-6, 59, 61, 79, 144

subconscious influence 25

suggestion 19, 24-5

Super PACs (Political Action
    Committees) 220

supply and demand

    and acceleration 164

    and blind questioning 105-6

    and bull markets 249-50

    and chart reading 11, 13-14

    and commonality 119-20, 252-6

    and consistency characteristics 98-
        100

    and consistent trends 114-19

and cost-averaging 159

and currency markets 252

and dynamics 128-9

and emotional intelligence 39

and MA 140

and market cycles 241-2

and price action 247-56

and psychological perception stages
45, 47-52, 54-6, 66, 70, 72-3

and ranging phases 78, 88-93

and stock market prices 249-50

and stops 150-1, 157

and type-3 endings 185-6, 189-91

and US Treasury bonds 250-2

vacuums of 87, 89-96, 116, 128,
167-8, 190-1

and volatility 250

supply inelasticity/rising demand 50, 256

supply of money 196-201, 204

support/resistance levels

and anticipating price action 116-18

and blind questioning 104-5, 108-9,
112

and mean reversion 138-9

and ranging phases 77-8, 79-81, 84-
5

and round numbers 146

and volatility 78

Swatch (watch manufacturer) 301

T

Taiwan Semiconductor (technology
manufacturer) 327

targets 142, 144-5

TARP (Troubled Asset Relief Program)
74, 203

Tata Consultancy (IT company) 330

technical stops 158-9

technology (as future theme) 261-3

technology autonomies 319-27

Templeton, Sir John 4, 24-5

Tesco (supermarket chain) 306

The Group Mind (book) 21

theme/fundamental value xiv, 1, 3-4, 367

Tiffany (luxury goods group) 300-1

TIPS (Treasury Inflation-Protected
Securities) 197

tobacco autonomies 317-18

Törngren, Gustaf 142

Toyota (auto manufacturer) 343

trailing stops 149, 155-6, 1 57

trend direction 140

trend endings

acceleration 163-5, 169-71

key reversals 163, 171-4

and market cycles 241-2

and massive reactions against trend
177-83

type-3 endings 185-93

trend mean 13, 17, 105, 131-2, 137-8, 170

trending phases

and anticipating price action 118-19

and blind questioning 103, 107,
111-12

as 'exciting' 77, 87-8, 179

and psychological perception stages
43, 54-8

triple vision 100-1

triple waterfall crash 49

turning point (psychological perception
stage) 43-4, 62-6

Tyco International
(engineering/manufacturing
company) 353

type-3 base formation 223, 232-4

type-3 endings 185-93

U

unconscious transmission 23
Uni-Charm (cosmetics/toiletries
    producer) 295
Unilever (consumer goods producer) 286
United Technologies
    (engineering/manufacturing
company) 348-9
upside key day reversals 171, 172-3
urbanisation 50, 56, 257, 265, 267, 272,
    339
US Treasury bonds 61, 106-10, 235-6,
    240-4, 250-2

V

vacuums of supply/demand 87, 89-96,
    116, 128, 167-8, 190-1
velocity of money 195, 200-1, 204
Visa (credit provider) 340
volatility
    and anticipating price action 118
    and commodities 197-9
    and stops 150-1
    and supply and demand 250
    and support/resistance levels 78
    and type-3 base formation 232, 234
    and type-3 endings 185-6, 191-2
Volcker, Paul 49, 197, 219
Volkswagen (auto manufacturer) 342

W

Wal-Mart (supermarket chain) 259, 305
Wells Fargo (bank holding company¬)
    229-30
West Texas Intermediate Crude Oil 145-6
wholesale banks 218

Woolworths (Australian supermarket
    chain) 93-4
WPP (advertising company) 330-1

X

Xstrata (mining company) 70-1

Y

yield curve spread 202-4
Yom Kippur War (1973) 48
Yum Brands 277